NO PICNIC

NO PICNIC

JULIAN THOMPSON

CASSELL&CO

Cassell & Co
Wellington House, 125 Strand
London WC2R 0BB

First published in Great Britain in 1985
Republished in a revised edition by Leo Cooper in 1992
This edition 2001

A CIP catalogue record for this book is available from the British Library

ISBN 0-304-35647-6

Printed and bound in Great Britain
by Cox & Wyman Ltd., Reading, Berks.

CONTENTS

ACKNOWLEDGEMENTS

I would like to thank everybody who has helped me to write this book, but in particular James Ladd for his help and encouragement and for casting a critical eye over the first four chapters; my Personal Assistant, Tricia Roberts, who typed most of the first drafts in her spare time, skilfully managing to decipher my writing; Mrs Shandra Keelan and Miss Betty Gershon who typed both first and second drafts; Corporal Latimer who drew the maps in his spare time; and last, but not least, my wife who for almost a year while I wrote endured being ignored on most evenings during the working week, at most weekends and through Summer leave, Christmas leave and most of Easter leave; and listened patiently to each chapter she was read.

I would also like to pay tribute to Chief Petty Officer Peter Holgate, Royal Navy, who took most of the photographs that appear in this book; but I must also thank 2 Para and 3 Para for providing some of the photographs, as well as Petty Officer Birkett, Leading Airman Ryan and Leading Airman Campbell.

LIST OF MAPS

GLOSSARY

Bandwagon	See BV 202
Basha/Bivvie	A shelter made from a poncho, a couple of sticks and rubber 'bungies'. More elaborate models have walls made of stones or peat blocks. Infantry in the British Service, which includes Commandos and Paratroopers, are not issued with tents. Some specialists, such as SAS, SBS and M & AW Cadre are supplied with two-man tents.
BV 202	Tracked, articulated, oversnow vehicle consisting of a tower and trailer built by Volvo. Although designed for oversnow work it was also highly successful on peat bog. Referred to as 'Bandwagon' or 'BV'.
Chinook	Large, twin-rotor helicopter with a payload of ten tons, about five times that of a Sea King helicopter. Built in the USA and used by both Argentina and Britain.
CVRT	Combat Vehicle Reconnaissance Tracked — Scorpion or Scimitar light tank.
Carl Gustav	84 mm medium anti-armour shoulder-held, recoilless weapon, known as 'Charlie G', or '84', or 'MAW'.
DF	Defensive Fire — pre-recorded and adjusted artillery, mortar or machine-gun fire by troops in defensive positions against attacking troops or patrols. Likely approaches, FUPs and so forth will be selected for such treatment.
Direct Fire Weapons	Weapons that have to be aimed directly at the target to hit as opposed to indirect fire weapons such as mortars or artillery.
FAL	Argentine rifle that fires automatic or single rounds. Looks similar to the British SLR. Some versions had a folding butt.
FOO	Forward Observation Officer, an artillery officer who directs artillery fire. Normally one with each forward rifle company commander; provided from the battery supporting the battalion or commando.
FUP	Forming Up Position — the area behind the Start

	Line in which assaulting troops form up for an assault. Preferably in dead ground, i.e. out of sight of the enemy and therefore unable to be fired at by direct fire weapons.
GPMG	General Purpose Machine Gun — belt-fed 7.62 mm weapon, normally one per section in every British commando or battalion. Can also be mounted on a tripod and equipped with a heavier barrel and dial sight to enable it to fire at night, or through smoke and mist, and hit pre-recorded targets. The kit to carry out the conversion is known as the Sustained Fire (SF) kit. There are three SF kits per rifle company.
H-Hour	The time at which the first wave of assaulting troops cross the Start Line (see Start Line) or leave their landing craft to assault a beach.
Individual Weapon Sight	(IWS) a British, first-generation image intensifier sight which can be clipped onto a rifle or GPMG for shooting or observing at night. The Argentines had second-generation night sights and excellent night vision binoculars.
L-Hour	The time at which assault helicopters touch down and the first wave of assaulting troops deplane.
LCU	Landing Craft Utility — a landing craft capable of carrying 200 men or 22 tons of stores, or four large trucks. Four LCU's were carried by each of the two LPDs (*Fearless* and *Intrepid*) in their docks.
LCVP	Landing Craft Vehicle and Personnel — a landing craft capable of carrying an infantry platoon (30 men), or a landrover and trailer.
Light Machine Gun	Magazine-fed machine gun based on Bren of Second World War design but firing 7.62 mm ammunition.
LPD	Landing Platform Dock — assault ship. Britain had, and still has, two, *Fearless* and *Intrepid*.
LSL	Landing Ship Logistic — roll-on, roll-off ships manned by the Royal Fleet Auxiliary.
MILAN	Wire-guided, anti-tank missile, very useful for bunker-busting.
NGFO	Naval Gunfire Observer — an officer provided by the artillery to observe naval gunfire.
NGFO Party	A gunner term to describe the NGFO and his radio operators.

OP	Observation Post — a small, well concealed position from which to observe.
OP Party	A gunner term to describe the FOO and his radio operators — see FOO.
PNG	Passive Night Goggles — image-intensifying goggles mainly used by helicopter pilots to fly at night.
Rapier	British surface-to-air missile.
Sangar	A protective wall built of stone or peat blocks constructed in ground too hard to dig, or when trenches are flooded.
Scimitar	CVRT — light tank built by Alvis equipped with 30 mm automatic cannon.
Scorpion	CVRT — light tank built by Alvis with the same chassis, drive and hull as Scimitar, but equipped with 76 mm gun.
Sea King	A medium-lift helicopter built by Westlands. The mark IV designed for troop lift can carry about twenty men depending on the equipment with which they are loaded. The anti-submarine version can carry about ten men.
Sixty-Six	66 — a shoulder-held light anti-armour weapon (LAW), anti-tank rocket in a throw-away launcher.
SLR	Self-Loading Rifle — adapted by the British from the original Belgian FN design. The British version does not fire automatic.
Staff Titles	Until January, 1982, the Commando Brigade, in common with its British Army counterparts, used the peculiar, but effective staff titles given below:

Brigade Major (BM) — A grade 2 staff appointment and the co-ordinator of the General Staff at Brigade level which deals with operations, intelligence, training, organization and air matters. Under him he had a number of General Staff Officers grade 3 (GSO3), such as the GSO3 Intelligence and so forth. The BM was de facto Chief of Staff.

DAA and QMG (DQ) — The Deputy Assistant Adjutant and Quarter Master General was head of the Brigade Personnel (A) and Logistics (Q) staff. Under him he had a Staff Captain A (personnel), Staff Captain Q (logistics) and a number of specialist advisers such as the Brigade Electrical and mechanical Engineer Officer (BEME).

On 1 January, 1982, the titles changed. The new system was intended to conform with that in use in NATO Armies. On 2 April, 1982, we instantly, and without any formal announcement, reverted to the old system. We intended going to war with a system we and our Naval opposite numbers understood, and which avoided wasting precious time while people worked out which title went with which staff officer — perhaps in the heat of battle.

The new system is summarized below and readers, if they are familiar with the NATO system, may judge for themselves how much it conforms to the NATO system.

Old	New
BM	Chief of Staff
DAA & QMG	Deputy Chief of Staff
Staff Captain A	SO3 G1 (Personnel)
GSO3 (Intelligence)	SO3 G2 (Intelligence)
GSO3 (Operations)	SO3 G3 (Operations)
Staff Captain Q	SO3 G4 (Logistics)

Start Line

A line in the ground, usually a natural feature, stream, bank or fence, preferably at ninety degrees to the axis of advance, which marks the start line for the attack and is crossed at H-Hour in attack formation. Can be marked by tape if there is no natural feature which lends itself to being used as a start line. (American term is Line of Departure [LOD].)

Time

All times in this book are local in the country in which the events being described take place. Falkland Islands Time is four hours behind Greenwich Mean Time and five hours behind British Summer Time. For a reason which is not clear to me to this day, the war was 'fought in "Zulu" Time', i.e. Greenwich Mean Time. Thus some accounts of the war, based on reports, official or unofficial, have dawn at about 10.30 am and dusk at about 8.15 pm in mid-winter at 52° 30 minutes south and all other timings seemingly out of kilter. To avoid readers puzzling over why, for example, night attacks were apparently being conducted at seven o'clock in the morning, I have stuck to local times throughout. Last light in the Falklands was at about 4.15 pm and first light at about 6.30 am local time.

When we arrived in Stanley, we found that the Argentines had imposed Argentine Time (three hours behind GMT) on the town, but left the countryside in Falklands Time. Having to operate in two times was bad enough, but this was ridiculous. The British Land Forces switched to local (Falkland Islands) time within a day or so of the surrender, and invited the citizens of Stanley to do likewise.

I have used am and pm instead of the 24-hour clock used by the military.

AUTHOR'S PREFACE

When I gave the orders for the landing at San Carlos to the Commanding Officers of the Units in 3 Commando Brigade I said, among other things, that the operation we were about to embark upon would not be a picnic. I was determined that no one in my Brigade would be under any illusion but that we would have to fight to win. Although the Falklands War of 1982 was both small in scale and short in duration it was indeed no picnic, hence the title of the book.

Mercifully the casualties, both at sea and on land, were light in comparison with many previous wars, long or short — although this is no consolation to the bereaved. The British fought this small, short war at a distance of over 8,000 miles from their home base, with only Ascension Island as a staging point just over half-way down the route. The problems imposed by distance alone were daunting enough. On top of this we were outnumbered both in the air and on the ground at all times throughout the war. Finally there was the terrain over which the land campaign was fought and the climatic conditions endured by marines and soldiers.

'No one who has not visited the Falklands, be he a Government Minister, Serviceman, Whitehall official, MP or journalist, can ever speak or write convincingly about them with any sense of conviction or degree of credibility,' wrote Major-General Edward Fursdon, the Defence Correspondent of the *Daily Telegraph*, after a visit in September, 1982.

'The Falklands are everybody's playground now,' said a cynical SAS officer after the campaign. But, both before and during the campaign few of those not down south and actually involved with land operations seemed to have much idea of the limitations imposed by the terrain and the climate on land operations. The climate was not as harsh as, say, Korea or Italy in winter, but it was unpleasant enough. The combination of wet weather and around freezing temperatures can produce as many, and sometimes more, injuries as a considerably colder but drier climate. There were few places where more than a handful of men could be brought in to dry out and, once the Commando Brigade was established in the mountains overlooking Stanley, none. There were few tents. As will become clear over and over again in the text, once a man was wet, he stayed wet, unless he could dry his clothes in the surprisingly frequent but usually short periods of sunshine.

But hanging out clothes to dry is not a recommended practice in forward positions and difficult when on the march. The best that could usually be achieved was a state of dampness, or not quite dry. Most men's feet never dried and many suffered from trench-foot. Although the worst trench foot cases were evacuated, many more had to march and fight while enduring a sensation described by somebody as like having one's feet screwed into a vice while dipping them into boiling water.

By Norwegian or Alpine standards the 'mountains' in the Falklands are hardly worthy of the name. Nevertheless for heavily laden infantry, rather than peacetime hill-walkers or ramblers out for the day, the stone runs, craggy summits and ubiquitous peat bogs made them formidable terrain to move and fight over. Living day and night in the mountains in peat- or rock-walled sangars, where the shallowest scrape filled with water within minutes, was far from pleasant. The complete absence of roads outside the immediate environs of Stanley and the surfaced track to Fitzroy meant that, once ashore, every round of ammunition, ration-pack and gallon of fuel for the handful of tracked vehicles and for the Rapier generators had to be carried on the backs of marching men, or by the gallantly flown, but far too small, helicopter force — and every casualty likewise.

It must have been difficult for anyone working off small-scale maps to have much of an idea what an infantryman's war in the Falklands would be like — the long pauses to drag up more supplies, the snail-like pace, the cold and physical exhaustion. The faces of many of my marines and soldiers as we tramped into Stanley were drawn and grey and, with the camouflage cream, looked like the faces of middle-aged chimney sweeps rather than those of teenagers and men in their early twenties. There is nothing new in this; look at pictures of infantry soldiers in any war. But it had been a long time since Britain had fought a war of this intensity and there were few serving officers, even of senior level at home, who had experience of a war of this type. The land campaign started with potentially the most hazardous phase of war — an amphibious operation. Since the Second World War most of the specialized equipment for amphibious operations has steadily been scrapped without replacement at the same rate. We were to carry out such an operation without the array of amphibious tanks, tracked amphibious armoured personnel carriers and gun-equipped landing craft commonplace in the latter half of the Second World War and still in the armouries of some countries today. The expertise in planning and conducting amphibious operations was in 1982, and still is, in the hands of a small number of officers in the Royal Marines and Royal Navy, and it soon became apparent that many of the imperatives of an amphibious operation were not understood outside this circle of *cognoscenti*.

Knowing these things, it is perhaps not surprising that some of the more perceptive among my Brigade left Britain in early April, 1982, not really expecting to return. There was a feeling that we would win, but many would die like the leading element of a besieging army that storms the breach — the forlorn hope. Several people whose judgement I trust have told me this, unsolicited, since we returned. When it ended so suddenly we blinked and said almost as one: 'We're alive!'

We were all surprised by the warmth of our welcome home. Newspapers were so late in arriving in the Falklands that many of us had no idea of the strength of feeling generated and were delighted with, but rather overwhelmed by, the regard in which we were held by our countrymen.

We were very lucky indeed — lucky to have so much support at home, so our families did not have to bear the burden of anti-war propaganda as well as anxiety for their loved ones. We were lucky not to have had more casualties. The media made much of what has incorrectly come to be called the Bluff Cove bombing of *Sir Galahad*, which actually occurred at Fitzroy. Sad though that incident was, there were several occasions when we were a whisker away from worse — but our luck held.

Last, but most important of all, we were lucky in the quality of the men throughout the Task Force, whatever the colour of their uniforms and wherever they served. Of course, for me, as Commander 3 Commando Brigade, the men in my Brigade were special, and this book concentrates unashamedly on their story. It was the Commando Brigade that landed in East Falkland on D-Day, marched and fought alone for the first twelve days of the land campaign and, having crossed East Falkland mainly on foot and by helicopter, marched into Port Stanley on 14 June, 1982, twenty-five days after the first amphibious assault. Without the courage, devotion and professionalism of the Royal Navy, the Merchant Navy and the Royal Air Force, the Commando Brigade would never have reached the shores of San Carlos Water or survived during the days which followed. But, when all was said and done, to win the war men had to close with and defeat the Argentine Army. There is nothing new in this and it was as applicable to the Falklands in 1982 as it was when Haig, writing about the campaign in France in March, 1915, said, 'We can not hope to win until we have defeated the German Army'.

It was to the Marines, soldiers, quite a few sailors and several airmen, whether permanent members or temporarily under command of 3 Commando Brigade that the lion's share of this task fell. In concentrating on 3 Commando Brigade this book does not set out to belittle the fine achievements of units not in the Brigade, but merely tries to tell the story of the Brigade's battles and marches the way they were. The Brigade was a close-knit family and, whatever our rivalries, had that special feeling that comes from shared experience, the prospect of facing a daunting task and seeing it through to the end.

It is therefore to all the Officers, Warrant Officers, NCOs, Marines, Soldiers, Sailors and Airmen of 3 Commando Brigade in the Falklands Campaign, be their berets green, red, blue, sand-coloured or khaki, and whatever their cap badge, that I dedicate this book with pride and affection.

PREFACE TO SECOND EDITION

Now that nearly ten years have passed since the events described in this book, I thought it was time to insert material which would have been impossible to include while I and the other major players were still serving. Since writing *No Picnic*, my first book, I have had two other books published, and completed several articles and contributions to other works, including a number of pieces for *The Observer*. I considered that the text of *No Picnic* would benefit from a good tidy up.

When I wrote the first edition, I tried to keep myself out of the narrative as much as possible. My aim: to write a book which would show just what the marines and soldiers of my Brigade had achieved. Very few accurate accounts of the Falklands War had appeared by mid-1983; only Max Hasting's *Battle For The Falklands* and Robert Fox's *Eyewitness Falklands*. Media publicity had concentrated on some units at the expense of others, often accompanied by ignorant comment. For example the brilliant battle fought by 42 Commando on Mount Harriet had gone almost unnoticed. The wrong interpretation had been put on many of my actions, and those of other commanders.

Writing in 1983/4, I was in a good position to put the record straight and sort out fact from fiction. My Brigade War Diaries, official documents prepared by every unit and headquarters in war, had at that time not been sent to the Public Records Office. They were sent soon after, and, under present legislation, will be closed to public inspection until AD 2012. The War Diaries contained much valuable material and, in particular, my Headquarters Diary had: copies of all my orders; the battle logs with timings and descriptions of all events, major decisions, and moves affecting every unit in my Brigade; copies of every signal sent and received by my headquarters from 2 April to arrival back in Plymouth on 12 July, 1982. At that time I also had access to the official reports from all other units in my brigade. Although I could not quote from any of these documents, I could refer to them for facts, figures, timings and other aids to establishing what did, and what did not happen.

In this edition I have included some information about the Argentine strengths. Most of this was taken from the maps attached to the Argentine Army Official Report on the War, of which I have photocopies, thanks to the kindness of Professor Virginia Gamba-Stonehouse, who taught Strategy and Civil-Military Relations at the Argentine Army Staff College, and is now at King's College, London.

I must thank my Publisher Leo Cooper for agreeing to publish this revised edition, and my Literary Agent Jane Gregory for her support. Jane Thompson was, as ever, a tireless assistant. Her advice and support were invaluable.

Julian Thompson
London 1991

PREFACE TO THIRD EDITION

Since the Second Edition, another nine years have passed, yet more books have been published (notably by Ewen Southby-Tailyour and Mike Clapp, both of whom figure prominently in this book), and more information has emerged about the Falklands War of 1982. I have also had the opportunity to discuss a number of issues with Admiral 'Sandy' Woodward. As a result it is now clear to me that the misunderstandings and friction that manifested themselves between him and the other two Task Group commanders forward in the Theatre of Operations in 1982, and alluded to in the Second Edition, would have been considerably less burdensome, or might never have arisen at all, had the command structure for Corporate, as the operation was codenamed, been better. This is explained as the story unfolds, and other than saying that the fault was lack of an overall commander in-theatre, I will not burden the reader by rehearsing all the arguments in the Preface. Suffice it to say that I sensed at the time that my staff found it troubling, although I did not discuss it with them, and some years later, a senior naval officer told me that, at one stage, he feared for the success of the operation. But all's well that ends well, and Corporate did end well. The lesson was learned, and afterwards plans were put in hand to ensure that there would be an overall commander in-theatre on future operations.

I must thank Angus MacKinnon for agreeing to publish this revised edition, and my Literary Agent Jane Gregory for her support and work on my behalf. Jane Thompson was always a source of encouragement and editorial advice in this endeavour.

Julian Thompson
London 2000

CHAPTER ONE

Alarm and Excursion

From the ships docked in the harbour
New horizons will appear.
I'm going Southbound.
So tonight after sundown
You must go from this place
Without a tear, without a frown,
Disappear without a trace.
I'm going Southbound.

From *Southbound* by Phil Lynott and sung by Band Corporal Henry Moneghan to large audiences on the voyage South.

'You know those people down south: they're about to be invaded. Your Brigade is to come to seventy-two hours' notice to move with effect from now.'

It was 3.15 am on Friday 2 April, 1982, and I had been woken by a telephone call. The caller was Major-General Jeremy Moore, the Major-General Commanding Commando Forces, Royal Marines.

At the time of this telephone call, my Brigade, 3 Commando Brigade, Royal Marines, was at its normal seven days' notice to move. Giving a military unit a specific notice to move is normal practice and in theory any shortening-in of the time should be a step-by-step process within the overall time scale. So, for example, a brigade at seven days' notice to move on 2 April should not be required to move before 9 April and a reduction to seventy-two hours' notice ordered on 2 April, but to take effect on 6 April probably couched thus: 'On 6 April you are to come to seventy-two hours' notice to move.'

However, 3 Commando Brigade RM was quite accustomed to theory being discarded in favour of practicality.

The people 'down south' referred to by General Moore on the telephone were the inhabitants of the Falkland Islands. Before 2 April, 1982, few people in Britain could have said with any accuracy where the Falkland

Islands are. But the Royal Marines' involvement with the Islands goes back over 200 years and for the last thirty years the Corps has provided a garrison of about forty-five men, known as Naval Party 8901.

The islands in the Falklands group lie about 400 miles (650 km) due east of Southern Argentina and 350 miles (550 km) north-east of Cape Horn. The land mass of 4,700 square miles is roughly three-quarters of the area of Sicily or the same as that of the state of Connecticut. The first recorded landing was made in 1690 by Captain John Strong from Plymouth in Devonshire who named the sound which separates the two main islands Falkland Sound after the then Commissioner of the Admiralty, Lord Falkland. In 1767 British Marines erected a wooden blockhouse at Port Egmont in West Falkland and from 1833 there has been a continuous British presence on the Islands. Argentina laid claim to the Islands on the break-up of the Spanish Empire in the early nineteenth century, and for five years, from 1826 to 1831, established a colony there. But the Governor foolishly arrested two United States fishing vessels for poaching and retribution, in the shape of the corvette USS *Lexington*, was swift. The Americans destroyed the Argentine settlement and the Royal Navy re-asserted Britain's right to the Islands on 2 January, 1833.

Argentina has never given up her claim to the Islands and it seems that from about December, 1981, when Galtieri took office, the ruling junta started planning to seize them. Whether planned or not, the spark that set off the train of events that followed was the landing of a group of Argentine scrap metal merchants in South Georgia in March, 1982. South Georgia lies 800 miles (1300 km) south-east of the Falklands and, until April, 1982, was permanently inhabited by only thirty members of the British Antarctic Survey.

The Argentines invaded the Falkland Islands on 2 April and South Georgia on 3 April, 1982.

Why the Commando Brigade was given so little warning is a mystery. It is now public knowledge that from 29 March, 1982, the Staff at Fleet Headquarters at Northwood had been taking precautionary measures in case the Argentines invaded the Falklands. On the same day Admiral Fieldhouse, the Fleet Commander, ordered Rear Admiral Woodward, the Flag Officer First Flotilla, then at Gibraltar exercising with sixteen frigates and destroyers, to prepare plans for the detachment of a task group to the South Atlantic. On 31 March intelligence was received in London that the Falklands would be invaded on 2 April. At Downing Street the Prime Minister conferred with the Secretary of State for Defence, John Nott, two Junior Foreign Office Ministers, and Admiral Leach, the First Sea Lord, standing-in for the Chief of the Defence Staff, who was out of the country. As a result of this meeting, Admiral Leach was ordered 'to prepare a force which he had advised would be required to retake the islands "without commitment to a final decision as to whether it should sail".'

On 1 April Major-General Moore, my immediate superior, was handing back command of the Royal Marines to Lieutenant-General Pringle, on the latter's return from convalescence after his severe injury at the hands of the Provisional IRA. This hand-over took place in the same building occupied by the Naval Staff, and one floor above the First Sea Lord's office, yet no hint of what was to come was given to the Royal Marines.

My Brigade, the force which would have to land and retake the islands, and without whom the sailing of a task force, except as a gesture, would be pointless, remained blissfully ignorant that our services might be required.

The commanding officer of 40 Commando, it is true, had been warned in vague terms that his commando might have to travel to the Falkland Islands to pre-empt an invasion. Soon the requirement was reduced to a company. But he was not allowed to make any preparations, including bringing his men to shorter notice, nor was it revealed how the commando, or the company, would get to the scene. Even in a ship steaming at 30 knots, the journey would take over eleven days, and a more realistic time would be fourteen to sixteen. The airfield at Stanley was too short to take long-range transports, and at that time British C-130 aircraft, capable of landing at Stanley airport, were not fitted with air-to-air refuelling probes. The only way to Stanley by air would have been via Argentina.

Soon the commando was stood down and part of the Commando Brigade Air Defence Troop, with their Blowpipe shoulder-launched surface-to-air missiles, was warned that they might be needed. Their method of transport to the Falklands was also left unresolved, leading to facetious speculation that they might travel on Argentine civil airlines, posing as musicians, with their Blowpipes in double-bass cases. By 31 March, the day of the Downing Street meeting, the Air Defence Troop had been stood down.

That evening I returned to Plymouth from a reconnaissance for a NATO exercise in Denmark. Major Gullan of my staff briefed me on the order, counter-order that had been imposed on units of my Brigade over the previous two days. On 1 April I was told over the telephone by my superior headquarters that none of the brigade was on anything other than the normal seven days' notice. On that day, two carriers HMS *Hermes* and HMS *Invincible*, were ordered to come to 48 hours' notice for sea.

I went to bed under the impression that no British reaction to Argentine military moves was being contemplated and, even if it was, my Brigade would not be involved. I was not alone in this; as Captain Gardiner noted in his diary:

At midday on Friday 2 April, 45 Commando was due to go on Easter leave. At 5 o'clock that morning I was informed by telephone that the Commando had been recalled. It was as well the Argentines had not invaded the day before; nobody would have believed it. It was a pretty peculiar feeling being called to war by telephone from one's bed. Time has not dimmed the memory of the sensation.

3 Commando Brigade Royal Marines forms the major part of the combined United Kingdom/Netherlands Landing Force contribution to the Amphibious Forces of the NATO Alliance. The three commandos which provide the infantry for the Brigade are roughly equivalent in size to British non-mechanized infantry battalions. Each commando has three rifle companies each of about 120 men, a support company and a headquarters company.

The rifle companies consist of a company headquarters and three troops each of about thirty men, which are further divided into a troop headquarters and three sections. A rifle troop in a Royal Marines Commando is broadly similar in organization to a platoon in a British Army non-mechanized infantry battalion. Rifle troops, and platoons, are commanded by second-lieutenants or lieutenants, like Lieutenant Dytor of 45 Commando and Lieutenant Bickerdike of 3 Para. The seconds-in-command of troops and platoons are sergeants like Sergeant McKay of 3 Para and Sergeant Collins of 42 Commando. Rifle sections are commanded by lance-corporals or corporals like Corporal Newland of 42 Commando, Corporal Siddell of 45 Commando and Corporal Bailey of 3 Para. We shall meet them, and others like them, later. Rifle troop weapons are the standard British self-loading 7.62 mm rifle, which does not fire in bursts like a machine gun; one 7.62 mm General Purpose Machine Gun (GPMG) for each section; a Carl Gustav (84 mm) Medium Anti-Tank Weapon (MAW) in each troop headquarters; and 66 mm Light Anti-Tank Weapons (LAW) in rifle sections. The two commandos earmarked for Arctic operations in North Norway also have one Light Machine Gun (LMG) in each rifle section. This extra automatic fire power was to prove invaluable in battle.

Each commando support company has a mortar troop equipped with six 81 mm mortars and an anti-tank troop equipped with fourteen Milan anti-tank wire-guided missiles. Once again these are broadly similar to their counterparts in the British Army. However, the Royal Marines differ from the British Army, at least at the time of the Falklands Campaign, in that support company also has a reconnaissance troop and assault engineer troop. The commando reconnaissance troops, although small in size, are commanded by a trained mountain leader officer and contain NCOs and Marine specialists in mountain work and sniping. The assault engineer troops are trained in combat engineer skills such as mine clearance and demolitions.

They provide each Commanding Officer with small teams of engineers in addition to any that may be allocated by the Brigade Commander from the Commando Engineer Squadron.

The Artillery Regiment, 29 Commando Regiment Royal Artillery, which supports the Brigade, has three gun batteries each equipped with six 105 mm light guns (the TA battery which provides the fourth gun battery in the Regiment did not take part in the campaign). The Regiment also has a battery trained and equipped to control and spot naval gunfire — 148 Forward Observation Battery. The observers and their teams in 148 Battery are trained to land ahead of the main force by helicopter, small boat, submarine or parachute in order to spot for the ships firing in support of the main landing. During the campaign they did just this, but their method of landing was by helicopter or small boats, not by parachute or submarine. The Commando Gunners are all volunteers from the British Army and have passed the same rigorous commando course as their Royal Marine counterparts. They are justifiably proud of their special role as an élite gunner regiment. Their links with the Royal Marines Commandos are close and based on years of working together on operations from Aden and Borneo to Northern Ireland (in the infantry role) and on frequent exercises from the Far East to Norway. The Commanding Officer of the Regiment was Lieutenant-Colonel Holroyd-Smith, Royal Artillery, a large, outspoken man with a genial manner and gruff voice who never seemed put out by anything. As the Commander of the Commando Brigade's Artillery Regiment he had been my gunner adviser for over a year. His direct, frank manner and sound tactical knowledge had been a considerable asset on exercises and reconnaissance over the past year and were to make him a tower of strength in the days that lay ahead.

Combat Engineer Support for the Commando Brigade is provided by 59 Independent Commando Squadron Royal Engineers of the British Army and the only independent engineer squadron in the United Kingdom order of battle. Bound to the Commando Brigade by the common experience of the Commando Course and its outward symbol, the green beret, the Squadron is fiercely proud of its independent status and ability to march and fight as infantry in addition to the wealth of engineer expertise it offers the Commando Brigade. The Squadron was commanded by Major Macdonald, Royal Engineers, a tall, prematurely grey-haired man, very fit and intelligent, with a great sense of fun. Macdonald was an ex-Para Engineer, a ski-mountaineer, the current Army Hang-Gliding Champion and lately Joint Services Hang-Gliding Champion. He was also a highly professional officer who planned ahead. 'As a result of studies I had made in 1981,' he wrote, 'I had already noted an operational weakness [in the Squadron], that of lack of specialist forward engineer recce troops for offensive as well as intelligence-gathering operations. As a result I had formed, on a trial basis, a recce troop in January, 1982, which had a Royal Marine Officer, Lieutenant Kendall Carpenter, as troop officer under the Troop Commander, Lieutenant Livingstone. This Recce Troop had been trained with Recce Troop 40 Commando for three months [by early April, 1982].' This planning by Macdonald was to pay dividends in the Falklands.

The Commando Brigade is unique in the British Services in that all its logistic sub-units are grouped into the Commando Logistic Regiment. The Royal Marines, soldiers and sailors in the five squadrons — medical, transport, workshop, ordnance and headquarters — are all commando-trained and knit together by their loyalty to the green beret. They are trained to march, shoot and dig like infantry and are just as fit. Another sub-unit with a mixture of Royal Marines, army and a few navy is the Commando Brigade Air Squadron. At the time of the campaign the Brigade Air Squadron was equipped with Gazelle and Scout helicopters. The Anglo/French Gazelle was brought into service in the British Forces as an unarmed reconnaissance and liaison helicopter. It is fast, easy to fly and provides a good observation platform, provided it is not flown into areas where it is likely to come under direct enemy fire. The metal construction and cramped space inside ('Built out of Bacofoil and designed by narrow-hipped Frenchmen' complain some pilots) does not make it particularly suitable for carrying troops festooned with personal equipment, radios and weapons, even when the back seats are removed.

The old Scout, affectionately referred to as being 'built like a brick shithouse', had been converted years before to fire the SS11 anti-tank wire-guided missile, and the anti-tank periscope sight, when fitted, provided an excellent viewing device. It allowed observation from behind cover with the helicopter fuselage out of sight and only the rotor head and periscope in view to the enemy. As it turned out, the Scout was to operate in the SS11 firing role only once in the Falklands campaign. However, its sturdy construction and flat rear floor, once the back seats were removed, made it very suitable for carrying small numbers of troops and particularly for casualty evacuation. Both types of light helicopter did sterling service in the campaign, although in the event some of the roles in which they were employed had not been envisaged for them before May, 1982.

The Headquarters and Signals Squadron provides the communications for the Brigade Commander to fight the battle and this is standard throughout the British Army. However, unlike Army brigades, the Headquarters and Signals Squadron in 3 Commando Brigade also includes an Air Defence Troop and a Raiding Squadron in its organization. The Air Defence Troop is manned entirely by Royal Marines trained to operate the Blowpipe surface-to-air missile and is the only air defence organization permanently part of 3 Commando Brigade. Similar troops in the Army are manned by the Royal Artillery.

The First Raiding Squadron Royal Marines (1RSRM) man both inflatable and rigid raiding craft. It was the latter they took to the Falklands. The coxswains of these craft are all Marines or corporals. As Royal Marines they are trained commando soldiers and capable of defending, camouflaging and concealing their craft in the small Forward Operating Bases (FOBs) which they set up ashore. Whether landing special forces, carrying out ammunition resupply or providing a means of transport for the Brigade Commander and his staff, these small craft driven by expert small boat seamen were to prove invaluable during the campaign.

The instructors in mountain and arctic warfare who train 3 Commando Brigade in its NATO role in Norway in winter and who provide the necessary mountain and climbing leaders in the commandos are trained by the Mountain and Arctic Warfare Cadre (M and AW Cadre). For at least one year before the Falklands campaign, I had used the M and AW Cadre as my Brigade Reconnaissance Troop. With training in morse and long-range communications added to their already confirmed skills of survival in adverse conditions, and the ability to reach and return from almost inaccessible positions in the mountains, the M and AW Cadre was ideally suited to the task of medium-range reconnaissance and surveillance both ahead of and on the flanks of the Commando Brigade. In this role they filled the gap between the local reconnaissance tasks performed for the commandos by their own reconnaissance troops and the long range, often strategic, reconnaissance, executed by SBS and SAS. The Commander of the M and AW Cadre, the ebullient Captain Boswell, was well known to me, having been my Reconnaissance Troop Commander in 40 Commando some years earlier. On 2 April, 1982, the Cadre was still running a course for grade-two Mountain Leaders (ML2). The course went to war with its instructors. When I visited them in their ship on the passage south, I asked them what they thought of this final exercise that had been organized for them.

1982 had started with a squeeze on defence spending which had resulted in fewer units of the Commando Brigade deploying to Norway for winter training than is usually the case. The only commando to go was 42 Commando and with it went one commando battery and elements from the other supporting units in the Brigade — such as engineers, logistics and air squadron. 45 Commando had settled down to mountain training in Scotland after a hard tour in Belfast in the latter half of 1981, but they sent one company to Brunei for jungle training, as part of the Royal Marines' policy of keeping the expertise alive. 40 Commando also embarked on a period of training in Great Britain.

For many years the Royal Marines had trained in the harsh environment of Norway both in winter and summer and 45 Commando with a battery and other supporting elements had exercised in Norway in winter every year since 1973. The numbers deployed to Norway had steadily increased until in 1980 and 1981 a brigade of 3,500 men trained there for two and a half months each year. The wealth of skills gained in operating in this harsh climate permeated the whole Brigade; officers, NCOs and older Marines with five to six Norwegian winters under their belts were commonplace. Many of the newcomers to the winter training scene, from units shut out of the 1982 winter training by the moratorium on defence spending, were included in special cadre courses run in Norway for their benefit. Even those with no winter experience had their commando course, with its demanding standards behind them. The well-remembered cries of the instructors, 'It's in the mind' or 'It's only pain', would serve to remind them that they could 'hack it'. The fruits of ten years' experience in Norway were to be seen in the kit with which every man was equipped and, as important, the knowledge of how to use it properly. Except for the boots, which failed to keep men's feet dry or warm, the equipment was excellent. It is hard to imagine a brigade more suited to the tasks that lay ahead. The quality of its men, the professionalism at all levels in operating in a harsh climate and years of practice in amphibious exercises meant that the moment of crisis found the men trained to meet it.

When that moment arrived in the early hours of 2 April, 1982, it found 40 Commando returning from personal weapon training near Liverpool, 42 Commando on leave, having just returned from Norway, and 45 Commando in Scotland about to go on leave that day, but with one company in Hong Kong en route home from Brunei. The rest of the Brigade was in the Plymouth area about to go on leave. However, most of the key Staff officers of the Brigade Headquarters were in Denmark on a reconnaissance for a NATO exercise later that year, and much of the heavy equipment that had accompanied the units in Norway was still at sea.

The initial few moments of surprise at the sudden news of the Argentine invasion of the Falkland Islands were soon overcome as well-practised procedures swung into action. For many of the older members of the Brigade, alarms and excursions at minimal notice had been the pattern of their lives for years. Among one and all was the feeling of intense satisfaction that there was a job to do and pride that they had been chosen to do it. This close-knit family, with differing cap badges in their green berets, set to with a will. As Gardiner noted in his diary:

> The next half hour was spent scarting (sic) around in torchlight trying to get some kit together. I was in camp, ready to go almost anywhere by 0600. ... In spite of the lack of notice and the fact that we should have gone on leave that very day (some had already gone), it is with

more than a little pride that I can say that the entire Commando could have deployed with its stores thirty-six hours after the button was pressed.

While the bulk of the Brigade Staff were returning to England from Denmark at best possible speed, I moved from my own Headquarters five minutes drive up the road to Hamoaze House, the Devonport Headquarters of the Major-General Commanding Commando Forces, Major-General Moore. I took those of my staff left in England, Captain Rowe, the GSO 3 Intelligence, Major Gullan (Para), the GSO 3 SD/Air and Major Baldwin, who had recently handed over as DAA & QMG and was recalled from leave at 3.30 that morning. All three were to play important roles in the days that followed. Rowe, a tall, good-looking Welshman with a dry sense of humour and a low tolerance for fools, had commanded a rifle company with distinction in the Sultan of Oman's Armed Forces during the Dhofar war. Gullan, on exchange from the Parachute Regiment, already decorated with a Military Cross and MBE, was a fine soldier, brave and enthusiastic. Not until 2 Para joined the Brigade did it emerge that his nickname was 'Hector the Corrector'. Baldwin's quick wit and well-developed sense of humour combined with his brilliance as a logistician made him a good officer by any standards.

The shift to Hamoaze House proved to be the right move, for my staff and I were thus on hand as the information flowed in to our superior Headquarters. In the first two days this mainly concerned shipping to move the Brigade. At first the allocation changed hourly, but remained inadequate to move even the manpower of the Brigade, let alone its combat supplies. There is no point in moving men and weapons to battle if they have no ammunition to fire at the enemy, no food to eat, no fuel for vehicles and aircraft, and no spares with which to repair or replace damaged weapons and equipment. This point is often overlooked by those who have no experience of war.

The breakthrough came during the afternoon of 3 April with the welcome news that the P & O liner SS *Canberra*, the second largest in the British Merchant Navy, was to be requisitioned. Soon other 'Ships' were 'Taken Up From Trade', inelegantly called STUFT, starting with the P & O Ferrymasters ferry MV *Elk*, to augment the RN ships providing the troop and stores lift for 3 Commando Brigade.

At first there was very little information on which to base planning. It was not until 10.30 am on 2 April that confirmation was received that the Argentines had invaded the Falklands. The major effort at this stage was to get everybody back from leave or duty to their unit bases, and start the movement of the Brigade War Maintenance Reserve out of the depots to the ports at which the ships would be loaded. Moving the men would be the easy part, moving the War Maintenance Reserve, the 4,500 tons of ammunition, food and spares, the combat supplies that a Brigade needs to sustain itself in battle, demanded considerable planning and skill. Few people had to be told what to do. Solutions to problems were worked out and then submitted for approval before being implemented.

As Macdonald wrote:

> The voice on the telephone was tense: it was Major Hector Gullan. He suggested that I should come down to HQ Commando Forces as quickly as possible to see the Brigadier. Within minutes I was down at Hamoaze House, there were maps of the Falkland Islands everywhere. ...
>
> The Brigadier explained to me that there was a crisis involving the Falkland Islands. We were to deploy to sea within 72 hours on medium scales, which I was to decide and was there anything I wanted. I replied immediately that I wanted three Combat Engineer Tractors (CET) and armoured engineer crews from Bovington.

It was decided at an early stage in planning to take the minimum number of wheeled vehicles. The going anywhere in the Falklands away from the settlements was so bad that even a lightly loaded Landrover would be lucky to cover four miles an hour. Vehicles loaded with ammunition and stores would be lucky to move at all. The Brigade did have seventy-six of its BV202 oversnow vehicles in England, the remainder being stockpiled in Norway. Although designed to operate over snow there was a good chance that these vehicles with a ground pressure of only 1½lbs per square inch, about that of a man on skis, would be able to motor across the peat bog. Events were to prove that they could.

At this stage it was important to get together as soon as possible with my opposite number the Commodore Amphibious Warfare (COMAW), Commodore Clapp. Clapp, an ex-Naval Observer and Buccaneer Squadron Commander, was a genial Westcountryman with wide experience as seaman, aviator and staff officer. He was a practical man with considerable moral and physical courage. He was to need both in the weeks ahead. On 2 April he was absent from his Plymouth Headquarters, visiting his immediate superior the Flag Officer 3rd Flotilla at Portsmouth. As the likely commander of the Amphibious Task Force which would include all ships which would transport and land the Commando Brigade, it was vital that the Commodore was co-located with the Brigade Commander as soon as possible. He was soon on his way and, with his Staff, joined us at Hamoaze House on the evening of 2 April.

With the arrival of the remainder of the Brigade Staff from Denmark, also on the evening of 2 April, the planning machinery, which had been gathering momentum during the day, moved into top gear. Units were soon being added to the Commando Brigade and very welcome they were too. A complete list of the units in 3 Commando Brigade is shown in the notes to this chapter on pages 161-2.

The first to join was the 3rd Battalion the Parachute Regiment (3 Para). The Commanding Officer, Pike, a Wykehamist, was known to me from our time at the Army Staff College at Camberley. It was good to have this tough, well-trained Battalion added to the order of battle of the Commando Brigade. Although fierce rivalry exists between the wearers of the green and red berets there is also a good deal of mutual respect. Parachute battalions are organized very much the same as commandos, the only — and quite significant — difference being that each parachute battalion has a patrol company divided into two platoons and commanded by an experienced major. In 3 Para, D Company was designated Patrol Company, in 2 Para it was C Company. These patrol companies, larger than commando reconnaissance troops, were to provide excellent information for their Commanding Officers during the campaign.

A very important and welcome addition to the Brigade at an early stage was T Battery (Shah Sujah's Troop) Royal Artillery, equipped with twelve Rapier surface-to-air missile launchers. Their inclusion in the Commando Brigade, despite the difficulty of finding shipping space for them, was greeted with enthusiasm as the details of the fighters and bombers the Argentines had available began to emerge. None of this information was coming from MOD at this stage, but Captain Rowe, his Second-in-Command, Colour-Sergeant Smith, and their team worked hard to cull an enemy air order of battle out of books available to the public, such as *The Military Balance* and *Jane's All The World's Aircraft*.

Another welcome augmentation were the two troops of the Blues and Royals (RHG/D) each equipped with two Scimitar and two Scorpion light tanks, with their Samson recovery vehicle making a total of nine light armoured vehicles. At about the same time the Band of Commando Forces Royal Marines was added to the Brigade. Trained as stretcher-bearers and in First Aid, the intention was for the Band to be based in SS *Canberra* initially and possibly come ashore later.

On Sunday, 4 April all Commanding Officers were summoned to Hamoaze House for a briefing. Concurrently, their adjutants and other staff were being briefed at a mounting meeting to give them details of which ships they would be loaded into, where and when. It was a remarkable effort by the Staffs that in just over forty-eight hours, without warning and with no contingency plan, they had prepared the staff tables for a greatly expanded Brigade to load into shipping, much of which had only been allocated a matter of hours before the mounting meeting. Although loading was to change in detail before the Force sailed and considerably at Ascension, this does not detract from the hard work and professionalism of the Staffs. Without years of experience in amphibious procedure behind them, it is doubtful that they could have achieved what they did in the time, the one commodity which was in short supply.

At the Brigade briefing, Commanding Officers were given as full an intelligence picture as could be gleaned from information available at the time, which was very little. Major Southby-Tailyour gave an excellent terrain briefing on the Falkland Islands. Southby-Tailyour, described by Max Hastings as an adventurer who found his moment, had spent much of his time during a one-year tour of duty in the Falklands some years before, conducting private surveys of the beaches for a yachtsman's guide to the Islands. If he had lived 400 years ago he might have sailed with Drake or Hawkins. He was to be a leading player in the business of defeating the descendants of the people the Elizabethan sea-dogs had harried so successfully 400 years before. Southby-Tailyour was followed by Lieutenant Veal, Royal Navy, who had just returned from the Joint Services' Expedition to South Georgia and gave a terrain brief. I then gave my views on how events were likely to unfold over the following weeks and said what training was to be carried out while the Brigade was on passage. I later followed this up with a signal to all units laying down the priorities for this training.

Immediately after the briefing the Commodore and I flew by helicopter to Admiral Fieldhouse's headquarters at Northwood, giving them plenty of warning. With us came Major-General Moore, whose headquarters was responsible for outloading my Brigade, and Southby-Tailyour. On arrival, we could see no helipad. The pilot consulted his helicopter landing site directory. Apparently this major NATO and national headquarters did not have a helipad. The pilot tried to put down in a playground adjacent to the headquarters. Frantic housewives dashed out of the houses bordering the playground as the rotor downwash blew away their washing and covered them with dust. Fearful of our treatment at the hands of the women, who by now were trying to hold down their skirts, retrieve their washing, cover their ears and shake their fists at us, we beat a retreat to seek another place to set down. A games field some distance away was the best we could find.

As we stepped out of the helicopter a Land-rover appeared. This was the landing-site for the headquarters, we were informed. The pilot's comment on organizations that fail to notify or mark the location of their helipads was unrepeatable. The atmosphere of farce which marked our arrival persisted. Nobody seemed to know why we had come. We explained that, as the commanders intimately involved with executing Britain's response to the Argentine invasion, we were trying to find out what was required of us.

We sat down with some of the staff and, after listening to administrative details which concerned the carriers, but appeared to have no bearing on the amphibious operation, we were asked for our views on how amphibious operations might be conducted. As at this stage we had not been given a mission, or any other direction other than to get the Brigade loaded and to sea as quickly as possible, this came as a surprise. At one stage we were taken to see Admiral Fieldhouse. We both made two points. First, that a head-on assault in the vicinity of Port Stanley, or anywhere else that was strongly held, should be avoided. The British did not possess the equipment to make this possible. This was agreed. Second, it was vital that air superiority, at least over the beachhead area, was achieved before any landing was attempted. This we were promised.

We followed up by asking if HMS *Intrepid*, sister ship to *Fearless*, could be made available as we might need more landing craft. We stressed the need for more assault helicopters. We were given little hope that these requests would be met, and were given the impression that we must cope with what was available at the time. We felt we would be at a severe disadvantage.

Present at the meeting was Rear Admiral Reffell, the Flag Officer Third Flotilla, normally the commander of all the amphibious ships and the carriers. He had commanded the commando helicopter carrier, HMS *Albion*, had been the Commodore Amphibious Warfare, and was now Clapp's immediate superior. He was the Flag Officer with the most amphibious experience in the Navy, and probably the most training for the type of conventional maritime warfare we expected. His staff consisted of the right mix of specialists for joint operations, including aviators. He whole-heartedly supported both the points we made at this meagre briefing. Both Clapp and I hoped that his presence at Northwood meant that his experience would be called on, while we prepared our forces for whatever was required. With luck, he would be appointed the overall commander.

We climbed back into our helicopter. It was some time before we voiced what was in our minds. We were not impressed.

The following day I flew by helicopter to Brize Norton to debrief the Royal Marine detachment captured in the Falklands and returned to England. This was a wasted trip, and in hindsight it should have been apparent to me that they would have nothing to offer about the Argentine order of battle, or anything else that would be relevant by the time we arrived in the South Atlantic. They were in sombre mood, and thoroughly depressed. It is hard to blame them. It is not pleasant acting as a trip-wire.

The only light relief was provided by the junior minister tasked with meeting them. He kept interrupting to remind us that if we persisted in our questioning, he and the detachment would be late for tea with the Prime Minister, a prospect that he clearly did not relish. I resisted the temptation to remark that as the politicians had got themselves into this mess, they might at least allow those of us who were tasked with extracting them the opportunity to glean as much information as we could.

The last of the troop and stores ships in the first wave to leave the United Kingdom sailed on 9 April — MV *Elk* loaded with vehicles, ammunition and stores and SS *Canberra* carrying the majority of 40 Commando RM, 42 Commando RM and 3 Para. In overall charge of the embarked troops in *Canberra* was Colonel Seccombe, brought in at the last moment at my request as Deputy Brigade Commander. Seccombe was an old friend. He was an experienced soldier who, among other things, had commanded a company in the Borneo campaign and a commando in Northern Ireland and Cyprus, always with considerable style and to great effect. On one occasion he carried a wounded Gurkha rifleman through the jungle on his back for two days after a battle with the Indonesians deep inside Indonesia. His sense of humour and abundant common sense were to be a priceless asset during the voyage south, controlling the three strong-willed Commanding Officers embarked in *Canberra*, who for days on end were not under the eye of their Brigade Commander. In the darkest moments that lay ahead after the landing he was a tower of strength. Except for those flying to Ascension most of the Brigade was now at sea. It would be substantially reinforced before the landings seven weeks later, as we shall see, but that was all in the future. What was needed now was to plan for what lay ahead, shake down in the ships and, above all, prepare physically and mentally for battle.

CHAPTER TWO

Mid-Atlantic Interlude

Ascension is a small, volcanic dustheap in the South Atlantic, over 4,000 miles from England, nearly 4,000 miles from the Falklands and situated about half-way between Brazil and Africa. The only greenery on Ascension is the tropical rain forest on the summit and upper slopes of Green Mountain. All else is razor-sharp rock that rips boots to bits and great conical mounds of dust and volcanic clinker. The long, South Atlantic swell beats ceaselessly on the Island's rocky coast. Deceptively calm when viewed from the deck of a large ship, the swell made any landing by conventional landing craft out of the question, except in a little cove at English Bay. Here the beach was wide enough for one Landing Craft Utility (LCU) at a time (1). There is no port on the island; all supplies arrive by air or are offloaded from boats at anchor offshore into lighters which brave the swell and the surf to land their loads on the small jetty at Georgetown, the capital.

The 11,000 foot runway at the island's Wideawake airfield is its most valuable asset. It was on this airfield and nowhere else that helicopters from the Amphibious Task Group could land. The risk of dust ingestion, and the consequent ruining of engines made helicopter landings elsewhere a non-starter. No training areas or ranges existed on the island. Great ingenuity and co-operation was shown by Mr Don Coffey, the Pan-Am Manager on Ascension, in suggesting areas for ranges and providing targets for firing live ammunition by the Commando Brigade. Valuable though this live firing was, there was no scope for manoeuvre, or any other form of training other than marching and shooting.

The Commando Brigade arrived at Ascension over a number of days, starting with X Company 45 Commando by air on 13 April. They and Y Company, who also flew in, made good use of the few days they had on their own before the rest of the Brigade arrived by sea and hordes of airmen and sailors poured in by air from the United Kingdom to operate this mid-ocean staging post.

'We enjoyed our stay ... the position was sufficiently chaotic for people to be glad not to be interested in us. So we conducted ourselves largely to our own satisfaction at the far end of the island and completed the most worthwhile training programme I think I have ever seen,' wrote Gardiner. Not everybody was so lucky!

As the Commando Brigade sailed south in eleven different ships (2) the command structure for the campaign ahead began to emerge.

Task Force Commander
Admiral Fieldhouse at
Northwood, Middlesex
(throughout the
Campaign)

Commander Carrier Battle Group Rear-Admiral Woodward	Commander Amphibious Task Group (Amphibious Ships (2)) Commodore Clapp	Commander Landing Force Task Group (3 Cdo Bde RM) Brigadier Thompson

South Georgia Task Group Captain of HMS *Antrim*   Sub-Surface Task Group

The Task Force was commanded from Northwood and the Task Group Commanders reported direct to that Headquarters. Major-General Moore, who became Land Deputy to the Task Force Commander during the planning of the operation, joined the Landing Force on D+9 (30 May, nine days after the landing at San Carlos) with the second brigade (5 Infantry Brigade). Until than I commanded all land forces on the Falkland Islands.

There was one key player missing from this chain of command: a three-star (Vice Admiral) operational level commander interposed between Fieldhouse, the Task Force Commander at Northwood, and the three group commanders tasked with the Falklands operation, Woodward, Clapp and I. We all reported back directly to Northwood, eventually 8,000 miles away. Woodward is sometimes incorrectly described as the Task Force commander, and this was entirely due to the 'woolly' command set-up. At times Northwood would treat him as the overall commander down south, asking him for opinions and decisions that were outside the remit of his role of commander of the Carrier Battle Group, but without informing us that they had done so. Clapp and I were repeatedly assured that as the senior, he would arbitrate over shared assets, deciding where they would be allocated if dissension arose. His role was described as 'Primus inter pares', but left control and responsibility firmly with the Task Group Commanders. It was an uncomfortable compromise, leaving much to personalities, requiring a degree of tolerance and understanding all round; two characteristics which are often in short supply under stress. Woodward was put in a difficult position by this imprecise command organisation, but to his credit refused to try to take charge of me, despite being ordered on one occasion to do so.

A three-star operational level commander, riding initially perhaps with General Moore, in a ship with the right communication fit, such as *Glamorgan* or *Antrim*, built with accommodation for a Flag Officer and staff, would have invaluable. Positioned forward in the operational area, he could have drawn together the strands of the carrier, amphibious and landing force battles. He could have decided on priorities, seen for himself what was happening and removed the sources of friction. Perhaps most useful of all, he could have taken the responsibility for speaking direct to Northwood off the backs of the busy group commanders.

Clapp and I hoped this task would fall to Reffell, who could have been given the appropriate rank. Instead, Refell had to send his Staff Aviation Officer to augment Woodward's staff. Clapp and I assumed that the submarine 'mafia' was responsible for this decision, Fieldhouse and Woodward being submariners. Later I learned this was not the case.

HMS *Fearless*, carrying Commodore Clapp and myself and our staffs, steamed ahead of the remainder of the Amphibious Task Group to meet the Task Force Commander, Admiral Fieldhouse, at Ascension. Admiral Fieldhouse brought with him his Air Deputy, Air Marshall Curtiss, and his Land Deputy, Major-General Moore, for what is best described as a Council of War in HMS *Hermes* on 17 April. The day before, Rear-Admiral Woodward, Commodore Clapp and I had met so that Woodward could be briefed on the progress of planning in the Amphibious and Landing Force Task Groups.

Neither Clapp nor I had had a chance to talk to Woodward earlier; indeed I had never met him. Before he arrived on *Fearless*, he was described in enthusiastic terms by Captain Larken, a fellow submariner. I now know that he is an intelligent and sensitive man, calm in the face of danger and unflappable in a crisis. He was, and is, highly regarded by some within his own service. Unfortunately, his style at that first meeting was totally at odds with mine, and Clapp's, and I now know why. Unknown to us at the time, he arrived on board having been told by Northwood to examine the feasibility of landing on *West Falkland* [author's emphasis], and establishing an airstrip capable of operating Phantom air-defence fighters there. The rationale behind this grotesque notion being that having established a foothold, negotiations could then be carried out with Argentina on the future of the islands. Apart from the fact that the proposed site for the airstrip was about as close to the Argentine mainland airbases as it was possible to get without actually being in the sea, my engineers had neither the plant nor the numbers to carry out such an ambitious scheme. Landing on West Falkland would also necessitate another amphibious operation on East Falkland, if the Argentines refused to budge, and this itself was reason enough not to contemplate such a move. Had we been put into the picture on the West Falkland option from the outset, we might have been in a position to thrash it out together and give a reasoned response, instead of greeting the idea with scorn and contempt. Having been invited to investigate the possibility, without knowing where it originated, we wasted a great deal of time in discussion, and my sappers spent hours examining the technical aspects in order to provide me with ammunition to kill the idea should it come up again. The responsibility for the ensuing acrimony rests largely with Northwood. It is simply not good enough to promulgate a structure of three co-equal commanders, and then arbitrarily, and without ever telling the other two, treat one of the commanders as if he was the overall boss on some occasions, which they did a number of times. Although to be fair, Northwood was faced at short notice with an amphibious landing followed by a land campaign, two phases of war of which they had no experience, even on exercises.

The air was considerably cleared at the Council of War the next day. The command chain, for all its imperfections, removed any doubts about who was subordinate to whom, at least as far as I was concerned. Another of Clapp's and my worries was also addressed: we were promised that the air battle would be won before a landing was attempted. This was the second occasion we were given such an assurance. Within hindsight, I was naive not to question such a bland statement, which a few moments' analysis would have exposed as being a fabrication, unless the Argentine Air Force was stupid, or we were to interdict Argentine mainland airfields.

Woodward stated that from about the end of May the severe South Atlantic weather and pace of operations would being to take their toll on ship serviceability. He forecast that by about mid to late June, equipment failure on the majority of warships with the original task groups would cause severe restrictions on their operational capability. This naval sustainability limitation was ultimately to have a profound effect on the land battle. Not least, it reduced the time for the pre-landing reconnaissance of the Falklands to a minimum.

I was told that the Commando Brigade would be reinforced by a further Parachute Battalion, 2nd Battalion The Parachute Regiment (2 Para). 2 Para was commanded by Lieutenant-Colonel H. Jones, whom I had first met when commanding 40 Commando RM in South Armagh. H. Jones had then been the Brigade Major (Chief of Staff) of 3 Brigade at Portadown (not to be confused with 3 Commando Brigade RM). I had considerable respect for Jones's quick wit, strong personality and soldierly qualities. H. Jones flew ahead of his Battalion to Ascension, bringing with him Major Miller as his Liaison Officer to Brigade Headquarters. We had last met in South Armagh when 40 Commando had relieved 3 Para and Miller was commanding the Battalion's patrol company. The Battalion would bring with it a number of attached sub-units including another light gun battery (29 Battery from 4th Field Regiment), the Parachute Clearing Troop of 16 Field Ambulance, a troop of 9 Parachute Squadron Royal Engineer's, two sections of Blowpipe from 32 Guided Weapons Regiment Royal Artillery and a flight of Scout helicopters from 656 Squadron Army Air Corps. This was good news indeed. The addition of 2 Para to 3 Commando Brigade merely increased the feeling that existed already among all ranks in the Brigade that the team getting ready to go south was the First XI. We were, we felt, second-to-none and although outnumbered by more than 2 to 1 by the enemy, we could 'hack it'.

However, military common sense dictated that if pitched battles were to be fought against what was estimated to be a total of 10,000 Argentine soldiers in the Falklands, including a reinforced Argentine Brigade defending Stanley, at least another brigade's worth of troops should be on hand. When asked, I said that five battalions or commandos was as much as I would wish to handle in battle. So 5 Infantry Brigade with another Brigade Headquarters would be needed. This would necessitate a Divisional Headquarters to command both Brigades. Even this force would barely equal the numerical strength of the Argentines, let alone meet the required three-to-one superiority for an attacking force.

Clapp and I, the Amphibious and Landing Force Task Group Commanders, had four requirements that must be fulfilled before a landing would take place. The first of these, a prerequisite to detailed planning, was intelligence on where the enemy was and in what strength. Not until the very end of the campaign were there any air photographs showing enemy dispositions, defensive positions, strong points, gun positions and so forth. Even they arrived so late and were so poor that they had no influence on planning. So, for the first time probably since Gallipoli in 1915, an amphibious operation was to be mounted with no air photographs of the enemy. Detailed intelligence would therefore have to be gleaned by the 'mark one eyeball'. Men would have to go in and land on the Falkland Islands and send or bring back the necessary information. The task would be carried out by the SBS and SAS. In addition to establishing sea control over an area 200 nautical miles around the Islands, known as the Total Exclusion Zone (TEZ), and attempting to establish Air Control in the TEZ, the most important, time-consuming and dangerous task for the Carrier Battle Group in the pre-landing phase would be to land the SAS and SBS reconnaissance teams so vital to the two Task Group Commanders who were planning the landing. Forward with the Carrier Battle Group was Colonel Preston, my liaison officer with Woodward. His task was the co-ordination of Special Forces insertion from the Carrier Battle Group, reacting to the requirements of Clapp and myself. Preston and I held daily secure-voice telephone conversations, so that, even while the Amphibious Group was still at Ascension and the carriers operating forward, thousands of miles away, the tasking of Special Forces to acquire the critical intelligence could go ahead as efficiently as possible.

As the intelligence picture built up, detailed plans could be made. But in addition to planning, the second of the four requirements, our combined Staffs had two more: to restow the ships and to carry out trials and work up the two Task Groups.

The normal sequence for an amphibious operation is: identify the tasks (the mission), find out all you can about the enemy (intelligence), make the plan, stow your ships so that men and loads will come off in the sequence you want to meet your plan; then land. There had not been the time or intelligence to make a plan or stow properly before the ships left the United Kingdom, so a massive re-stow of loads was necessary. Some of the LSLs arrived at Ascension up to eighteen inches over their loading marks. An additional LSL arriving empty at Ascension from Belize provided the opportunity to redistribute loads. It was also found that *Canberra* and other ships could take many more men than they had sailed with from Britain.

Concurrently with the restow of ships, there was a need to test and work up the various parts of the Amphibious and Landing Force Task Groups. How, for example could men be loaded into LCUs from *Canberra*? Only trials by day and by night would establish a drill to get heavily-laden men, possibly in choppy sea and almost certainly in the dark, quickly into an LCU. Should the ship be at anchor, lying still or steaming slowly forward?

Could Scorpions and Scimitars be loaded into the bow of the LCU and fire over the lowered ramp on the run-in to the beach, to provide a poor man's version of the Landing Craft Gun that had been found so essential in the Second World War to suppress enemy fire on the beach in that critical stage after naval gunfire has to lift? How long would it take ten helicopters, landing two at a time one on each of the two helicopter decks on *Canberra*, to lift a rifle company, form up into a wave and land them?

Nobody knew the answers to these and a host of other questions. But the answers had to be found before detailed planning could be done. For example, it would be foolish to plan on a major lift by landing craft if men could not be loaded into them from the civilian ships. All the answers were found and tried out both by day and by night. However, these trials and work-ups needed helicopters and landing craft, which were also in urgent demand for the restow of ships. The problem of the restow was aggravated by *Fearless'* dash south for the Council of War. She had run her fuel stocks so low that she could not dock down for lack of fuel for ballasting. Without docking down, she could not get her LCUs out to start the restow. A tanker for refuelling was not available for two days after her arrival.

The best possible compromise between the demand on craft and helicopters for restowing the ships and for trials, training and working-up resulted in one helicopter-training day for each commando, battalion and battery, and a day and night landing craft session for each commando or battalion. Each commando, battalion and battery also got one day ashore to fire its weapons. The only exceptions to this were 2 Para and the Rapier Battery. 2 Para arrived only twelve hours before the Amphibious Task Group sailed and only achieved a day and a night landing craft training period. This hurried training period for 2 Para and especially the crew of their ship, MV *Norland*, was evident on D-Day. In Falkland Sound, in the dark, the lack of practice in night embarkation in full kit so slowed up the loading of craft that, through no fault of the Battalion, 2 Para were to be over an hour late. When I visited *Norland* at Ascension to watch the short training session, I met Major Keeble, the second-in-command, for the first time. His quiet, courteous manner and firm grip on his job made an immediate impression on me. I also met the company commanders, among them OC A Company, Dair Farrar-Hockley, who H. Jones introduced by remarking that when he heard him on the radio he always stood to attention, an allusion to how similar OC A Company sounded on the air to his father, General Sir Anthony Farrar-Hockley, then Commander-in-Chief Allied Forces Northern Europe.

The Rapier Battery, having landed on Ascension and about to start firing, was recalled. A signal had arrived from Northwood which resulted in the Amphibious Task Group being put at a shorter notice to sail. This cancellation was to bear fruit on D-Day when problems that should have been ironed out at Ascension cropped up at the San Carlos beachhead under air attack.

None of the training included a proper rehearsal of the whole Brigade landing plan in darkness, laid down as a 'must' in all the manuals based on bitter experience in two World Wars. Had there been such a rehearsal, many of the snags which arose on D-Day might have been avoided. However, it was not to be, there were no suitable beaches on Ascension, no training areas, no helicopter landing zones (except the airfield) and, most critical of all, insufficient landing craft and helicopters to restow and do such a rehearsal, even had there been time, which there was not.

Meanwhile, the planning process in HMS *Fearless* continued. Starting with nineteen possible beaches on East Falkland, each one was examined in detail by two Staffs and eventually five possible areas were selected for closer examination by Special Forces patrols. The results of their reconnaissance had a major part to play in the decision on which beach to select. There were many factors which steered us towards the eventual choice made by Clapp and myself. Each had to take account of the other's particular requirements and there was no room for selfishness or a unilateral approach to planning. Early in the planning process we discarded the idea of landing anywhere other than East Falkland. Landing on another island would mean another amphibious assault, unless the Argentines agreed to leave the Falklands after the first landing, which was becoming increasingly unlikely.

An assault anywhere in the vicinity of Port Stanley would probably run into well-prepared defensive positions, wire, mines and beaches covered by gunfire both direct and indirect. The Amphibious and Landing Force Task Groups simply did not possess the firepower and, more important, the armoured amphibious vehicles and close-support, direct-fire assault guns in ships or amphibians to contemplate such a plan. Furthermore, the casualties to the civilian population and damage to the buildings would be such that an assault on Stanley was ruled out almost from the beginning. Finally we had been told to avoid heavy casualties to our own side. Therefore, any beach selected had to be out of range of the guns defending Port Stanley, and if possible be far enough away so that any Argentine reaction, even by heliborne forces, would arrive after the beachhead had been built up sufficiently to hold and beat off such a counter-attack. Conversely, a landing too far from Stanley, which must be the ultimate goal, would involve a long approach march with all the difficulties, particularly resupply, attendant upon such a choice.

The beach or beaches selected must have gradients suitable for the LCU and the Mexeflote to land men and vehicles. The terrain behind the beach must provide good exits for vehicles because even the few tracked and wheeled vehicles taken by the Commando Brigade needed to get off the actual beach and disperse, although of course the terrain would not permit loaded wheeled vehicles to drive more than a few hundred yards inland, therefore a beach with sand dunes, cliffs or high tussock was not suitable.

The Brigade would need to defend the beach against a possible enemy counterattack, the terrain behind the beach must lend itself to defence. Furthermore, there must be sufficient elbow-room in the area around the beach not only to deploy the Brigade to defend it, but in which to land and, if possible, disperse, the thousands of tons of ammunition, fuel and rations which the Brigade would need to fight a battle of any size.

The weather in the Falklands is notoriously fickle; the only almost constant feature is very high winds. Therefore it was vital to find a beach that could be used whatever the wind direction. The landing and build-up would be dangerously slow anyway, given the scarcity of landing assets, without the added complication of hours or even days of delay caused by bad weather. As important was to find an anchorage that would be difficult to attack by submarine or from the air and impossible to attack with air-launched Exocet.

As the days passed it dawned on us that one of the prerequisites for carrying out an amphibious operation, achieving air superiority, was not to be accomplished. This was nobody's fault, least of all Woodward's. Clearly, it would be politically unacceptable to withdraw at this stage. We were committed whatever the outcome. In marine language, it was 'shit or bust'.

Woodward expressed his concern in a signal to Northwood which he copied to me. The last sentence read, 'a ticket on the train about to leave Ascension will be very expensive'. There were no marks for guessing that he meant the amphibious group would take heavy casualties.

This caused me to send a letter back to Northwood by hand of a staff officer who was visiting Ascension. After stating that we would of course do whatever we were ordered, I pointed out that gaining air superiority, even locally over a beachhead, was not a new idea, but a 'must' arrived at after bitter experience gained in such places as Crete, Norway, and other disasters in the Second World War. We could therefore expect to take very heavy casualties before we even put a foot ashore. I was told not to worry, which is no answer at all. Apart from anything else it could be taken as a hint that something was about to be done about the Argentine mainland air bases within range of the Falklands. It would have been better, and more honest, to say something on the lines of: 'We are not going to gain air superiority; get on with it'. That is the kind of order I would have understood, and if it had been passed early enough, we could have made some provision in the logistic plans to cope.

In the event it was not until 6 May that we worked out the true situation for ourselves. This was six days after the LSLs had sailed and one day before the remainder of the Amphibious Task Group sailed, and thus too late to restow again.

The adverse air situation was to force many changes of plan after D-Day, not least that of having to land the Field Dressing Station and all the Brigade's ammunition and other supplies, instead of keeping them afloat. It was fortunate that the beachhead chosen had just enough space to accommodate these vital assets — but only just.

On 29 April Major-General Moore flew out to Ascension and boarded *Fearless* to see Clapp and myself. We gave him a briefing on our plans and three outline operation orders, with marked maps prepared by our Staffs, for the three landing options selected by us from the nineteen possible beaches. These three were Cow Bay/Volunteer Bay, Berkeley Sound and San Carlos.

Cow Bay/Volunteer Bay and Berkeley Sound were only possible if the Argentines looked as if they wanted to surrender and a face-saving reason had to be found. The beaches at Cow Bay and Volunteer Bay were exposed to north-easterlies and easterlies and the anchorages would be difficult to defend against submarines or air attack. The beachhead itself could not be easily defended and was, in any case, uncomfortably close to Stanley. Berkeley Sound was even closer to Stanley and as an added hazard the seaward approaches might well be mined. The Argentines really would have to be on their last legs for this option to be chosen. San Carlos was the favourite. It provided everything that Clapp and I wanted. Its only drawback was the distance to Stanley.

Moore returned to Northwood bearing these three outline operation orders with him. Presumably they were presented to the Chiefs of Staff and the Cabinet and formed the basis for the decision to support our preferred option, San Carlos.

Later, after the Task Groups left Ascension, and San Carlos had been chosen, we and our Staffs privately agreed that Port Salvador was a possible alternative to San Carlos, should the latter be found to be held in strength or the sea approaches mined. Port Salvador was overlooked from the east and south-east by Mount Kent, Mount Estancia and Long Island Mount, as well as by other hill features to the south and west of the complex of inlets. I had every intention of using Port Salvador at some stage in the campaign as a stepping stone to advancing on Stanley from the west and north-west, having first seized the high ground, or at least having established OPs on it, after clearing it of enemy. As events at San Carlos were to demonstrate, had the main initial landings been at Port Salvador, the casualties in ships and men would have been very heavy.

However, all the options, Berkeley Sound, Cow Bay/Volunteer Bay and Port Salvador had a common theme in that they led the attackers, 3 Commando Brigade, on to the high ground overlooking Stanley from the north and west, avoiding an approach from the south and south-west. After considerable thought, I and my Staff concluded that any line of approach that resulted in breasting up what would probably be the main Argentine defensive positions on Sapper Hill, Mount William and positions south of Stanley from the south or south-west was to be avoided if possible. The intention was to come at them from the north-west in the hope that this would be the least expected direction. As will be seen, Port Salvador was a key factor in this plan.

The members of my Staff in this planning process were my Brigade Major, John Chester, my logistician the DAA & QMG, Major Wells-Cole, and the members of my Rover Group. A brigade commander's Rover Group consists of his supporting arms commanders, in this case my gunner, Lieutenant-Colonel Holroyd-Smith, commanding 29 Commando Regiment Royal Artillery, and my sapper, Major Macdonald, the Officer Commanding 59 Independent Commando Squadron Royal Engineers. The Rover or R Group was well practised in working together and for over a year this same team had been taking part in reconnaissances for several exercises and possible operations; as a result they were totally 'in the Brigade Commander's mind' — an ideal situation. Added to this team was Major Baldwin, lately the DAA & QMG and so an experienced planner and staff officer. As an 'extra' he was put in charge of the work-up programme at Ascension with

Major Gullan and generally assisted in the planning process. Major Southby-Tailyour, the Falklands expert, and Captain Rowe, the GSO 3 Intelligence, completed the planning team that was summoned either as individuals or together to spend hours in my cabin in *Fearless* poring over the maps and dissecting the options before being sent away to prepare yet another outline plan. It would be hard to overstate the achievement of the R Group and the Staff. Their hard work, professionalism, flexibility and abiding cheerfulness under great pressure for seven weeks before D-Day and throughout the campaign was second to none. No Brigade Commander could have been better served.

Since 1982 a number of people have claimed that the choice of San Carlos was theirs, and furthermore they planned the amphibious operation. No doubt, as the years pass, others will make this claim. The facts are that the selection was arrived at after a long and searching examination of beaches, ground and enemy locations. This, combined with the ship-shore movement assets available, and the tactical requirements of an ill-armed and almost defenceless hotch-potch of ships, led to the detailed planning. It is not sufficient merely to say, 'Land at place X'. The staffs must draw up the helicopter and surface assault tables, together with a mass of other detail, so that the plan fits together like a watch, yet is flexible enough to be changed at short notice. It must be put together by the people who have to carry it out. Only in *Fearless*, and nowhere else, were the necessary information, expertise, and decision-makers gathered in one place: Commodore Clapp and I, and our staffs. Higher headquarters may have approved our selection of beachhead, but there their responsibility ended. Neither at Northwood, nor in the Carrier Battle Group, was there the capability to do anything other than rubber-stamp the work done by the amphibious staffs.

It was also fortunate that Clapp and I got on so well. In each other's company almost constantly and involved in long discussions until late each night, there was plenty of scope for bickering and recrimination, but harmony was the order of the day. While the Staffs planned, training went on, both ashore and on board. In the cramped LSLs and stores ships and on the long promenade deck and open spaces of *Canberra* the fitness and other training went on all through daylight hours. Troops ashore for the day force-marched from English Bay to the firing ranges and back again. The first ever static line parachute descent from a Sea King Mark IV helicopter was carried out by a stick which included: the youngest soldier in 3 Para, whose birthday it was; Major Macdonald, Captain Boswell and Major Gullan. It was a double first because the Parachute Jumping Instructor (PJI), Flight-Sergeant Roberts RAF, conducted the trial — the first such trial to be conducted by an NCO. The CVRT of the Blues and Royals practised firing over the lowered ramps of the LCUs — the heaving vehicle decks presenting a very different proposition from firing points at the Castle Martin or Lulworth Cove tank gunnery ranges. Everywhere one looked the anchorage was a bustle of activity by day and for much of the night. Ashore the clatter of helicopter blades at Wideawake and the roar of firing from the improvised ranges seemed incessant, while Corporal Pascoe and his welders cut the port bulwarks off MV *Elk* to allow her deck to be used by helicopters.

At 8 pm on 7 May the Amphibious Task Group, less the LSLs which had left on 1 May, sailed from Ascension and headed south in an atmosphere of increasing tension, awaiting orders from Northwood. On 12 May the signal from Northwood arrived at last, giving the task. No matter, the Brigade Operations order was already in print and on 13 May the Brigade Orders Group of all Commanding Officers and Officers Commanding was summoned to HMS *Fearless* and I gave my orders for the landing at San Carlos.

CHAPTER THREE

South Georgia

While the Commando Brigade was pausing at Ascension to restow and practise landing techniques with what one wag called 'The British Rail Ferry Assault Ships', South Georgia was retaken. The catalyst for the invasion of the Falklands was the illegal landing on South Georgia of Argentine scrap metal workers accompanied by Marines. The island is crescent-shaped, 105 miles long, eighteen miles across at its widest point and lies 800 miles to the south-east of the Falklands. Much of South Georgia is snow-covered throughout the year and numerous glaciers run down from the central mountain spine. The wind on South Georgia is even more violent and unpredictable than in the Falkland Islands. A particular feature is the rolling, turbulent wind which blows down the mountainside, rather like a waterfall, or rushing surf. This 'katabatic' wind roars down the fjords, can gust up to 100 knots and will blow small boats, particularly inflatables, out to sea despite outboards being pushed to full power. Violent changes in wind direction follow in quick succession. Ice blown out to sea by the katabatic wind can suddenly be blown back up the fjord by the wind changing 180 degrees in direction, trapping inflatables and piercing their fabric sides.

As the Brigade Staff was embarking in HMS *Fearless* on 6 April, it became apparent that an operation was being considered to recapture South Georgia, quite independently from operations against the Falklands. The Argentine garrison in South Georgia was estimated to consist of about sixty Marines and the island was beyond the range of Argentine land-based air cover. Because of the severity of the terrain and climate it was highly likely that the Argentines would be located at the British Arctic Survey Base at King Edward's Point, Grytviken or at the old whaling station at Leith. Climate and terrain were the overriding factors in deciding the composition of the force to retake South Georgia — it must be mountain — and arctic warfare-trained and equipped. Therefore it was decided that it should come from 42 Commando, the only commando to deploy to Norway for winter training in 1982. The force assembled had to be limited in numbers because of the shipping space available. It was commanded by Major Sheridan, the second-in-command of 42 Commando, a very experienced snow and ice mountaineer. The story goes that when a very senior Army general heard that the Force Commander was the Commando second-in-command, he expressed doubts about the wisdom of selecting a pear-shaped administrator whose only recent experience was likely to be running the Officers' Mess. It was quietly pointed out that Sheridan's recent experience included the first ever traverse of the Himalayas on skis.

The force selected was M Company, 42 Commando, commanded by Captain Nunn. He took with him two 81 mm mortars, a section of the Commando Reconnaissance Troop, a small logistic and medical party, two Naval Gunfire Observer parties from 148 Battery and one SBS Section. Later, an SAS Squadron was added to the Force, bringing its strength up to about 230 men. They all flew to Ascension Island on 7 April, embarked in RFA *Tidespring*, a Fleet Oiler, and sailed south. Although the strength of the landing force might appear weak for the task that lay ahead, the Task Group as a whole had the ability to deal with an isolated Argentine garrison out of range of land-based air support. Nuclear submarines (SSN) were deployed to prevent the Argentine's aircraft carrier or any other surface unit from providing support to the garrison and the main threat to the Task Group was thought to be submarines. Before leaving England Sheridan was briefed on the options for dealing with the Argentines. In view of the virtual certainty that they would be located in Leith and Grytviken and nowhere else, it was suggested to him that he should contain the enemy by occupying dominating ground in the vicinity of each position and use naval gunfire to persuade them to surrender.

The Task Group, which included HMS *Antrim*, HMS *Plymouth* and, eventually, HMS *Brilliant* as escorts, reached the area of South Georgia on 21 April and spent several days attempting to conduct reconnaissance. Several problems then arose. The SAS, who were under the operational control of the Naval Task Group Commander, the Captain of HMS *Antrim*, and not of the Landing Force Commander, landed their reconnaissance patrols on the Fortuna glacier against the advice of Sheridan, despite his far greater experience in battle, including commanding a company in the Dhofar War, and his expertise in such hazardous conditions both as a Mountain and Arctic Warfare officer and as a mountaineer of repute. Within twelve hours they asked to be evacuated immediately to avoid casualties from the severe cold, having made no headway across the crevasses on the glacier. Two Wessex Mk 5 helicopters and one Wessex Mk 3 were sent to extract them, but both Wessex Mk 5s crashed, one after the other, on the glacier when the pilots became disorientated and lost the horizon which merged with the sky in 'white-out' conditions caused by the falling snow and overcast sky. The pilot of the remaining Wessex, the single-engined Mk 3, making two trips, embarked the passengers and crew of each of the crashed aircraft, and each time loaded well over the maximum permitted weight, and managed a hard but successful landing back on HMS *Antrim*. Once committed to his landing, in a gale and a snow storm, the pilot did not have the power to make a second attempt. It was a brilliant piece of flying by Lieutenant-Commander Stanley in white-out conditions and high, turbulent winds. His gallant rescue of the SAS was the only bright spot at the end of a disastrous day which had seen the Force's only troop-lift helicopters destroyed.

Other SBS and SAS patrols were unable to reach their targets because of appalling weather and ice which punctured boats or blew them off course out to sea. *Tidespring*, with the main body of M Company on board, was steamed away from South Georgia because of a report that there was an Argentine submarine in the area. As the captain of the *Endurance* remarked later, 'in military terms the whole operation had become a monumental cockup'. This was partly due to back-seat driving by Northwood, and not for the first nor last time. The orderly progression of land operations had already been severely disrupted when, on 25 April, the Argentine submarine *Santa Fe* was sighted on the surface five miles out from Grytviken by Lieutenant-Commander Stanley. He attacked her with machine-gun fire and depth charges, somehow keeping her from diving and escaping until help arrived in the form of helicopters equipped with AS12 missiles which are more suited to attacking a vessel on the surface. Eventually, as she was returning to Grytviken, the *Santa Fe* was attacked by helicopters armed with AS12 missiles and limped into Grytviken harbour badly damaged and listing heavily.

Although there were now thought to be up to 140 Argentine Marines and sailors ashore and Sheridan had only seventy-five men immediately available, the bulk of M Company being in *Tidespring* about 200 miles away, he pressed the Naval Task Group Commander to be allowed to attack Grytviken without delay and without any reconnaissance. He would rely upon the shock effect of the attack on the *Santa Fe* and the use of naval gunfire support to offset his inferior numbers. In deteriorating weather an ad-hoc Company made up of SBS, SAS, M Company Headquarters, the Reconnaissance Section and *Antrim*'s and *Plymouth*'s Royal Marines detachments landed in *Antrim*'s, *Brilliant*'s and *Plymouth*'s anti-submarine helicopters, while *Antrim* and *Plymouth* started a bombardment. In order to avoid unnecessary damage to the British Antarctic Survey Base, the bombardment was arranged as a creeping barrage starting across the valley from the enemy position and slowly moving closer. When the fall of shot was within a few hundred yards of the Argentines the white flag was run up. The following day, 26 April, the Argentine garrison at Leith also surrendered, making a total of 137 prisoners of war. One Argentine sailor in *Santa Fe* lost a leg in the missile attack by the helicopters and another was killed by a Marine who thought be was about to scuttle the submarine, but there were no other casualties on either side.

The recapture of South Georgia had been an almost bloodless victory. It proved, if it needed proving, the value of naval gunfire support. The two Naval Gunfire Forward Observation parties had earned their spurs and done splendidly. Why this method of attack, to which the Argentines had absolutely no response, and which Sheridan had favoured from the outset, had not been tried on the arrival of the South Georgia Task Group, is a mystery. However, the easy victory created in some quarters a mood of dangerous over-optimism that the operation to recapture the Falklands would be a 'push-over', a mood not shared by 3 Commando Brigade.

CHAPTER FOUR

Approach to Battle

Since early May, 1982, Special Forces had been operating ashore in the Falkland Islands, their most important task being to provide the detailed intelligence without which Clapp and I could not plan any landing. We both needed two sorts of intelligence: first, beach information; what were the beach gradients, was there any surf, what were the approaches, how many landing craft could the beach accept at a time, where the exits possible for tracked and wheeled vehicles? A great deal of this information was already contained in Major Southby-Tailyour's notes and without them the planners would have had little inkling of where to start looking for suitable beaches along the thousands of miles of deeply indented coastline. The notes, and Major Southby-Tailyour's personal knowledge and advice, made it possible to gather in three weeks the sort of detailed information that had taken months to collect before the Normandy landings in 1944. At least from the start Special Forces could be tasked to look at only a few beaches.

The second category of intelligence the planners needed was information about the enemy. Were there any enemy on the beaches, or near enough to react quickly, where were his main concentrations of strength, what was he doing, how alert was he and what was his morale like? In some cases Special Forces patrols, whose job it was to find out as much as possible about a beach and the adjacent country, could also report back on the presence or absence of enemy in the vicinity. Other Special Forces patrols were sent to places in which it was likely that there would be large concentrations of enemy, to watch them and report on their activities.

The open moorland which makes up all but a tiny part of the Falklands is devoid of foliage to provide cover. Special Forces patrols could, therefore, move only at night. In daylight they either had to find a cave or rocks to hide among or, more usually, dig small holes in the peat. They brought ashore with them chicken wire which could be shaped to go over the holes they had dug, placing turves over the top for camouflage. In these damp holes they would lie for days, watching. The going across country was so bad in places that, at times, patrols only moved at 250 metres an hour. To avoid compromise, patrols were usually landed up to four nights' march away from their targets and they would move at least one night's march away before pick-up. So with anything up to five nights having to be allowed merely for the approach to and withdrawal from the target, let alone the time spent observing and perhaps moving closer, or to another position, the gathering of intelligence was a long and painstaking business, a point not readily appreciated by those who forecast that it could be done in two weeks. In the event it took three weeks and even that was barely enough.

The means of getting the patrols ashore on the islands was another limitation on the speed at which intelligence could be gathered. Because of the adverse air situation and to avoid detection by the enemy, patrols were landed at night and mainly by helicopter. Only four of the Sea King helicopters were fitted with Passive Night Goggle (PNG) equipment, which allowed the pilots to fly the helicopters at night low enough to avoid enemy radar and to find the right spot on the ground in the dark without previous reconnaissance or lights to guide them in. With so few helicopters and considerable distances to fly, it was not possible to land many patrols each night. Fog at sea, or ashore, caused further delays and several nights passed without any patrols being landed or withdrawn. Had a conventional submarine been used to land SBS patrols, time would undoubtedly have been saved and the risks reduced, but no such submarine was available. To ease the strain on the helicopters and to attempt to diminish the risk of compromise incurred by nightly helicopter sorties inserting Special Forces, frigates and destroyers were used towards the end of the pre-landing reconnaissance phase to land SBS patrols by boat; this practice continued after D-Day until the end of the campaign.

The skill and dedication of SBS and SAS patrols was severely tested during the days before D-Day and they did all that was expected of them and more. The planners in HMS *Fearless* waited anxiously for their reports and, as it became clear that San Carlos was the favourite for the landings, every report of enemy activity in or near the area was carefully analysed. The question was, would the Argentines start preparing defences at San Carlos settlement, Port San Carlos and Ajax Bay and around the complex of inlets and hills in the area which the planners just referred to as San Carlos? Almost unbelievably, except for visiting patrols, it seemed to be devoid of enemy. Meanwhile enemy patrols and helicopters searched for the SBS and SAS teams all over the Falkland Islands, but none was found until Captain Hamilton's SAS team were discovered and attacked just before the surrender. Special Forces patrols saw plenty of enemy activity but space prevents an account of these busy three weeks in detail. As well as seeing ground troops and helicopters, at least one SBS patrol, overlooking Ajax Bay, was treated to the sight of an almost daily flight by one or more Argentine C130s southbound over Falkland Sound in the morning, often in formation with two Pucaras. Later in the day the C130, this time on its own, would return, flying north over Falkland Sound. As D-Day approached it was clear that air control over the Falklands had yet to be wrested from the Argentines. Supplies were coming in by air and would do so until the morning of the Argentine surrender on 14 June. The enemy was building up his Pucara strength on the islands, the C130 apparently acting as navigation leader for pairs of Pucaras flying in from mainland Argentina.

The tasks for Special Forces patrols during the pre D-Day period were chosen by Clapp and I, consulting each other and the SAS and SBS Commanders, who, correctly, were all travelling in the same ship. The subsequent tasking signal was sent to Woodward who moved his ships so that helicopters from *Hermes* and *Invincible* and frigates or destroyers could land and recover the SAS and SBS patrols. Because Clapp and I spent several hours each day together, were totally frank in exchanging our views and understood the problems of amphibious operations, we were able to allocate and re-allocate priorities for Special Forces operations without acrimony. It was upon Clapp that the burden of responsibility would fall for getting the Commando Brigade to the right beaches in one piece, landing its combat supplies and providing air and sea protection during and after the landings.

So important was the acquisition of intelligence that Special Forces, and particularly the assets to insert them, could be spared for only one direct-action task during the run-up to D-Day — the Pebble Island raid. Preceded by a party from D Squadron's Boat Troop, who carried out a three-day reconnaissance of the air-strip, the remainder of D Squadron, including one 81 mm mortar team, was landed by Sea King helicopter into a Landing Zone marked out by Boat Troop on the night of 14/15 May. The Squadron was landed late, touching down at midnight with a pick-up time of 5 am, to enable HMS *Hermes* to be well east again by first light. Although the Squadron force-marched to the target, they had very little time to spare for their attack which started at 2.45 am. The Argentine garrison was kept pinned down by naval gunfire from HMS *Glamorgan* and by the GPMGs of the covering party dropped off by the Squadron for this purpose, while the 81 mm mortar team fired illuminating bombs. The assault party, led by Captain Hamilton, then destroyed all eleven aircraft on the strip, using prepared charges, and started withdrawing at 3.30 am. While the Squadron was withdrawing, a half-hearted counter-attack was put in by the Argentine garrison. The officer leading the attack was shot by D Squadron and the remaining Argentines fled. The Squadron continued its withdrawal to the Landing Zone unopposed and was lifted back to HMS *Hermes* by helicopter. HMS *Glamorgan*, which should have left the gunline at 3 am, stayed on to provide fire support — not the last time that the gallant destroyers and frigates risked themselves to help troops ashore. The raid was a brilliant success, destroying six Pucaras, a Shorts Skyvan and four Mentors — the largest concentration of enemy aircraft close to Falkland Sound and San Carlos. The destruction of the Pucaras was particularly important. This Argentine-built, twin-propeller aircraft was designed for counter-insurgency. It could carry rockets, bombs and cannon and because of its manoeuvrability and slow speed was considerably feared by British helicopter pilots. So anything that reduced this threat was to be applauded.

Another part of the Commando Brigade was also operating in and near the Falkland Islands during the weeks before D-Day — the Naval Gunfire Support Teams of 148 Commando Forward Observation Battery, Royal Artillery. Having played a major part in the re-capture of South Georgia, Captain McCracken and Captain Brown, with their teams, joined up with other Naval Gunfire Support Teams in the ships of the Carrier Battle Group in the Total Exclusion Zone on 29 April. Between 1 and 20 May ships of the Carrier Battle Group, under Woodward, carried out thirteen bombardments of Argentine positions on the Falkland Islands. These included the daylight bombardment of Port Stanley on 1 May and support for the SAS Pebble Island raid on 15 May. On many occasions the bombardments were observed by the naval gunfire observer in a Lynx helicopter, and at Pebble Island Captain Brown landed with D Squadron 22 SAS to spot for HMS *Glamorgan*.

Naval Gunfire Observer Teams were landed before D-Day in the San Carlos area to be on hand to spot for naval gunfire during and after the main landings. Captain McCracken led one of them. His Observation Post (OP) was on Sussex Mountain, where he was to wait for the arrival of 2 Para on D-Day, prepared to call down naval gunfire to support them. He tells the story that one night before D-Day, having been landed by boat near Rookery Point, he saw large numbers of Argentine soldiers approaching his hide position and thought that the game was up. But he had been deceived by a Falklands phenomenon; the clear, unpolluted atmosphere and lack of trees or other feature to provide a reference point for scale or size had tricked his eyes into believing that a flock of penguins was the enemy. Although not officially part of Special Forces, the Naval Gunfire Observer Teams proved their contention that they are capable of operating with them and are, at times, an important ingredient in Special Forces operations. Naval gunfire support played a notable part in the campaign before and after the landing. Fourteen different ships conducted sixty-three bombardments on thirty-two days between the recapture of South Georgia on 25 May and the Argentine surrender on 14 June. The ships on the gunline came under attack at least twelve times, resulting in one ship sunk, five badly damaged and four slightly damaged.

By 13 May the intelligence that had been gleaned indicated that the Argentines occupied both East and West Falkland, with their main strength in the Stanley area. They had a reinforced brigade round Stanley consisting of a brigade headquarters, six infantry regiments, including a marine unit, supporting arms and logistic units. This brigade was thought, correctly as it turned out, to be commanded by Brigadier-General Joffre, the Commander of 10 Infantry Brigade. The exact composition of the Argentine infantry regiments was not known to the British Intelligence staffs at the time, but they were believed to consist of anything from 700 to 1,000 men. The bulk of 10 Brigade's artillery was estimated to consist of a battalion and a half of Italian 105 mm pack howitzers — about thirty-eight guns. These pack howitzers were out-ranged by the British 105 mm light gun, but could be lifted by smaller helicopters and were therefore more mobile. It was not confirmed at this stage but it was believed that the Argentines also had several of the heavier 155 mm guns on the islands. These could be towed equipments of French design with a range of 22 km or M109 self-propelled guns with a maximum range of only 14.5 km. One set of decent air photographs would have been of inestimable value, but there were none.

In addition to infantry and artillery, Joffre had engineers, an unknown quantity of armoured cars and possibly American amphibious armoured personnel carriers (LVTPs) and abundant air defence guns and missiles. His air defence guns were the Oerlikon twin 35 mm K63s and the single-barrelled 30 mm Oerlikons; the missiles the Tiger Cat (the land-based version of the Sea Cat), the Franco-German Roland and the British hand-held Blowpipe. His air defence system was thought to include good radars, both for early warning and for fire control. Joffre also had sufficient helicopters to move about 200 men in one lift, including Chinooks which could lift wheeled 155 mm guns.

At the twin settlements of Goose Green and Darwin the garrison was estimated as an understrength infantry regiment of about 300-500 men, possibly supported by some artillery, but certainly including air defence guns and, it was thought, some surface-to-air missiles; a gun or missile had shot down a British Sea Harrier on 4 May. There were likely to be a number of Argentine airforce personnel at Goose Green, which had one of the bigger airstrips outside Stanley, and a sizeable logistic organization at either Goose Green or Darwin, because the isthmus provided a convenient stepping stone by which supplies carried in helicopters or small vessels could be taken to West Falkland, the latter perhaps using the protected waters of Choiseul Sound and Brenton Loch. Despite the need to off-load sea-transported stores at Darwin and transport them across the isthmus before sending them on their way, this route avoided the British frigates that prowled each night off the northern and southern entrances to Falkland Sound. Enemy troops had been sighted at North Arm Settlement, Port Louis and Green Patch. There was a possibility of an airmobile reserve based at Fitzroy or thereabouts, possibly consisting of all, or part, of an infantry regiment, some artillery, a commando company of Argentine Special Forces and some helicopters to provide mobility.

It was believed that on West Falkland the Headquarters of 3 Argentine Infantry Brigade commanded the Garrison consisting of an infantry regiment at Port Howard, possibly with artillery in support (18 guns), and a further infantry regiment with some engineers at Fox Bay. At Pebble Island, north of West Falkland, there was intelligence of Naval Air Arm personnel, radars and aircraft.

Most of the thirty-four airstrips on the Falkland Islands were assessed as being capable of operating Pucaras, Aermacchis and other light aircraft; some of them could accept C130s and all of them helicopters. Which airstrips were being used and for what was not clear at this stage and never was right up to the end. What was clear when I gave my orders to my Brigade on 13 May, was that the 11,000 or so Argentine troops on the islands outnumbered 3 Commando Brigade by more than two to one. The enemy had more helicopters, had air superiority and the added bonus of T34C Mentors, Pucaras, Aermacchi M339s and Augusta A109A attack helicopters positioned at various points, many unidentified, throughout the islands. They had more guns, at least as good a helicopter lift as the British and by D-Day would have been in position for seven weeks, only 350 miles from home. If the enemy had their wits about them and used the time to good effect, their positions would be well-sited and prepared; counterattack plans, with well-recced routes and landing sites, would have been made and rehearsed; a quick reaction force, including artillery, would be ready to at least harass the beachhead to delay the break-out and then, having identified the British route or routes to Stanley, establish blocking positions to further delay the advance. Finally, with six regiments around Stanley in prepared defence positions the break-in battle and subsequent fighting facing the British would be 'something else'.

Although reports from Special Forces patrols indicated a militarily inept enemy, sloppy, disinterested and dozy, only contact between the British and Argentine main bodies of ground troops would show how good, or bad, the enemy really was. Special Forces patrols, by their very nature and given the short time for reconnaissance, could only 'sample' parts of the Argentine positions and it would be a foolish commander who based his assessment of 11,000 men and their likely reactions on a few patrol reports. Furthermore, without air photographs, it was not possible to locate the enemy positions with the sort of accuracy required by soldiers fighting a land battle. Knowing, for example, that there were six infantry regiments around Stanley, supported by guns, went only a small way towards building up the intelligence picture. Until patrols could 'eyeball' the enemy positions, prisoners be taken and interrogated, captured documents and maps be scrutinized and observation posts (OPs) be established to keep a continuous watch on the enemy, the positions that regiments and batteries might occupy had to be arrived at by an educated guess. In making the guess, I was relying on the standard of education in the military art of my Staff and principal advisers (the R Group) being pretty high. I was not disappointed.

By the time the Commanding Officers of commandos, battalions and other units in 3 Commando Brigade had assembled in HMS *Fearless'* wardroom on 13 May, they had read the Brigade Operation Order which had been given to them twenty-four hours before. On two occasions before that, I had given an outline of my options to my Commanding Officers so that they could familiarize themselves with the relevant maps. At these meetings I did not, as related in some accounts, conduct councils of war to seek my Commanding Officers' opinions of the plans. The Brigade Operation Order ran to forty-seven pages. I did not intend to read through the whole Operation Order, but rather to treat it as confirmatory notes to what my Staff and I were going to say.

An Orders Group, or colloquially, O Group, is the process by which a commander, at any level, gives his orders to his subordinates to carry out the tasks he has set them in order to achieve his mission. Getting the O Group right is so important that considerable pains are taken and much time is spent on teaching and practising the art of giving orders at all Schools of Instruction in the Royal Marines and British Army dealing with leadership and command, from courses for budding corporals to the course for majors at the Army Staff College at Camberley. It is an art well understood in the Royal Marines, the British Army and those Armies trained by the British. It is a method of command often misunderstood by those who do not need to conduct such business face to face, doing so instead by signal.

The way in which an O Group is stage-managed will depend upon the personality of the commander, the level of command and the circumstances. At platoon or company level the orders for a quick attack given face to face or over the radio will not require much stage-management. The forthcoming amphibious assault would be the first carried out by the British since Suez in 1956 and one would have to go back to the Second World War to find an example of a landing on this scale being conducted by the British alone, without allies. The orders would therefore need careful stage-management if the mass of information was to be got across clearly and concisely and I was to ensure that everyone was in no doubt what I, the Commander, required of them. In this case by using the comprehensive operation order as confirmatory notes, much of the factual information that the order contained, such as beach locations, helicopter landing sites and times of sunrise and sunset could be digested before the O Group, or afterwards, leaving the minds of the Commanding Officers uncluttered to absorb the essentials — how the operation was to be conducted and my 'design for battle' (a brief résumé of what the Brigade was to achieve), followed by some basic points of soldiering that I wished hammered home at all levels.

The buzz of conversation among the audience that sat in rows of chairs in *Fearless'* wardroom was quickly stilled as Clapp and I entered. Captain Rowe opened the O Group by giving the latest intelligence picture of the enemy, which was as already described, and the air threat. Chester then gave a résumé of the British Naval and Naval Air Forces in support of the operation. I followed to give the mission and my design for battle, which was: to conduct a silent night landing by landing craft so that by first light the Brigade would have secured the high ground overlooking Port San Carlos, San Carlos Settlement and Ajax Bay. As quickly as possible after first light one Light Gun Battery would be flown in, followed by the Rapier Battery and then the remaining light guns, the design being that as soon as possible the Brigade should be in a good defensive position on reverse slopes ready to fight off Argentine attacks from the air or on the ground, or any combination of these two. I impressed upon the Commanding Officers that the landing was not an end in itself, merely the beginning and that this point was to be made clear to everyone. All ranks were to be quite sure what the Brigade task in this phase was, so that if leaders at any level became casualties, companies, troops, platoons and sections would use their initiative and press on to their objectives unless specifically ordered not to. Soldiers, and especially infantrymen, in a complicated operation such as an amphibious landing, need to know the plan in the sort of detail that, for example, the junior officers and ratings of a warship do not. Leaders at low level may be required to take up the reins of command from dead or wounded superiors and carry on to achieve the objective. They must know, among a host of things, what the objective is, how to get to it, what fire support is available, how to call for it, what neighbouring sub-units are supposed to be doing; to be able to use radios correctly, and control their newly acquired command. Once battle is joined it will be too late to try to find out this sort of information.

The individual tasks for each Commanding Officer were then given by me, addressing each Commanding Officer by name and prefacing his orders by the phrase, 'I want you to ...'. The landing plan was in three phases. In phase one 40 Commando and 45 Commando were to land simultaneously by landing craft at night to secure San Carlos Settlement and Ajax Bay. In phase two, 2 Para and 3 Para were to land, using the landing craft that had returned from landing 40 Commando and 45 Commando, and secure Sussex Mountain and Port San Carlos. Phase three, starting at first light, was to see the first use of helicopters to move the Rapiers and guns ashore. Most of the

THE BEACH HEAD

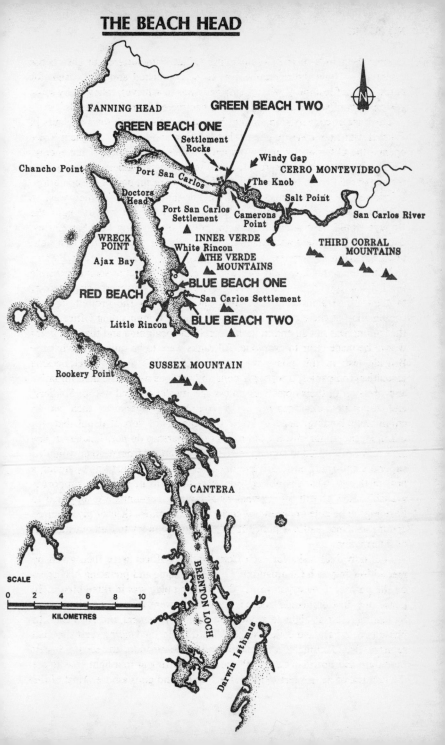

FANNING HEAD

GREEN BEACH TWO

GREEN BEACH ONE

Settlement Rocks

Windy Gap

CERRO MONTEVIDEO

Chancho Point

Port San Carlos

The Knob

Salt Point

Doctors Head

Port San Carlos Settlement

Camerons Point

San Carlos River

WRECK POINT

INNER VERDE

White Rincon

THIRD CORRAL MOUNTAINS

Ajax Bay

THE VERDE MOUNTAINS

RED BEACH

BLUE BEACH ONE

San Carlos Settlement

Little Rincon

BLUE BEACH TWO

Rookery Point

SUSSEX MOUNTAIN

CANTERA

BRENTON LOCH

Darwin Isthmus

SCALE

0 2 4 6 8 10

KILOMETRES

guns and the complete Rapier Battery were embarked in LSLs. The LSL forward helicopter spot, situated between the bridge and the fo'cs'le, could not be used at night and guns could not be re-located on the after spot behind the upperworks which could be used at night. 42 Commando was to remain afloat as Brigade reserve and would be landed at a time and place that I thought fit to meet the situation as the landing progressed. As soon as phase two was complete, the offload would start of some stocks of gun ammunition, fuel, rations and those unit first-line stores not carried ashore by the men, such as spare batteries (battle batteries) for radios, water jerricans, the immediate resupply of ammunition, more mortar bombs, more grenades, more linked belt for machine guns and so forth.

The tasks were given to unit after unit, commandos and battalions first, then the two troops of Blues and Royals, a troop to 40 Commando and a troop to 3 Para. 29 Commando Regiment's tasks followed, then those for 59 Independent Commando Squadron Royal Engineers, until all the units in the Order of Battle had been covered. One Commanding Officer was missing from the O Group: Lieutenant-Colonel Hellberg, the Commanding Officer of the Commando Logistic Regiment, a quiet, tough Everest and Alpine mountaineer, was ahead in the LSLs with his Regiment. His place at the O Group was taken by his second-in-command, the freckle-faced, red-haired Major Knott, who had won a Military Cross in the Radfan fifteen years before.

Having given the Commanding Officers their tasks, I handed over to my Chief of Staff, or Brigade Major, Major Chester, to cover the coordinating instructions, details that affected all or most of those present collectively. He pointed out that the timings of H and L hour, and indeed the date of D-Day itself, would follow in the signal known as the OPGEN Mike, to be sent by the Commodore when the details were firm. This signal would come out in a set format and Chester issued a copy of this format to all Commanding Officers. He reminded them that in an amphibious operation H hour was the time that the first wave of landing craft would beach and L hour the touch-down time for the first wave of helicopters. Easy to remember, he said, because, illogically, H hour was for landing craft and L hour for helicopters, which drew a laugh. The allocation of craft and helicopters to units and their loading times would also be sent in the OPGEN Mike. Major Chester, a tall and highly intelligent man who concealed an acid, short-fused temper under a quiet exterior, was my right-hand man and unreservedly trusted by all Commanding Officers in the Brigade. One by one he covered the points in his part of the orders: beaches and boundaries; marked maps were not to be taken ashore; nobody was to take photographs, letters, or personal documents with them; the recognition of friendly special forces, the priority of work in the Brigade defence position, the Brigade OP screen; and a host of other details.

The Naval Gunfire Support plan was explained, followed by the outline helicopter and landing-craft plan. The Commodore's Staff Officer Operations (SOO) then gave a brief description of the movements and grouping of the amphibious ships, escorts and civilian troop-carriers on the day preceding D-Day (D-1) and on the night of D-Day itself, so the troops on board would have some idea of what was going on, although many of them would be below decks and see nothing until they boarded their landing craft or helicopter. The SOO then explained that the timing for launching and loading the landing craft just outside San Carlos Water had been chosen so that the final approach to the north end of Falkland Sound would be in darkness to lessen the risk of air attack. I had wished to start landing as soon as possible after last light (the onset of darkness following sunset) to avoid the traditional dawn landing and have the maximum darkness in which to get the Brigade on to the high ground and clear any enemy off the sites from which the Rapier would defend the anchorage against air attack. However, a last light H hour would have meant a sea approach in daylight, which was clearly hazardous, given the adverse air situation. Clapp would have preferred a first light (the onset of daylight before sunrise) H hour with the maximum amount of darkness for the approach. However, with the usual spirit of co-operation a compromise solution was agreed within a few minutes of the problem being put to us both some days before the O Group. Even so, the SOO explained, at least half of the passage through the TEZ on D-1, and all within range of Argentine mainland-based air attack, would be in daylight. It would, the SOO promised, be the longest day.

The final speaker before I stood up again was the Deputy Assistant Adjutant and Quarter-Master General or DAA & QMG (DQ for short), the Chief Logistics Staff Officer, Major Wells-Cole. He had relieved Baldwin one week before the Argentine invasion and was a large, smiling, Navy and Combined Services cricketer with six children. He was a man of considerable physical and moral courage, and not afraid to face me with unpalatable news — his unenviable lot for at least the first ten days after the landing. He quickly highlighted the salient points in the fifteen pages of the logistic annex to the Operation Order which covered a great range of detail from resupply to the burial of the dead. I then concluded the O Group by reminding all Commanding Officers that the timings for D-Day would be in Zulu time, ie Greenwich Mean Time, not the local Falklands Time which was four hours behind GMT. I repeated the order that they were to instil into all their men the need to press on to their objectives, past their own casualties if need be. Once in position they were to exercise tight fire discipline if enemy patrols probed their positions and not to fall into the trap of allowing the enemy to draw their fire to disclose their machine guns. I concluded by saying that the campaign would not be a picnic, but, given the quality of the men in the Brigade, I was absolutely confident that they would succeed. I then told them that there would be questions in five minutes. There was none; an unspoken tribute to Chester, Wells-Cole and the Staff whose meticulous planning and crystal clear orders had left no room for doubt or ambiguity in anyone's mind.

As the Commanding Officers dispersed by helicopter back to the ships in which they were travelling, I went down to the flight deck of *Fearless* to see them off, thinking that it was unlikely that I would see them again before meeting them ashore on D-Day. The sun shone, but there was already a nip in the air as the ships ploughed steadily south and through the roar of helicopter engines and clatter of rotor blades we shouted the traditional pre D-Day parting, 'See you on the beach'. The Commanding Officers nodded and grinned before running to the waiting helicopters.

In fact I was to see them all again before D-Day, in order to explain to them personally a change of plan necessitated by late intelligence. On 16 May it became apparent that the Argentines had positioned a force of about company strength on Fanning Head overlooking the entrance to San Carlos Water. Furthermore the mobile, or strategic, reserve that had been thought to be at Fitzroy, was reported as being north of Darwin, nothing more precise than that. Clapp in particular was worried about the Fanning Head Mob, as they came to be called. A few rounds from a 105 mm anti-tank recoilless rifle could easily sink or damage a ship or landing craft if the Argentines took a leaf out of Lieutenant Mills' book. His men had nearly sunk an Argentine Corvette with an 84 mm medium anti-armour weapon during their spirited defence of South Georgia. Therefore, Clapp said, he wanted the Fanning Head Mob taken out, or at least kept busy, during the landing. The Commander of the SBS came up with a bold plan that fitted with the pre-H-hour Special Forces tasks. A reinforced section of SBS, twenty-five men, armed with twelve GPMGs, would land by helicopter near Fanning Head after dark on 20 May, taking with them a Naval Gunfire Forward Observer. The section would attack the Fanning Head Mob from the east, on the assumption that this would take them in the rear because their task was to observe to the west and south-west. Using naval gunfire and a heavy weight of fire from their twelve GPMGs, they would keep the Argentines busy while the landing went on in darkness. The SBS Commander included an added refinement in his plan: with my permission, he suggested that they test the resolution of the Argentine defenders by inviting them to surrender in the face of superior firepower. If his ploy worked, it would, he reasoned, give a good indication that the Argentines were ready to throw in the towel without fighting. This line of argument was a last vestige of the post-South

Georgia pushover syndrome. To persuade the enemy to surrender he would send Captain Bell with the SBS Section armed with a loud-hailer. Bell, born in Costa Rica, the son of a British UN official, had joined the Royal Marines speaking better Spanish than English. He was the Adjutant of the Brigade Headquarters and Signals Squadron, an organization he was to see little of until well after the surrender. His talents were in constant demand, a courteous, good-looking man with a shrewd judgement of the Latin-American thought process. He was not sold on the surrender idea but was gamely prepared to give it a try.

The reports of the enemy strategic reserve being north of Darwin worried me more. If they got an inkling of the landing, even on the night of D-Day, and moved fast they could get up on to Sussex Mountain, which overlooked the whole of the eastern arm of San Carlos Water, containing the major anchorage and three of the four beaches. Clearly Sussex Mountain must be seized as soon as possible, so I changed the order of landing. There were enough landing craft to land only two commandos or battalions simultaneously, so I brought 2 Para forward from phase two to phase one to land alongside, but slightly before, 40 Commando. 45 Commando would land in phase two and not in phase one, otherwise the plan remained unchanged. Commando and battalion objectives, beaches and landing-craft allocation remained as before. The risk in this change of plan was that if there were enemy at Ajax Bay they would shoot into the backs of 40 Commando and 2 Para landing opposite Ajax at San Carlos Settlement on Blue Beach One and Blue Beach Two respectively. For this reason I had wished to land at Ajax simultaneously with the landing at San Carlos Settlement. However, the possibility of the Argentines seizing Sussex Mountain before the Commando Brigade arrived had to be considered and was a higher priority. If enemy did open up from Ajax they would have to be dealt with by gunfire from the frigate *Plymouth* which was to accompany the first wave of landing craft right into San Carlos Water. Having made the necessary changes to the plan I visited Commanding Officers on 17 May in their ships to brief them: H. Jones, the CO of 2 Para, in *Norland*, Whitehead, the CO of 45 Commando, in *Stromness*, Hunt (40 Commando), Vaux (42 Commando) and Pike (3 Para) in *Canberra*.

By 17 May the main group of amphibious shipping had joined up with the LSLs which had left Ascension seven days ahead, so I was able to brief Hellberg personally on the plan and subsequent modifications. All was set, or nearly so. Now that all the amphibious ships, including merchant ships, were together and had made their rendezvous with Woodward's Carrier Battle Group, the final adjustments to the troop dispositions could be made. For the landing and during the subsequent land battle, an important part of any orders given would include the groupings of units and sub-units to carry out the task. A commando or battalion could have attached to it: the Battery Commander (BC) of the Battery in support as the Commanding Officer's artillery adviser; artillery Forward Observation Officers (FOOs) to spot for and correct the fire of guns allocated in support; engineers to clear mines and obstacles; armour; Blowpipe air defence; tactical air control parties to direct Harriers in the ground-attack role; light helicopters; and Naval Gunfire Observers to direct naval gunfire. All these would be listed in the grouping or task organization annex of the Operation Order or confirmatory notes. The Task Organization is the bane of students at Camberley, because it has to be scrupulously accurate to avoid confusion and double-booking of the valuable supporting arms and services. The Task Organization in a brigade amphibious operation can be complicated, involving considerable numbers of men and equipment. For example the grouping for just one commando, 40 Commando, for the initial landings was as follows, written in military abbreviations in the Operation Order, but in full here with explanations in brackets:

40 Commando — Phase One
8 Battery in Direct Support (including BC and FOO parties)
3 Troop B Squadron Blues and Royals in Direct Support
2 Scouts (Anti-Tank Guided Weapon/Reconnaissance Helicopters) in Direct Support from first light.
2 Troop 59 Independent Commando Squadron Royal Engineers in support and under command for movement (including)
One Royal Engineer Reconnaissance Section, one Combat Engineer Tractor (a tracked, amphibious, armoured engineer vehicle)
Number 1 Air Defence Section (Blowpipe) in support and under command for movement
Naval Gunfire Observer (NGFO) Party in support and under command for movement
Two Frigates (Naval Gunfire Support) in support

Every commando or battalion had other sub-units and specialists grouped with it, the grouping probably changing with every phase. Many of the men to be grouped with a particular commando or battalion had, until 18 May, been travelling in a different ship to the unit they were to support. Until the plan was firm and to avoid spending weeks at sea with the ships at overload, group elements were not married-up, to use the military phrase, with their supported units. Some of the men required for tasks before and during the landings were on ships of the Carrier Battle Group which were not to take part in the assault, or come near San Carlos. These men, mainly Special Forces and NGFO parties, needed to be transferred to the ships from which they would land. Others, who had been with the amphibious group all the time, similarly needed to marry-up with their units or go to ships from which they could be collected by the same wave of landing craft transporting their supported unit. This process, known as pre-D-Day cross-decking, a United States Navy and Marine expression and common parlance in NATO amphibious forces, was planned for 19 May, using helicopters, which, provided the wave height was less than about twenty-five feet, was feasible even from LSL flight decks; whereas it was highly unlikely that the wave height would be less than six feet and allow landing craft to be used.

Furthermore, orders had to be passed right down to the men who needed the information, so Commanding Officers of units split between several ships had to get across to see them.

'Giving orders was quite a complicated matter. I had to cross-deck to *Sir Lancelot* to give orders and then arrange for my men and their equipment to be cross-decked to join their battalions and commandos before the assault. This is no fun in a South Atlantic gale,' wrote Major Macdonald.

The cross-decking plan had, of course, to tie in with the landing plan. Both had been prepared by our Staffs working in concert. The degree of skill demonstrated by these Staffs and particularly my GSO3 Operations, Captain Samuelson, Royal Marines, and Major Minords, Royal Marines, of Clapp's Staff, was tangible proof of the need for expertise in the nuts and bolts of the amphibious art — something not acquired overnight.

While the final touches were being put to the cross-decking plan on the evening of 18 May, an order from Northwood caused a last-minute change to be made. Both of us were under the impression that we had made it clear that any cross-decking of large numbers of men, say a commando or battalion, given that every man was carrying between 50-70 pounds of personal kit and ammunition plus another 20 or so pounds of 81 mm mortar bombs or 84 mm MAW or 66 mm LAW, would have to be done by landing craft, because the tiny helicopter force would be unable to cope. As it was highly unlikely that the sea state would allow landing craft to be used in the open sea down south, Clapp and I had maintained that commandos and battalions would have to load into landing craft for the assault from the ships in which they had travelled south from Ascension. So 40 Commando, 3 Para and 42 Commando were told that they would load into their craft from *Canberra*, which they had assiduously practised at Ascension.

The other options were to stop at South Georgia to cross-deck, or find a sheltered spot in the Falklands, well away from San Carlos, in which a cross-decking could be achieved, perhaps in the guise of a landing and as part of the overall deception plan. The latter had been vetoed by Northwood and neither Clapp or I liked the idea of the two LPDs steaming the four or so days' passage from South Georgia, possibly pounding into heavy seas carrying 700 to 1,000 men over their maximum overload figures. There would be no room for men to sleep anywhere, except on the steel decks in compartments and passages throughout the ships, on the tank decks and in landing craft, and four nights with minimum sleep was not an appropriate start for men about to march and fight for an indeterminate number of days. So, apart from the cross-decking already described to achieve the correct grouping of units, no major cross-decking would take place, or so we thought. However, somewhere, either in MOD or at Northwood, someone had been calculating the losses to enemy air attack that might, and indeed were highly likely to be, sustained on the run-in on D-1, and these losses included at least one major ship. This information was not vouchsafed to us at the time and we were merely told to spread the troops around more and, in particular, two of the three battalions or commandos now in *Canberra* were to transfer to other ships. It was pointed out by both of us, to no avail, that cross-decking so many men would require landing craft and that days could pass before the sea state was right for such an evolution, thus postponing the date of D-Day with all the risk attendant upon such a delay. The SBS and NGFO parties, now in place near the beaches, might be discovered; the Argentines might 'twig' and move troops on to the beaches and mine the approaches. But cross-decking there was to be, so the two Staffs quickly assembled and it became clear that, to avoid wrecking the landing plan, 40 Commando and 3 Para should be transferred to *Fearless* and *Intrepid* respectively. While they were about it, Zulu Company of 45 Commando, in *Canberra*, would also go to *Intrepid*, because her craft would be lifting the remainder of 45 Commando from *Stromness* in the second wave on D-Day. With the sea state as it was that night, as the Staffs wrestled with the figures, there was only one way that such a large body of men could be transferred, in daylight in one day. This was by steaming one LPD each side of *Canberra* on the same course and rigging a light jackstay to each LPD and transferring the men one at a time. If the operation started at first light, it might just be completed by darkness. Meanwhile the helicopter cross-decking would go ahead as planned. There is always a temptation for those in the field, or at the sharp end at sea, to be critical of higher headquarters. But it is important to bear in mind the pressures on those at home, so much so that many of them must have wished that they were down in the South Atlantic and away from it all. They guarded our backs well and for that we were extremely grateful.

Fearless and *Intrepid* were warned to stand by for the operation and to prepare for a massive influx of men. The Captains and ships' companies of both LPDs responded in their usual swift and flexible way. In *Fearless* Captain Larken, the tall, ex-submariner whose calm and well-reasoned good sense had been such a blessing to all who came into contact with him over the past weeks, did not turn a hair, but merely added that if the sea state on 19 May looked at all possible he would give it a try by landing craft, but that the light jackstay method could and would be made to work. The Executive Officer of *Fearless*, Commander Kelly, the delightful, ex-Commando Wessex Pilot and ex-Squadron CO, quickly got to work to have every available space turned out so the troops would have somewhere to stretch out, preferably under cover. Feeding these extra men would also be a problem, but not one to defeat Kelly or *Fearless*.

As day dawned on 19 May the sea state looked good for a landing craft cross-decking. The LPDs docked down by pumping sea water through four ballast pumps into tanks in the ship's bottom. As the dock floor reached sea level, the stern gate was partially opened to allow sea water to flood in. Ballasting was continued until the water in the dock was at the required depth and the stern gate then opened fully. LCUs could then float out, collect troops from *Canberra* and return to the dock to disgorge their load onto the apron, a steel ramp leading up from the dock into the tank decks crammed with vehicles. With bated breath and fingers crossed, we watched the craft plough back and forth. The troops on *Canberra* exited through the large door in her side, swinging on a rope across to the narrow catwalk on the LCU's top side. Even in that sea state, the LCUs heaved and bobbed so that at one moment the catwalk was a couple of feet above the door sill in *Canberra*'s side and then dropped sickeningly away ten or so feet below the door; the grey-green sea seethed between the hulls of the LCUs and *Canberra*, while the basket-work fenders, bow and stern lines creaked and groaned. One man from 40 Commando fell between the craft and *Canberra* and the watchers thought that he would be crushed between the craft and ship's side, or sink beneath his loaded equipment. However, he was fished out, wet but unharmed. The hours of practice in loading craft from *Canberra* paid off in the speed with which this evolution was completed. Without favourable weather it could not have been achieved by landing craft; even so conditions in the open sea were on the limits for dock operations and, as lumpy sea swashed in and out of the LPD docks, small breakers surged in and broke on the ramps. The big LCUs, crammed with men, lurched and heaved as their Royal Marine colour-sergeant coxswains gently eased them skilfully forward into the narrow space between the dock bulkheads and the dolphins which divide the dock into two. Despite their skill, the loaded craft weighing over 100 tons smashed into and splintered parts of the wood cladding on the bulkheads and the dolphins. No one, except perhaps the Almighty, can claim any credit for arranging that 19 May, alone in the days that preceded and followed should produce an acceptable sea-state.

The helicopter cross-decking went without a hitch until the very last Sea King transferring men of D and G Squadrons 22 SAS from *Hermes* to *Intrepid* ditched, killing twenty-two Warrant Officers, NCOs and troopers, including the air crewmen. It was the only time I saw Lieutenant-Colonel Rose, Commanding 22 SAS, upset or moved, other than by excitement at the prospect of action or irritation at the inability of others to match his quick brain. Speaking quietly and obviously under deep strain, he asked for and got a helicopter to visit *Intrepid* to speak to his men. He returned to assure me that the Squadrons would fulfil all their tasks, despite sustaining the heaviest loss in one day since the Second World War. I had expected nothing less from these brave and highly professional men.

Both LPDs were now at an overload never dreamed of by their designers or the authors of the technical books which laid down how many troops each could accommodate. *Intrepid* had about 1,000 men and *Fearless* about 700 men over the top. Everywhere one looked there were men in various states of undress with their equipment, weapons, packs and radios. A treat for some of them was *Fearless'* CCTV system on which a succession of video cassettes of films and ITV and BBC newsreels sent south in the mail and dropped by C-130 were shown non-stop. B Company 40 Commando, crammed into *Fearless'* wardroom, normally 'officers only country', and now stripped of every vestige of furniture, cleaned their weapons, slept, read, or avidly watched the TV news of the past few weeks right back to early April. A series of street interviews conducted with random passers-by in various parts of the UK provoked shouts of laughter when the question, 'Where do you think the Falkland Islands are?' produced answers that ranged from 'Somewhere in the West Indies' to 'Near the Azores' and 'Off the coast of Scotland'.

CHAPTER FIVE

First Foothold

'Gentlemen, do not be dismayed if chaos reigns and these plans go awry, because chaos undoubtedly will reign' — Brigadier James Hill, Commander 3 Parachute Brigade, addressing his Brigade on the eve of the Normandy landings in 1944.

Before dawn on 20 May the ships' companies in the Amphibious Task Group came to action stations and they and the embarked troops waited with interest to see what weather the day would bring. The longest day, so cheerfully promised by the Commodore's staff, was here at last. Daylight revealed a gloriously, marvellously foul day, a heaving lumpy sea, drizzle and rolling banks of mist that drifted like smoke beneath a low cloud base. If that weather continued through the daylight hours it might foil any Argentine attempts to locate the ships approaching the Falklands, and the massed air attacks that all on board were bracing themselves to receive would not materialize. Seen from the upper decks of HMS *Fearless* the Amphibious Group was a brave sight and inspired all who saw it with the feeling that nothing was going to stop them. It was a unique amphibious group: among them the grey LSLs, a bright red civilian ferry, *Europic*, with Townsend Thoresen painted on her side in big white letters, the North Sea ferry *Norland* and the great white whale, *Canberra*, steaming majestically through the bucking, rolling, brave merchantmen. Frigates steamed through and around the convoy, which zigged and zagged to thwart Argentine submarines. Radio silence was imposed and signal lamps were used to pass messages from ship to ship. Aboard *Fearless* the staffs were worried because 2 Para had not acknowledged the receipt of the OPGEN Mike signal sent out on 19 May giving the final timings including D-Day itself, by now little more than twelve hours away. Important signals of this kind always included the cryptic 'Ack', for 'Acknowledge', as the last word of the text, and everybody else had 'Acked'. It was possible that 2 Para and their ship *Norland* did not know these vital timings or indeed the mass of other important detail contained in the signal. *Norland*'s reply by lamp to the query flashed from *Fearless* revealed that *Norland*'s literalizer, the equipment that decodes highly classified messages, had broken so the OPGEN Mike could not be read and would *Fearless* please re-transmit the signal. Quite rightly, *Fearless* refused. One signal passing through the ether would be quite enough to give the listening Argentines a 'fix' on the Amphibious Group's position and possibly enable them to vector submarines and aircraft, including the dreaded Super-Etendards with the air-launched Exocet, to attack the British ships. The message would have taken hours to transmit by light. So HMS *Broadsword* was called up by lamp and told to shoot a copy of the OPGEN Mike across to *Norland* by Costain gun line. Meanwhile, aboard *Norland*, 2 Para also were understandably very worried; clearly something was afoot: so many ships around them in close formation, steaming purposefully in a generally westerly direction. *Broadsword* was asked, as she approached, 'Do you know something we do not?' She carried the answer and shot it across.

As the day wore on the bad weather held and only at dusk did the amphibious ships and their escorts steam out from under the low clouds into a clear evening with a mass of stars pricking through the darkening sky. Thanks to the bad visibility the Argentine Airforce had failed to find the ships; the next few days would show what they could have done if the weather had been in their favour.

H-hour, the time when the first LCUs would drop their bow ramps on Blue Beach Two, was timed for 2.30 am local time on Friday 21 May. To meet this H-hour the LPDs must enter Falkland Sound from the north at 11 pm local time on 20 May and anchor outside the entrance to San Carlos Water, west of Wreck Point. The craft for 40 Commando in the first wave could load in *Fearless'* dock, the men filing their way down through the narrow passages, out through the tank deck, onto the ramp and into the craft, those men for the after two craft having to climb up the dolphin that divided the dock in half lengthways, up on to the narrow catwalks on the crafts' bulwarks and walk along these until they arrived at the after craft, then down into their LCU. Some of 40 Commando would land in LCVPs carried at *Fearless'* davits. These would be loaded while still hanging from the davits and then be lowered full of men. To reach the LCVP loading position involved a similar journey to that endured by men going to the dock, a long snake of sweaty, heavily laden, softly cursing men scrambling down ladders and narrow passageways, tripping over obstructions and bumping into each other in dim red light or total blackness. They had not rehearsed in this ship in the dark, because, until the last minute cross-decking had been ordered, they were to have loaded from *Canberra* into craft alongside. 3 Para, in the second wave, would load similarly from *Intrepid*, but in *Fearless'* craft which would have come into *Intrepid*'s dock and to her davits after landing 40 Commando in the first wave.

The craft for 2 Para in the first wave would float out from *Intrepid*'s dock empty and go across to *Norland*, loading the men through the ship's side door. 45 Commando, in the second wave, would load from *Stromness* down scrambling nets into *Intrepid*'s craft, returning empty from landing 2 Para, with the exception of Zulu Company who would start from *Intrepid*, where they had been since cross-decking on 19 May.

Few people got much sleep between the onset of darkness on 20 May and just before midnight when they started to move down to their craft. 'I spent much of the night talking to my sappers from 2 Troop on *Fearless* as they armed up with grenades and 66mm rockets. The atmosphere in the red light of the tank deck was professional and expectant,' wrote Major Macdonald.

As the men of 40 Commando filed on to the ramp leading into the LCUs, company sergeant-majors issued grenades, 84 mm and 66 mm rounds and, to some men, two 81 mm mortar bombs. The mortar bombs would be dumped on the beach for use by the Commando's Mortar Troop until a resupply could be arranged. The slowly moving files of Marines with blackened faces snaked seemingly endlessly into the craft. The hum of machinery in the tank deck and dock sounded so loud that it must surely alert any enemy on the shore. Through the gap between the top of *Fearless'* stern-gate and the after edge of the flight deck the night sky, although starless because of the overcast, was surprisingly light. From the upper decks the flashes of 4.5 inch shells could be seen bursting among ribbons of tracer on Fanning Head where Captain McManners, Royal Artillery, was spotting for HMS *Antrim* and Captain Bell and 3 SBS were engaging the Fanning Head Mob.

3 SBS had been landed by helicopter east of Fanning Head earlier that night and, before moving off, had detached a small party which was to move down to Green Beach One as quickly as possible to check that it was clear of enemy before 3 Para landed. It was. On their way to the beach they quickly scouted through Port San Carlos, but saw no enemy, who were, as it turned out, all asleep in the houses. An attempt some five days before to land the reconnaissance team for Green Beach One had been foiled because the insertion point in Foul Bay was occupied by enemy. So Port San Carlos had gone unwatched by the SBS since the OP parties had been withdrawn for briefing about seven days before D-Day. The risk of compromising the intended landing area at this stage was so great that it was decided by Clapp and myself to put the Green Beach One reconnaissance party in only a few hours before landing. The Ajax Bay SBS team had been in position since early May and the San Carlos Settlement SBS team had successfully re-inserted some five days before D-Day. South of San Carlos, well beyond earshot and out of sight, D Sqn 22 SAS, supported by HMS *Ardent*, were attacking Darwin to keep the strategic reserve pinned down and provide a diversion from the main landings. The Squadron had been landed by

helicopter that night north of Darwin and had approached their objective at a furious pace before starting their attack.

The amphibious group anchored about one hour later than planned because of navigational difficulties caused by mist at the northern entrance to Falkland Sound. One of HMS *Fearless'* ballast pumps chose this moment to break down which slowed up her docking-down process. Captain Larken boldly decided to continue with flooding despite the inherent risk that, until he could pump out on completion of dock operations, the ship would be able to steam only at slow speed with the stern gate open and the dock awash.

As 40 Commando in their landing craft chafed at the delay, the watchers on *Fearless'* bridge were far more worried by the long time that 2 Para were taking to load into their LCUs alongside *Norland*. The Battalion had not had the opportunity to take part in the many night-landing rehearsals carried out at Ascension by the other commandos and 3 Para. To compound the problem, a soldier fell between the craft and ship's side, suffering a crushed pelvis in the process. These two mishaps and the earlier navigational problem were to delay H-hour by about an hour. I was asked if I wanted to let 40 Commando go ahead in their craft without waiting for 2 Para, but rejected the suggestion because Major Southby-Tailyour was to lead 40 Commando's and 2 Para's craft in one formation into San Carlos water down the western side, splitting into two groups a few hundred metres or so east of Ajax Bay and leading 2 Para's craft into Blue Beach Two, before ordering 40 Cdo's craft into Blue Beach One. Any tinkering with the plan at this stage, in the dark and with the need to keep chatter on the radio to the minimum, might bring all manner of unforeseen chaos in its train. Seccombe, travelling in the craft with Southby-Tailyour, also advised against changing the plan at this juncture.

At last two groups of craft containing 40 Commando and 2 Para were shepherded together by Southby-Tailyour, riding with the CO of 2 Para in LCU Tango One. After consultation with Jones, Southby-Tailyour ordered Colour-Sergeant Garwood, the coxswain of LCU Tango Three, to catch up as soon as he had finished loading the last of 2 Para. The group of craft then set off. Southby-Tailyour ordered full speed instead of the planned six knots. Tango Three must have removed his engine governors because he arrived off Blue Beach Two on cue. The watchers on *Fearless'* bridge saw the dark mass of craft move into the gap between Fanning Head and Chancho Point, losing sight of them when they turned south to transit south down San Carlos water. There were eight LCUs and four LCVPs in all. 40 Commando needed the four LCVPs to carry A Company because two of their LCUs were carrying a Scorpion and a Scimitar, both vehicles side by side in the bows ready to blast at any enemy on the beach over the bow ramp lowered just before the start of the run-in. The men of B Company, Commando HQ and most of Support Company were crammed in behind the armoured vehicles in these two LCUs. C Company had a third LCU to itself, while the attached Royal Engineers and remainder of Support Company shared the fourth *Fearless* LCU with a Combat Engineer Tractor. 2 Para filled the four LCUs from *Intrepid*, a rifle company to each of three craft and Battalion HQ with Support Company in the fourth. HMS *Plymouth*, commanded by Captain Pentreath, 'rode shotgun' on the convoy ready to fire at opportunity targets if help was requested by the NGFO travelling with the Commanding Officer of 40 Commando. The NGFO for 2 Para, Captain McCracken, was waiting for the Battalion on its objective.

At the appointed place, off Ajax Bay, the formation of craft split, 40 Commando's craft stopping, while 2 Para's craft were led towards Blue Beach Two by Southby-Tailyour. The craft touched bottom about five metres offshore and the ramps dropped. 2 Para waded ashore. Their feet would remain wet until after the capture of Goose Green and Darwin nine days later. After a pause to shake out, the Battalion began its eight-kilometre approach march to its objective on Sussex Mountain. Four hours had been allocated for the move, allowing time for clearing light opposition on the way. It took twice that by men heavily laden with rucksacks; particularly those men from 32 Guided Weapons Regiment Royal Artillery attached to 2 Para and carrying the Blowpipe. They were not as fit as their Royal Marine counterparts in 3 Commando Brigade Air Defence Troop and, loaded down with their cumbersome Blowpipes and missiles, had great difficulty keeping up with the Battalion. Early experiences of moving at night in the Falklands were to lead the whole of 3 Commando Brigade into using the planning figure of a rate of advance of 1 kilometre per hour at night for large formed bodies of heavily laden men not in contact with the enemy. This was a figure that did not surprise those who know, or came to know, the Falklands, but which was greeted with ill-disguised disbelief by some back in England when the subject came up in radio conversation during the campaign.

In response to the all-clear red torchlight signal flashed by the SBS, 40 Commando landed a few minutes after 2 Para on Blue Beach One. A Company cleared White Rincon and then moved east to take up a defensive position on the western slopes of Verde Ridge. B Company, having cleared Little Rincon, also moved onto the western slopes of Verde Ridge. C Company cleared the Settlement, hoisted the Union Flag, then moved to its allocated defence position south of the Settlement. Like 2 Para, and indeed all the battalions and commandos of the Brigade, 40 Commando started digging in on their objectives immediately after arrival. All the positions chosen were on 'reverse slopes' and out of sight to any would-be attacker observing or approaching the anchorage from outside the rim of hills surrounding it. Therefore, the enemy would not know exactly where defended localities were, unless he patrolled properly or took air photographs. To attack reverse slope positions he would need to cross the skyline under fire. Meanwhile the Commando Brigade could dig, move about and carry out resupply reasonably secure in the knowledge that they were not being observed and could not be engaged by direct-fire weapons such as heavy machine guns, which would not be the case if they were deployed on the long, bare, forward slopes. The crest lines would be occupied by Observation Posts, both to observe the ground to the battalion or commando front and flanks and to bring down mortar, artillery and naval gunfire on enemy movement or attacks. Regular patrolling should ensure that enemy OPs looking in would not last long. Some Rapier launchers would also have to occupy positions on the crest in order to get an effective field of fire.

After landing 2 Para and 40 Commando, the craft returned to collect 3 Para and 45 Commando. The planned loading time for the second wave was between 3.30 am local and 4.15 am, with landing times of 6.05 am for 3 Para and 5.45 am for 45 Commando. The first wave had not landed until about 4.30 am and clearly the second wave would be correspondingly late. To add to the problem the radios from the Commando Brigade HQ in the Amphibious Operations Room (AOR) in *Fearless* to Commandos and battalions were not working well. On *Stromness* 45 Commando was waiting to embark:

> The moment for embarking passed and no boats had appeared. I went to the Operations Room to find news. Of course, that was when communications had broken down between us and Brigade. The poor Colonel was desperate for news too. Two hours later we scrambled over the guardrail down the scrambling net. Further delays waiting for the fourth landing craft. It had broken down somewhere. Back alongside to cram the remaining people into three landing craft. The sky was getting grey as we sailed. The landing went as planned, except, being daylight, there were too many people too close together. There simply was no way to change the plans at that stage. We secured our objectives unopposed and quickly deployed to the hill. It was a beautiful morning. We tramped off feeling a great deal better — we were now in our own element.

So wrote Captain Gardiner of 45 Commando in his diary. Every marine and soldier in the Brigade felt the same, with his feet back on land at last.

The only enemy encountered by the Brigade on or near their beaches was in Port San Carlos, west of 3 Para's Green Beach One. This enemy, about forty strong and the other half of the Company providing the Fanning Head Mob, had woken from their slumbers in the houses and settlement buildings to find a British parachute battalion landing two kilometres away and wisely decided to withdraw. Driving the fleeing Argentines ahead of them, 3 Para captured Port San Carlos and the dominating high ground of Settlement Rocks and Windy Gap. It was about 7.30 am when 3 Para landed and about 11.30 am before their objectives were secure.

With the onset of day the amphibious ships, STUFT and some escorts weighed anchor and steamed into San Carlos Water and the helicopters started flying. The first priority was to get the six light guns of 79 Commando Battery off the upper vehicle decks of LSL *Sir Geraint* and lifted ashore. Once the upper vehicle deck was clear, the twelve Rapier firing posts of T battery could be hoisted to the deck by crane and flown ashore. They had travelled south in the lower vehicle deck to minimize corrosion and damage to their electronics from salt spray. They had not fired during the stop at Ascension and their mechanisms might need some adjusting after landing and before they could be relied upon to fire accurately. The positions they had been assigned ashore had been selected after considerable thought by Major Smith, the Battery Commander, who had consulted a computer back in England to produce the best positions from which to cover the anchorage against air attack. Commandos and battalions had been told to clear all these positions before the Rapiers were landed. But, because of the delays to first and subsequent waves of troops, it would now be mid-day before all the intended sites could be cleared. It was critically important to get the Rapiers in as soon as possible to assist the warships in providing air defence of the anchorage and beachhead. The Rapier Battery reconnaissance parties would therefore have to fly in Sea King helicopters to some uncleared sites escorted by pairs of Gazelles armed with SNEB rockets and a GPMG. This was a risky decision to make, but, given the air threat, absolutely necessary.

Each reconnaissance party had the important job of checking that the site for their firing post, selected off a map, would indeed be suitable and then wait to guide in the helicopter carrying the Rapier slung underneath. Once the Rapier firing post had been deposited by Sea King, it was immobile and it would require the Sea King again to move it even a few yards. There were no roads or even tracks, so there was no question of using a towing vehicle to move a badly sited Rapier. It had to be right first time. Major Smith, a beefy, calm and cheerfully competent man, had earlier warned me that, once in their positions, it might take until nightfall before all the 'black boxes' in the Rapier firing posts were adjusted and all twelve were 'in', to use the technical expression. No one was quite sure what seven weeks in the lower vehicle deck of a vibrating, heaving LSL would do to the Rapier firing posts. This warning had been passed on upwards by Brigade HQ well before D-Day but had either been forgotten or ignored, because Rapier was seen in some quarters as the main defence of San Carlos Water against Argentine air attacks from soon after first light on D-Day.

Admiral Woodward had been briefed by his own staff, incorrectly, that Rapier would be extremely effective from early on D-Day, and furthermore that it was a land equivalent to the highly sophisticated shipborne Sea Wolf missile. In fact the Rapier with the landing force had an optical system (ie no radar) and was designed for the point defence of targets such as bridges and other high value *small* positions, where it would be faced by aircraft mainly attacking a single target, almost head-on and therefore with a small angle of deflection. It could not cope with the fast, low-flying, crossing targets, very difficult to see against a land background, and often several degrees below the horizontal so the Rapier was shooting at a sharp angle downhill. To begin with, several days were spent resiting most of the launchers to make best use of their limited capability. None of these problems were the fault of the Rapier crews who found themselves in a situation for which none of their training had prepared them. Worried at the high loss of escorts, which had it continued at the same rate as on D-Day, would have left him with none, Woodward sent me a terse signal. Stupidly, I reacted angrily. Friction of this kind would have been avoided had an operational level commander been able to come to see the situation for himself.

The ship losses and damage in and around San Carlos were a direct result of failure to gain air superiority and, in the circumstances, were unexpectedly light. This was luck, not good judgement on anyone's part.

At 8.00 am the Sea King with the Rapier reconnaissance party for the site on The Knob, east of Port San Carlos, was fired at. The Sea King swung away but both of its escorting Gazelles were hit. One managed to get back to the LSL on which the Flight was based, but one bullet hit the pilot of the other Gazelle, Sergeant Evans, Royal Marines. By a brilliant piece of flying, although dying of his wound, he managed to put his aircraft down in the water. His aircrewman, Sergeant Candlish, was the first to surface from the sinking helicopter, followed after a few seconds by Sergeant Evans, who was still conscious. Sergeant Candlish pulled Evans to him and inflated his lifejacket before realizing they were being shot at, although helpless in the water. The Argentine soldiers retreating from 3 Para along the northern back of the San Carlos River were responsible for the fire. Sergeant Candlish, still under fire, swam dragging his pilot with him to Port San Carlos about 500 metres away. As he neared the Settlement he shouted for help to people he could see by the houses, but the beach shelved steeply and, lacking a boat, they merely shouted encouragement. The fire continued until Sergeant Candlish's feet touched bottom and the watching people rushed forward to assist the two men.

As Candlish was pulling his mortally wounded pilot and friend from the water, he saw another Gazelle fly over Cameron's Point towards The Knob. It was hit by fire from the same group of enemy that had engaged Evans and Candlish. The bubble of the second Gazelle disintegrated under a hail of bullets and the aircraft fell like a stone into the hillside. Both the pilot, Lieutenant Francis, and the crewman, Corporal Giffen, were killed instantly. Sergeant Evans later received a posthumous Mention in Despatches for carrying out a successful ditching while mortally wounded, thus saving the life of his aircrewman.

The three aircrew were the only men of 3 Commando Brigade killed in action on D-Day. But out in Falkland Sound and in San Carlos Water many more sailors were to die under Argentine air attack. The first enemy aircraft to attack the anchorage and beachhead was a naval Macchi which attacked *Argonaut* at 8.45 am with rockets and cannon. This was followed by a pair of Pucaras at 9.38 am which attacked 2 Para on Sussex Mountain and D Squadron 22 SAS who were withdrawing from their successful diversionary raid on Darwin. The Argentines at Darwin reported that they had been attacked by a battalion. D Squadron rounded off a thoroughly satisfying night's work by shooting down one of the Pucaras with their American Stinger, heat-seeking, shoulder-fired, surface-to-air missile.

The next aircraft to appear were three Mirages which attacked the anchorage at 9.35 am. Thereafter raids seemed continuous, except for a short break for lunch. The helicopter pilots, landing-craft and Mexeflote crews bravely continues with the offload. It was uncanny to see a Sea King helicopter, with a gun or pallet of ammunition slung underneath, purposefully flying to its appointed landing site, while a pair of jets flashed by pursued by missiles and streams of tracer. The scenery and the bright sunshine, like a glorious day in the Western Islands of Scotland, added to the air of unreality.

While the first air attacks were hitting the ships in the San Carlos anchorage and on the gunline in Falkland Sound, the action at Fanning Head had come to a close after a frustrating and, at times, hazardous seven hours. Although nine Argentines were captured — six who surrendered and three wounded — the majority of the Fanning Head Mob, after fighting all night, ran off into the darkness just before dawn. During this sharp little engagement, some of the Argentines, hearing Bell on the loudspeaker, had attempted to surrender but had been stopped by their comrades. Perhaps the loudspeaker was not powerful enough for the invitation to surrender to be clearly heard, but more likely not all the enemy were in a mood to submit without a fight. However, the SBS action together with *Antrim*'s gunfire had achieved its main purpose — to prevent the Fanning Head Mob from interfering with the landing in any way. Had they been left to their own devices, they might have used their 105 mm recoilless anti-tank gun with devastating effect against the unarmoured LCUs packed with troops.

One effect of the almost continuous air attacks on D-Day was to frustrate my efforts to get ashore to see my Commanding Officers until late afternoon. Every time my Scout helicopter approached *Fearless* to collect me, another Air Raid Warning Red resulted in the deck being closed. Larken, quite rightly, did not want helicopters buzzing round his ship distracting his Bofors gunners and Sea Cat operators. Because radio communications from the AOR to commandos and battalions were fragmentary, and being unable to get ashore, I moved to *Fearless*'s bridge where I could at least see something of what was going on. Seccombe was already up there, as were three of *Fearless*'s young officers, including the Navigator, lolling in the Captain's chair with his feet up on the control panel while his Master was on the Gun Direction Platform above him fighting his ship. All three young Naval officers were in tremendous form and clearly enjoying themselves watchkeeping in action for the first time. Seccombe was as cool as usual.

By late afternoon, with the sun still shining, all the frigates in and near the anchorage had been hit and damaged, one of them, *Ardent*, mortally. With about two hours of daylight left, I remarked to Seccombe that it would be our turn next and that of the LSLs, sitting like fat ducks at the southern end of San Carlos Water. But, amazingly, no further attacks came that day. This was the first of many opportunities that the Argentine Air Force missed to cripple the Commando Brigade by sinking our supplies. On D-Day all of the Brigade's ammunition, fuel and rations were still embarked and the loss of the LSLs would have resulted in the Brigade being without any of its combat supplies, other than those carried on the belts of the men ashore.

I got ashore by Scout helicopter as the evening drew on and, before nightfall, managed to visit 3 Para, 42 Commando and 40 Commando. 42 Commando had been landed when it became clear that leaving them on board *Canberra* might result in the loss of part, or all, of the Commando if this prime target was hit and set on fire or sunk. Furthermore, because reports of 3 Para's contacts with the enemy in the Port San Carlos area were confused, it would be as well to reinforce this part of the beachhead in case the enemy should be in the vicinity in large numbers. It was, at this stage, inconceivable to anyone in 3 Commando Brigade that the Argentines would not mount at least some kind of harassing attack. On both counts 42 Commando would be of more use ashore, and at about 11.00 am they had been ordered to land.

I met the CO, Lieutenant-Colonel Vaux, as the Commando was moving east through Port San Carlos and told him to pursue the enemy, who had last been seen retreating eastwards, but not to advance further than Cerro Montevideo, eight kilometres east of Port San Carlos, and thus stay within range of friendly artillery. The Commando was in a jubilant and confident mood, released from the ship at last. The Regimental Sergeant-Major, Chisnell, a mountaineer and skier, greeted me warmly. Vaux, a small, shrewd and aggressive soldier, was transparently very happy that the hours of waiting as Brigade Reserve were over and he had a task at last. 3 Para were also in good heart and busily digging in. After the day's demonstration of what the Argentine Air Force could do, no one needed any second bidding to dig.

40 Commando, around San Carlos Settlement and on the western slopes of Verde Mountains, were also well in. The Commanding Officer, Lieutenant-Colonel Hunt, was his usual cheerful self. Hunt, a strong, outspoken character, had come in the first twenty of his Commando in their marathon within two days of taking over command. As well as being super-fit, he had a good brain and tactical ability and I had considerable respect for him. As an ex-CO of 40 Commando myself, it had a special place in my affections. Hunt and 40 Commando were to have a bitterly disappointing war through no fault of their own; but all that was in the future.

Darkness fell before I could get round to see 2 Para and 45 Commando. Until pilots were familiar with the ground, the beachhead was no place to be flying around at night, especially with the location of some units still uncertain, thanks to the poor radio communication. However, even the brief visits to part of the Brigade had been a tonic, seeing the cheerful faces, many well known to me, under their camouflage cream and topped by helmet, or green or red beret. The landings had been successful — that much was clear. It was also absolutely plain that the Brigade ashore could not be effectively commanded from *Fearless*. This came as no surprise and had been proved frequently on exercises. Indeed because of this, the Tactical Headquarters, from which I could command until my Main Headquarters could be got ashore, had been stood by to land from soon after first light that morning. The Tactical Headquarters eventually got ashore at last light about ten hours late, thanks to the delays caused by air attacks. A Brigade Commander must be able to get forward to see his Commanding Officers, or summon them back to see him or speak to them on the radio, when he chooses and the practical situation allows it. Command in war is complicated enough without trying to exercise it out of touch for hours at a time and unable to get off a ship fighting for its life. Without the amphibious ships and particularly the LPDs, with their specialized equipment, the landing could not have been done, but the day's events had convinced me, if I needed convincing after years of practice on amphibious exercises, that the whole Headquarters must be got ashore as quickly as possible. This feeling was reinforced when I heard, on returning to *Fearless*, that, on orders from Northwood, *Canberra* and *Norland* were to be out of San Carlos Water as soon as possible that night and that there was talk of the LPDs leaving the anchorage each night in case of submarine attack. Whatever happened and whatever the ships did, or did not do, the Headquarters with all its communications must get ashore so that, by the next dawn, the Brigade could be under the hand of its Commander to face whatever the day might bring. Although years later I learned that Clapp felt that I should have stayed on board, in hindsight, it was right to go ashore, and I would do the same again today.

The landing had gone well that first day, despite the air attacks, thanks to the devotion of the helicopter pilots, the landing craft and Mexeflote crews. One of the Mexeflote coxswains, Staff-Sergeant Boultby RCT, described this and subsequent days thus:

We had only been in San Carlos Water an hour before we received our first air raid. It was then we realized how many men can climb a rope ladder at once. We endured a further three air raids during the building of our 66 foot raft ... At one stage we were alongside RFA *Stromness* when we were attacked by Argentine aircraft. As they flew between us and RFA *Fort Grange* four 1,000 lb bombs were dropped. We completed loading and started on our way and were just passing HMS *Broadsword* when the next wave came in using rockets to attack *Broadsword*. So there we were surrounded by a raft load of Rapier missiles, grenades and other ammunition. Under these conditions, one is tempted to place one's head between one's knees and kiss one's rear good-bye.

Staff-Sergeant Boultby was later awarded the Military Medal for his gallantry in rescuing men from the burning *Sir Galahad* in Fitzroy.

The three commandos and two parachute battalions were ashore, as were all the Rapier firing posts and all four light gun batteries, with some ammunition. The Brigade was dug in and ready to protect the beachhead while its combat supplies — the bullets, beans and fuel to feed guns, weapons, men, vehicles and helicopters — were being unloaded. The plan to keep combat supplies afloat in the LSLs and offload them when required had to be discarded after the experience of the first day's air attacks. If they stayed in the LSLs they would risk being lost. They must be unloaded as quickly as possible and the only place that looked like having enough room in which to dump the thousands of tons of ammunition, fuel and rations was Ajax Bay and the disused mutton factory. The beach was close to the factory and would take several craft at a time; it was a short haul for the Eager Beaver forklift trucks to transport the pallets from craft to dump.

Other than pushing out patrols, there was no point in the Brigade moving out of the beachhead until a substantial part of its bullets, beans and fuel was ashore, and achieving this would use up most of the medium helicopters and all the landing craft for several days to come. If the Brigade did advance out of the beachhead, the distances over which it would need to be kept supplied would increase with every kilometre it moved away from the anchorage. Contact with the enemy would result in ammunition being used and having to be replaced immediately. As the Brigade moved away from the protection of its own artillery, the guns and their ammunition would have to be shifted forwards to catch up. To lift one light gun battery and 500 rounds per gun, enough for one battle, takes eighty-five Sea King helicopters, or eight Sea King helicopters flying almost eleven times each, or any permutation thereof — and there were four light gun batteries. It is a fact of military life that the deeper you advance into enemy territory, your needs expand accordingly; more and more has to be transported further and further.

As the Brigade moved away from the air defence umbrella round San Carlos Water it, but, more critically, its line of supply, would be exposed to air attack. Infantry on the ground, well dispersed, dug-in, or taking cover and aggressively firing back, would not be too vulnerable to attack from the air unless the enemy used cluster bombs, which the Argentines did not have, or napalm, which they did possess but fortunately used only once. On the other hand, the Brigade's arteries, along which the bullets, beans and fuel had to flow, were totally reliant on helicopter lift and the enemy possessed air superiority. Resupply in daylight would lead to helicopters being shot down and, with only eleven Sea Kings and five Wessex helicopters available for medium-lift tasks at this stage, even small losses would be a major set-back. Night helicopter resupply with only four PNG-equipped helicopters would have been impossible. The helicopter force was totally inadequate for the needs of a large brigade in contact with the enemy. After flying most of each night, the four PNG-equipped helicopters had to be maintained during the day and their crews rested, and one Sea King had to be dedicated to Rapier support. This left a puny force of only six Sea Kings and five Wessex available on a daily basis to the 3rd Commando Brigade.

The crucial battle of the whole campaign, starting on D-Day and lasting for the next five days, was for control of the air, so that large-scale operations outside the air defence umbrella could be conducted. The battle, on the British side, was fought by the Harriers, the escorts and other warships, indeed every ship that mounted a gun of any kind, and the Rapiers, Blowpipes and GPMGs ashore. This battle of attrition, which cost three warships sunk and the lives of seventy-seven men, mostly sailors, whittled down the Argentine Air Force to the extent that after 26 May it

EAST FALKLAND

MOUNT ROSALIE

FALKLAND SOUND

DOUGLAS SETTLEMENT

NEW HOUSE

PORT SAN CARLOS SETTLEMENT

BOMBILLA HILL
ARROY PEDRO RIVER

SAN CARLOS SETTLEMENT

CARLOS WATER

AJAX BAY

BULL HILL
BALL MOUNTAIN
THE ONION

MOUNT SIMON

CAMILLA CREEK HOUSE

DARWIN
GOOSE GREEN

BRENTON LOCH

LAFONIA

CHOISEUL SOUND

TEAL INLET SETTLEMENT

EVELYN HILL

THE "BABY"

LOWER MALO HOUSE

TOP MALO HOUSE

SMOKO MOUNTAIN

PORT FITZROY
FITZROY SETTLEMENT

LONG ISLAND MOUNTAIN
MOUNT ROUND

MOUNT LOW

MOUNT ESTANCIA
MOUNT VERNET

ESTANCIA HOUSE

STANLEY AIRPORT
STANLEY
SAPPER HILL

MOUNT WILLIAM
TUMBLEDOWN
MOUNT LONGDON
MOUNT HARRIET
TWO SISTERS
MOUNT CHALLENGER
MOUNT KENT
BLUFF COVE PEAK

SCALE

0   5   10   15   20   25
KILOMETRES

failed to pose a major threat to the conduct of land operations. Control of the air was never completely wrested from the enemy right up to the end, but, given the odds before D-Day, what was achieved was a major victory and most of the credit for that victory goes to Commodore Clapp, to the ships' companies who fought the inshore battle and to the Harrier pilots and Carriers that operated the aircraft.

It was a magnificent fight. Not since Crete in 1941 had the Royal Navy faced such odds from the air. Clapp received scant recognition. On his return home, no one at Fleet Headquarters showed sufficient interest to debrief him, and he was retired on completion of his tour as COMAW, reverting to the rank of Captain.

The policy of keeping the Carriers so far from the Falkland Islands was criticized by the ill-informed at the time and subsequently. Max Hastings was right to say that Admiral Woodward was the only person who could have lost the war in an afternoon. Admiral Woodward's skilful handling of the Carrier Battle Group kept them safe and thus our air support intact.

While the Brigade waited to move out, the time was spent in trying to find out where the enemy actually was and in what strength along the Brigade's projected route to Stanley. At last light on D-Day two patrols from the M and AW Cadre were put out by helicopter, one on Bull Hill and one on Evelyn Hill. During daylight, in good weather, the clear Falklands atmosphere would enable them to see for miles and report on enemy movement towards the beachhead, by helicopter or any other means. The OP on Evelyn Hill would also be able to keep an eye on Teal Inlet Settlement, which I intended to use as a main staging post on the route to Stanley. Commandos and battalions also patrolled their fronts and flanks to search for enemy and give early warning of his approach.

The precipitate departure of *Canberra* and *Norland* caused a major turmoil. The plans to use *Canberra* as a floating Field Dressing Station (FDS), to which men would be evacuated (casevaced) and treated before onward movement to the Hospital Ship *Uganda*, would have to be abandoned. But before she sailed as much of the FDS as possible had to be unloaded to the mutton factory at Ajax Bay, which provided the only building large enough in the beachhead. *Norland* was also carrying the Parachute Clearing Troop (PCT) of 16 Field Ambulance. They too had to be unloaded before she sailed. There was insufficient time to get all the stores off *Canberra* and *Norland* and the men of one complete Field Surgical Team (FST) were left on *Canberra*. Surgeon Commander Jolly, Royal Navy, commanded the Ajax Bay FDS. Jolly, a large, jovial and extrovert man who has described the work of his FDS in his excellent book *The Red and Green Life Machine*, was another of those who found his moment in the Falklands Campaign. No Brigade can have been better served by its Senior Medical Officer and the teams he led.

Canberra and *Norland* also took with them the unit stores of 40 Commando, 42 Commando, 2 Para and 3 Para. They would not see many of them again until after the campaign was over. These stores ranged from vital replacement radio batteries to the immediate re-supply of ammunition — the first-line stocks not carried on the men, such as mortar, Milan and Wombat ammunition and a complete resupply of small arms ammunition. Also in *Canberra* when she sailed were 90,000 rations, enough to feed the Brigade for eighteen days. The Logistic Regiment would immediately have to start meeting the urgent demands of units deprived of their own back-up supplies, while at the same time working round the clock to offload the LSL and STUFT.

Putting the valuable assets of the FDS and the Brigade Maintenance Area so close together at Ajax Bay has since been criticized by some pundits with the advantage of hindsight. There was simply not the time or resources to site and dig in the Brigade Maintenance Area and FDS anywhere else. The FDS in particular needed floor space, protection from the weather and a place where bright lights could be used to operate at night. A search for an alternative location after the Brigade Maintenance Area and FDS were bombed later on did not produce anything better in the whole San Carlos beachhead area.

As day dawned on 22 May my staff and I stepped ashore at San Carlos Settlement on Blue Beach Two. We found the Headquarters set up and camouflaged near the Settlement Manager's house, right by the white flagpole up which the Union Flag had been hoisted twenty-four hours before. The flag was no longer flying, having, wisely, been lowered to avoid providing an aiming mark for the Argentine Air Force. However, the pole itself was conspicuous enough and might provide a reference point for a sharp-eyed Argentine forward air controller. The pole was hacked down. The nerve centre of the headquarters consisted of seven BV202 (Bandwagons) backed into a specially constructed Command Post (CP) Tent. The back of each Bandwagon contained radios and small tables at which the staff worked and all could look into the central, covered area formed by the CP tent. The whole complex was covered by camouflage nets and difficult to see from the air, or the ground at a distance. The Headquarters was set up in exactly the same way as it had been on many an exercise from north of the Arctic Circle in Norway in winter to summer exercises on Salisbury Plain. The complex of vehicles did not, as described in one published account, 'pass for the Headquarters'; it *was* the Headquarters and, thanks to the officers and men who ran it, highly efficient.

I immediately flew to visit 2 Para on Sussex Mountain. They were in good heart and still improving their positions. Everywhere they dug they struck water about a foot down, and sometimes even less. In these cases the only solution was to build up with peat bricks or rocks. Every man had wet feet, but cheerful, confident smiles greeted questions as to their state of health. The Battalion had seen HMS *Ardent* sink the day before and had come under attack from the air a number of times, but aggressively returned fire with all the GPMGs that could be brought to bear. Major Crosland's B Company, many of them copying their Commander's habit of wearing a black, woolly hat, were full of ideas for firing airbursts from the 105 mm light guns into the head of the Bay Brook Valley behind the Battalion's left flank, a favourite approach for the Argentine aircraft. If they got the timing right, they reasoned, the approaching aircraft would find shells exploding about 100 feet above the valley floor. 'At least it might make their eyes water,' they joked.

I joined Jones in his Forward Observation Post up with B Company, which looked south over the rolling, peaty hills, covered with white grass, that lead to Sussex Creek, Cantera, Camilla Creek and the Darwin Peninsula. The Peninsula was out of sight from the OP, but parts of Brenton Loch could be seen. Although it was a grey, overcast day, the cloud base was high enough for aircraft to operate and the visibility was good. There seemed no reason why the Argentine Air Force should not appear, but it did not and no attacks were made on the beachhead or anchorage that day.

Moore's directive to me which he had issued on 12 May, by signal, read as follows:

You are to secure a bridgehead on East Falkland, into which reinforcements can be landed, in which an airstrip can be established and from which operations to repossess the Falkland Islands can be achieved.

You are to push forward from the bridgehead area so far as the maintenance of its security allows, to gain information, to establish moral and physical domination over the enemy, and to forward the ultimate objective of repossession. You will retain operational control of all forces landed in the Falklands until I establish my Headquarters in the area. It is my intention to do this aboard *Fearless*, as early as practicable after the landing. I expect this to be approximately on D+7. It is then my intention to land 5 Infantry Bridge into the beachhead and to develop operations for the complete repossession of the Falkland Islands.

Moore had embarked in the liner *Queen Elizabeth II* at Ascension on 20 May, D-1. At the same time the command chain was altered by Northwood to reflect Moore's arrival in the beachhead with another brigade, 5th Infantry Brigade, but ten days before he actually appeared.

This would have been just acceptable if the communication fit on *Queen Elizabeth II* had allowed him to talk to me or send me signals. Unfortunately, it did not. Northwood sent signals to him, including, among other things, instructing him to break out of the beachhead, and merely copied them to me. I assumed that I should carry out what he had been told to do, but without being able to discuss it with him to ensure that it was actually what he wished done.

As far as I knew the nearest enemy positions to the beachhead were those at Darwin and Goose Green, some nineteen and twenty-one kilometres respectively as the crow flies, from where I sat with Jones. Infantry, even commandos and paratroopers, cannot fly like crows or walk on water, so the marching distance was nearer twenty-three kilometres and twenty-five kilometres. However, the enemy at Darwin and Goose Green looked like providing the only possible target that the Brigade could take on without either conducting another amphibious operation on West Falkland or closing up to Stanley. While the combat supplies were being offloaded, a battalion raid on the Argentine garrison of Darwin and Goose Green looked the most promising way of fulfilling Moore's directive to 'establish moral and physical domination over the enemy'. The aim of the raid would be to cause as much damage as possible to the garrison and its equipment, including air defence guns and missiles.

2 Para was the nearest and, from their main positions on Sussex Mountain and their C Company patrol OPs forward, overlooked some of the ground approaches to the Darwin isthmus. 2 Para was the logical choice for this operation. Using anyone else would have involved a longer approach march or using the scarce helicopter or landing craft resources to make the move. I therefore warned Jones that it was likely that he would carry out this raid and that he would receive confirmation of this and orders later. I then flew on to visit 45 Commando dug-in on the eastern slopes of the high ground overlooking Ajax Bay and had a long talk with Lieutenant-Colonel Whitehead, the Commanding Officer. We had known each other for over twenty years and I had considerable respect for Whitehead's intellect and quiet determination. Few people crossed Whitehead's path twice, although his somewhat forbidding exterior covered a warm and compassionate man with a sense of humour. The Commando was well in hand and busily improving its positions. The lower slopes of the hillside were covered in fern and it was very difficult to see the well-camouflaged companies 'tucked away like chameleons in little holes in the hill', as Captain Gardiner described them.

The next day, 23 May, a formal warning order was sent to 2 Para that they were to raid Darwin and Goose Green. Jones came to Brigade Headquarters for a briefing and was told to submit his detailed plan to me for approval. He was briefed by D Squadron 22 SAS on what they had found during their diversionary raid on the night of 20/21 May. Lieutenant Thurman, Royal Marines, was attached to 2 Para to provide local knowledge. Thurman had been second-in-command of the outgoing Royal Marines Falkland Island detachment (NP8901) captured when the Argentines invaded, but had himself avoided capture on 2 April because he had been in Venice on leave at the time with his fiancée, the Governor's daughter. Thurman had spent much of his time in the Falkland Islands walking for settlement to settlement and knew the routes to, and layout of, many of them well.

The air attacks on the beachhead and anchorage started again on 23 May with renewed ferocity. On many occasions the attack patterns and routes differed from those of D-Day. Rapier, now well 'in', claimed a number of hits, as did ships in the anchorage, raising roars of cheers from the troops on the hillsides. 42 Commando had by this time arrived at Cerro Montevideo; when I visited them, I ordered them to halt and dig in. They were already outside the air defence umbrella. From their positions we could see the pairs of Mirages and Skyhawks swoop in low from the north-west on the 'goalie', the frigate guarding the entrance to San Carlos Water, and then lift over Doctor's Head to drop down low over the inner Verde and the Third Corral Mountains, before banking sharply to fly west along the course of the San Carlos River and Port San Carlos and attack the gallant 'goalie', on this occasion HMS *Antelope*, for a second time. The visit to 42 Commando convinced me that the Commando was achieving nothing outside the beachhead perimeter except to throw an extra strain on the already over-worked logisticians and the helicopters needed to keep the Commando supplied, so 42 Commando was ordered back to Port San Carlos to join 3 Para in its defence. 42 Commando was picked up that night from Salt Point in LCUs navigated by Southby-Tailyour and returned to Port San Carlos — a good example of the use of LCUs exploiting the water lines of communication within the beachhead.

That night, as Brigade Headquarters was moving its Bandwagons and Command Post (CP) into a large hole dug for the purpose by the Combat Engineer Tractor, HMS *Antelope* exploded in a mass of flames a few hundred metres offshore from the Brigade CP. The majority of the troops round the anchorage thought that most, if not all, her crew had gone with her. Explosion after explosion crashed out in the darkness. But, thanks to the bravery of the helicopter crews and the landing craft crews, only three men died, one of them a gallant Royal Engineer bomb disposal NCO who was trying to defuse the unexploded bomb deep in the ship. Corporal Dimmick RCT, a Mexeflote raft commander, expressed what we all felt when he later wrote:

We watched with lumps in our throats as *Antelope* raged with fire and finally sank. She was our escort and everybody felt a great loss as she was more than just a ship to us. She had so long been our guardian and protector.

The next day, 24 May, she broke in half and sank, but not before the air attacks started again.

During another day of air attacks the plans for the raid on Darwin and Goose Green firmed up. An approach by sea down Brenton Loch, which Jones favoured initially, was ruled out after consultation with Southby-Tailyour. The difficulties of navigating LCUs down Brenton Loch at night made the idea far too risky. Furthermore nobody knew what forces, if any, held the western side of the Loch. An OP had reported, wrongly as it turned out, seeing an LVTP swimming across the loch and then climbing out on the western bank; but it was not until at least a week after the capture of Goose Green that the whole of Lafonia was cleared and it was known exactly where enemy positions had been located. A helicopter approach was also out; there were simply not enough helicopters. The only answer was a night approach on foot, from Sussex Mountain, past Camilla Creek and on to the northern end of the isthmus. Jones's plan was that D Company would secure the area of Camilla Creek House that night so that three 105 mm light guns and some ammunition could be flown in before dawn. Any attempts to fly guns in by day would be a signal to the enemy that something was up. It was established that only three guns and 200 rounds of ammunition for each gun could be lifted during the hours of darkness by the four PNG-equipped helicopters. The remainder of the Battalion would move down the following night and carry out the raid, supported by the guns at Camilla Creek House and gunfire from a ship. D Company set off at last light.

The first helicopter task that night, however, was to fly reconnaissance elements of D Squadron 22 SAS to Mount Kent overlooking the key ground around Stanley. No sooner was this completed then the weather over the whole of East Falkland closed in and the visibility became so bad that the next helicopter sorties, to fly the guns to support 2 Para to Camilla Creek, became impossible. The raid was not tactically sound without artillery support so, to Jones's intense annoyance, I cancelled it. It was either that night or not at all as far as I was concerned. The main objective was still Stanley, so establishing a strong force on the vital ground of Mount Kent and the nearby features was the most important task ahead. As a precursor to seizing Mount Kent, several attempts had been made to get D Squadron's reconnaissance group up there by helicopter, with the aim of following up with the remainder of the Squadron and 42 Commando on successive nights. By the morning of 25 May the weather had been so bad at night that only the helicopter insertion of the Squadron reconnaissance party had been achieved, but not the Squadron main body or 42 Commando.

Another operation that was repeatedly frustrated by the bad weather at night was to search for and destroy the suspected Argentine OP on Mount Rosalie on West Falkland. It was thought, correctly as it transpired after the war, that the enemy on Mount Rosalie were directing the Argentine aircraft on to the ships in Falkland Sound and the entrance to San Carlos Water, which they could see clearly. For several nights the M and AW Cadre attempted to get patrols across Falkland Sound by rigid raider and finally, in desperation, by LCVP. But the weather at this stage proved too rough, even for the LCVP. Eventually, as the energies of the Commando Brigade were directed eastwards, the attempts to get to Mount Rosalie were abandoned.

Unfortunately the weather had been fine by day, giving no chance of any respite from the Argentine Air Force. That night *Atlantic Conveyor*, carrying five big Chinook helicopters and six more Wessex, was expected to arrive in San Carlos Water. With these helicopters added to the eleven Sea Kings and five Wessex already ashore, the Brigade would be some way towards getting the mobility it needed to lift not only the men but, more important, the guns and ammunition to start investing Stanley. Once these helicopters arrived, the Brigade's energies must be concentrated on getting to Stanley. Darwin and Goose Green did not lie on the route I intended to take; any effort in that direction would be a diversion from the aim.

At about 6 pm on the evening of 25 May the R Group with Chester, Wells-Cole and Dixon, the Officer Commanding the Headquarters and Signals Squadron, were at the usual evening conference with me in the small tent behind my bandwagon making the final adjustments to plans to get the Brigade forward. We were interrupted by Captain Eddington, the GSO 3 Signals, who stuck his head through the tent flap and told us that a signal had just arrived saying that *Atlantic Conveyor* had been sunk, taking all but one helicopter, a Chinook, to the bottom of the sea. Earlier that evening the bad news that HMS *Coventry* had been sunk had also been received, making 25 May a black day.

I ordered a full staff conference for the following day to include the CO of 22 SAS, the Commander of 846 Squadron, Commander Thornewill and Major Minords from Clapp's staff. They were to be tasked with investigating what, if anything, could be done to salvage the wreck of the plan using the existing helicopter and landing craft assets. As the R Group dispersed, somebody said, 'We'll have to bloody well walk.'

CHAPTER SIX

Goose Green

The sinking of *Atlantic Conveyor* left 3 Commando Brigade and Commodore Clapp's Amphibious Task Group with the eleven Sea King Mark IV and five Wessex helicopters with which they had carried out the amphibious landing on D-Day. Although one Chinook had survived from *Atlantic Conveyor*, it was not made immediately available. Out of the eleven Sea Kings, one was permanently allocated to the Rapier Battery every day during daylight hours, to carry fuel to the firing post generators, and REME fitters to maintain the equipment. The firing posts could not be allowed to go out of action for lack of fuel or maintenance. Of the remaining ten Sea Kings, the four PNG-equipped aircraft were not available for daylight tasks except in an emergency and then only for short periods, because the aircraft must be maintained and their crews rested after the exhausting and dangerous business of nightly sorties. The remaining six Sea Kings and five Wessex were all that were available for all troop, equipment and logistic movement ashore by the Brigade and the continuing offload being carried out by the Logistic Regiment and by Clapp's amphibious ships and STUFT. Clapp retained operational command of all the helicopters because, rightly, he judged that the offload must have priority.

This was the helicopter situation that faced the Staff as they met in a cowshed at San Carlos Settlement on the morning of 26 May to work out how the aim of getting forward to Stanley might be achieved. The most cheerful man there was the Commanding Officer of 22 SAS, whose D Squadron had managed to get their reconnaissance teams up on to Mount Kent during the night of 24 May. Also on the night of 24 May 6 SBS had been inserted by boats from a frigate into Port Salvador to carry out the necessary reconnaissance towards fulfilling my aim of using Teal Inlet as a stepping-stone on the route to Stanley. This at least was a beginning. However, the remainder of D Squadron who should have gone in to secure the landing site below Mount Kent the preceding night, 25 May, had been prevented from doing so by the bad weather that again had stopped helicopter flying.

The plan had been to follow up the fly-in of D Squadron with the whole of 42 Commando and a battery of guns by a night helicopter move to the landing site secured by D Squadron. This would be followed by the move forward of the whole Brigade, also by helicopter. Now, even if the one surviving Chinook were added to the helicopters already ashore, the move of just 42 Commando would be a laborious and lengthy process. Each night would see little more than one rifle company, some medium mortars, half the gun battery and a small quantity of ammunition lifted forward. Without the means to get the remainder of the Brigade up quickly to reinforce 42 Commando, who would be sixty-six kilometres from the beachhead, as the crow flies, the move being planned for the Commando was tactically so risky as to be foolhardy. The Staff and I could see no alternative to the remaining commandos and battalions walking, and if the Argentines counterattacked, 42 Commando, out on a limb without proper support, would be in trouble. Therefore I favoured waiting for the arrival of 5 Infantry Brigade and, far more important, more helicopters, before moving anybody other than D Squadron. Certainly there was no question of flying 42 Commando and the guns until the Landing Zone on Mount Kent was in the hands of our own reconnaissance. If the enemy was sitting, waiting, the losses in helicopters would be unacceptable. So swanning off to 'un-recced' landing zones was out as far as I was concerned, despite the scorn heaped on such caution by those at home.

I had just told my Staff to examine the feasibility of providing logistic support with the tiny helicopter force for an overland move on foot, when a message arrived summoning me to the Satellite Communication Terminal which had been set up at Ajax Bay that night. Until then conversations with Northwood had been over the secure voice radio telephone in HMS *Fearless*. The trip to Ajax Bay was about the same distance as that to HMS *Fearless*, but more convenient because at least Ajax Bay did not stop helicopter flying during air raids, or leave San Carlos water each night to avoid submarines. Ajax Bay had been selected for the Satellite Communication Terminal rather than San Carlos Settlement alongside Brigade Headquarters, because the Headquarters would eventually move forward and the Satellite Terminal could not move except by helicopter and should in any case be safer within the defence perimeter of the Brigade Maintenance Area (BMA) at Ajax.

The radio-telephone was as clear as if the call had been coming from next door. As clear and unequivocal were the orders from Northwood. The Goose Green operation was to be re-mounted and more action was required all round. Plainly the people at the back-end were getting restless. I returned to my Headquarters and summoned Jones. Chester informed me that the only way that the Brigade could go anywhere, other than 42 Commando's move to Mount Kent, was on foot. It had become quite clear to 3 Commando Brigade that, apart from the whole-hearted support from the Royal Navy, the Brigade was on its own: no assistance or support of any kind would be forthcoming from anyone, either close at hand or at home. It was, as they say in the French Foreign Legion, a case of *'de merde toi legionnaire'*.

Jones was told to seize Darwin and Goose Green using the same plan that had been agreed before. He was updated on the intelligence available to the Brigade at the time. It gave the assessment of enemy strengths in Darwin and Goose Green as two companies of 12 Infantry Regiment, one company of 25 Infantry Regiment, a platoon of 8 Infantry Regiment and possibly an amphibious platoon. The guns were assessed as possibly two 105 mm howitzers, up to six 35 mm anti-aircraft guns or 30 mm anti-aircraft guns and up to six 20 mm anti-aircraft guns. There were also estimated to be one platoon of engineers and one support helicopter. Jones then went on board *Intrepid* to see the SAS Squadron that had attacked Darwin on D-Day and they told him that, in their opinion, the whole isthmus was held by about one company. After further discussions with Holroyd-Smith, Jones returned to his Battalion to brief them for the forthcoming operation.

Whitehead was then summoned and told to move out of his positions above Ajax Bay by first light the next morning, 27 May, move by LCUs to Port San Carlos and march via New House to Douglas Settlement. Pike was told to be prepared to follow 45 Commando on foot and then swing down to Teal Inlet Settlement. Subsequently these orders were modified by me after Pike had discussed the route with a local from Port San Carlos, who said that the best way to Teal was south of Bombilla Hill and then due east to Teal Inlet Settlement. I also delayed the move of 42 Commando to Mount Kent because I did not want helicopters tied up which might be required to support 2 Para. 42 Commando would remain as Brigade reserve ready to reinforce that part of the Brigade needing assistance — most probably 2 Para. 42 Commando was warned accordingly. 40 Commando would send one company to relieve 2 Para on Sussex Mountain.

As night was falling on 26 May Jones led his Battalion south off Sussex Mountain and down towards Camilla Creek House. Soon after first light the next day, 27 May, 45 Commando, having landed at Port San Carlos, set off, very heavily laden, on their 'yomp'. 3 Para moved out soon after and set off in two columns towards Teal Inlet Settlement. By this time 2 Para was installed in the three small buildings of Camilla Creek House. Jones had decided to lie up in and around the buildings to provide concealment from the enemy air and satellite reconnaissance.

At 9.30 am a pair of Harriers attacked Goose Green. Squadron-Leader Iveson gallantly made three passes and was shot down on the third. He ejected and managed to hide in Paragon House, a deserted farmstead about ten kilometres north-west of Goose Green. He was eventually picked up after the battle by a Gazelle from 3 Commando Brigade Air Squadron flown by Lieutenant Scott.

Two patrols from C Company sent out by 2 Para reported that there were enemy positions on Darwin Hill, south-west of Darwin, south of Boca House and on ring contour 50 on the north-western part of the isthmus. Although Boca House was marked on maps as such, and was useful as a reference point, it consisted solely of the foundations and a jumble of stones. The patrols were, however, spotted and forced to withdraw under fire. At about midday someone in the Battalion tuned into the BBC's World Service and heard the announcement that 2 Para were advancing on Darwin, while 45 Commando and 3 Para were advancing on Douglas Settlement and Teal Inlet Settlement respectively. Jones was furious and ordered the Battalion to disperse and dig in to face the attack that must surely follow this gross breach of security. However, no attack came and despite the alertness of the enemy at Darwin, who had forced the withdrawal of the C Company patrols, the Argentines mounted a highly unprofessional vehicle patrol in a blue civilian landrover up the track to Camilla Creek House. They were jumped by the FAC Party returning from controlling the Harrier strike who allowed the vehicle to close their position and captured all three occupants before they could radio back to base. Interrogation by Bell, who had been sent to accompany the Battalion, revealed that the Officer in the party was the commander of the Argentine reconnaissance platoon and that the garrison was fully alert. Some days after the battle a prisoner incorrectly told General Moore that the garrison had been reinforced using part of the strategic, or mobile, reserve carried in helicopters from the Mount Kent area at very short notice when the Argentines had been alerted by the BBC World Service broadcast.

Just before dusk the BMA at Ajax Bay was attacked by Skyhawks dropping parachute retard bombs, killing five men and wounding twenty-seven. Three 400kg Matra bombs hit the Field Dressing Station itself without exploding, one passing through the roof and bouncing on the ground outside. The two others remained in the Dressing Station until after the end of the war. The bombs that did explode in the BMA started fires among the piles of ammunition stacked close by, mainly 81 mm mortar bombs and Milan missiles. These exploded all night a hundred metres or so from the Dressing Station and Logistic Regiment Headquarters, sending shrapnel whining through the darkness and destroying all of 45 Commando's Milan firing posts. The netted loads of gun and mortar ammunition waiting on the helipad to be lifted forward to 2 Para were also destroyed. These had to be replaced quickly before 2 Para's battle started. Hellberg, although tired and drawn, calmly restored order to the BMA, while the doctors worked on with their unpleasant 'lodgers' close by. 40 Commando's echelon area at Blue Beach Two was also hit, killing one man and wounding others.

Towards the end of the afternoon Jones gave orders to his assembled

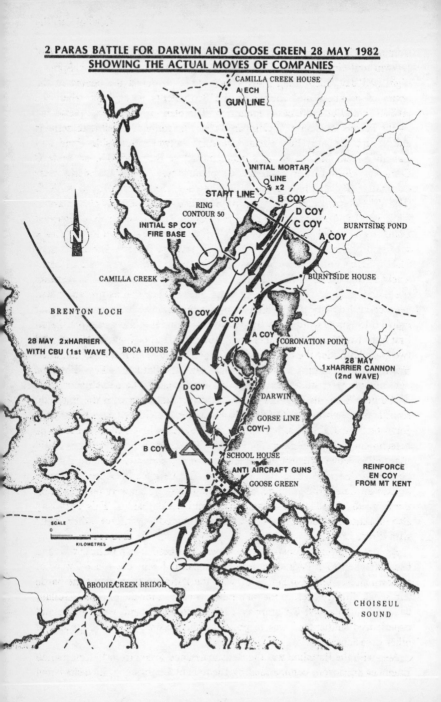

2 PARAS BATTLE FOR DARWIN AND GOOSE GREEN 28 MAY 1982
SHOWING THE ACTUAL MOVES OF COMPANIES

CAMILLA CREEK HOUSE
A ECH
GUN LINE

INITIAL MORTAR
LINE
x2

START LINE

B COY

RING
CONTOUR 50

D COY

INITIAL SP COY
FIRE BASE

C COY

A COY

BURNTSIDE POND

CAMILLA CREEK →

BURNTSIDE HOUSE

BRENTON LOCH

D COY

C COY

28 MAY 2xHARRIER
WITH CBU (1st WAVE)

A COY

CORONATION POINT

BOCA HOUSE

28 MAY
1xHARRIER CANNON
(2nd WAVE)

D COY

DARWIN

GORSE LINE

A COY(-)

B COY

SCHOOL HOUSE

ANTI AIRCRAFT GUNS

GOOSE GREEN

REINFORCE
EN COY
FROM MT KENT

SCALE

0   1   2

KILOMETRES

BRODIE CREEK BRIDGE

CHOISEUL
SOUND

Company Commanders. The mission was to capture the settlements of Darwin and Goose Green. The concept of operations was for a six-phase, night and day, silent then noisy attack aimed to defeat the enemy in the hours of darkness and then take the Settlements in daylight when the civilians could be more easily identified. The plan in outline was: phase one — the Patrols Company (C Company) clear the route of possible minefields and secure the start line astride the track between Burntside Pond and Camilla Creek: phase two — A Company clear Burntside House while B Company cleared ring contour 50; phase three — A Company clear Coronation Point; phase four — B Company clear Boca House while C (Patrols) Company clear the Airstrip; phase five — A Company clear Darwin while Band D Companies clear and hold Goose Green; phase six C (Patrols) Company seize and clear Brodie Creek Bridge. The fire support for the attack consisted of three guns from 8 (Alma) Commando Battery, Royal Artillery ('Black Eight' to the Commando Brigade because of their crest with its black shield behind it), provided the guns could be flown in that night. In addition the Battalion had two of its own 81 mm mortars, the bombs for which had been carried down by the riflemen in the Battalion. Until just before first light HMS *Arrow* would also be available with naval gunfire support. From first light two Scout helicopters under the command of Captain Niblett and two Gazelles under the command of Captain Pounds, all from 3 Commando Brigade Air Squadron, would be on task with the Battalion. Two Blowpipe detachments were under command of the Battalion. The detachment from 32 Guided Weapons Regiment Royal Artillery had been with the Battalion since landing with it on D-Day. However, for the Goose Green operation, Jones had, in addition, asked for and been given, a Royal Marine Blowpipe detachment from the Brigade Air Defence Troop. He wanted the fitter Royal Marines to move with the Battalion, reasoning, correctly, that they would be able to keep up. The Royal Artillery Air Defence detachment was to remain to protect the gun line. Support Company 2 Para were positioned on the flank to 'shoot in' the assaults by A and B Companies. This Company also subsequently followed up the assault, prepared to reinforce either thrust with direct fire.

As well as Captain Constance, the Royal Marines Liaison Officer who had been attached to 2 Para since leaving England, I sent down a member of my own staff, Major Gullan, to be with the Battalion throughout the battle and speak directly back to me on a radio he carried for the purpose. Gullan, who had commanded B Company 2 Para before Crosland, was a brave and experienced soldier and was to prove invaluable on this and a number of other occasions.

Also with the Battalion was the Reconnaissance Troop from 59 Commando Engineer Squadron, commanded by Lieutenant Livingstone, its tasks being to find and clear minefields and booby traps, particularly at the two entrances to the isthmus, and destroy captured enemy equipment. Most of their kit had been left on board LSL *Sir Lancelot* when she had been abandoned, after being bombed on 25 May, and kept empty of passengers while an unexploded bomb was being cleared.

The three guns of 8 Battery were flown in that night by the Sea Kings of 846 Squadron, before the Battalion moved off. Originally it had been planned that 200 rounds per gun would be taken in, but, because of the reports that the Argentines were alert and might have reinforced the garrison, the number of rounds per gun was increased to 320. The helicopters, flown by pilots using PNG, were handled with great skill.

Jones had asked for a troop of Scorpions and Scimitars to support him, but I refused his request because I did not consider that these armoured vehicles would be able to negotiate the boggy ground between Sussex Mountain and the Darwin Isthmus. The going on the isthmus is reasonable, but the maze of streams and rivers en route would, I thought, result in these vehicles becoming bogged down in the open and vulnerable to air attack once day dawned. I was wrong as it turned out, because their later exploits showed what they could achieve.

I made two other mistakes: I should have taken my tactical headquarters and another commando or battalion and fought a co-ordinated battle. Had I done so, it would have been over far quicker, at less loss. I do not imply any criticism of 2 Para, only that I asked more of them than I should have.

A Company 2 Para, commanded by Major Farrar-Hockley, crossed the start line at 2.30 am on 28 May and by 2.50 am was in contact with the enemy who speedily withdrew. 'There was no call for Sapper work,' reported Livingstone with A Company, 'but we all gained valuable experience and confidence. We then waited for the bright and fascinating tracer criss-crossing the sky to our right front to cease, indicating that the other Phase Two operation (B Company) was complete. All the time we were trying to avoid the by now uncomfortable rate of indirect enemy fire about us. Rain began to pour down to add to our discomfort.'

B Company on the Battalion's right began its attack at 3.10 am, making contact with the enemy thirty minutes later, and, after fighting through aggressively in a well-controlled series of section attacks, the Company secured Ring Contour 50. D Company, in reserve and moving up the boundary between A and B companies, also engaged the Argentines and killed some; the remainder must have fled into the darkness. At 3.14 am, in the middle of this battle, HMS *Arrow*, who was supporting the attack with naval gunfire, developed a fault in her turret which stopped her firing.

At about 4.00 am, and before B and D Company objectives were secure, A Company pushed forward to occupy Coronation Point. The enemy artillery fire was increasing, the planned timings were already slipping past and HMS *Arrow* was supposed to leave the Fire Support Area at 4.30 am in order to regain the safety of the air defence umbrella at San Carlos before daylight. Having repaired her gun, she gallantly remained until 5.20 am — typical of the frigates and destroyers that fought the inshore battle, whose first thought was always for the troops ashore. In spite of the effects of the illuminants lighting up the sky on A Company's right, making them feel exceedingly vulnerable on the bare features, the Company continued its 3000-metre advance. Encouraged by the initial successes and reports of minimal casualties to other companies, the objective was reached without opposition, except for the ever-present harassing fire from the enemy artillery. Gullan was keeping me in the picture on the radio with pithy, rapid-fire comments: at 4.27 am 'A Company pushing on — Naval Gunfire Forward Observer reckons he is under machine-gun fire'; at 5.45 am and 'B Company holding, D Company pushing through, going well'.

At first light, about 6.30 am, A Company was ordered by the CO to advance again, to assault Darwin. The Company Commander left one platoon on Coronation Point to give covering fire; the remaining two platoons and company headquarters were ordered to follow the track round the west side of the inlet. There was a feeling of great confidence and the expectation of breakfast in Darwin, the Company's final objective. As the two platoons reached the open ground a stream of fire from heavy and medium machine guns was unleashed on the company from Darwin Hill, a distance of about 400 to 500 metres. The platoons pushed on and reached a re-entrant which enabled them to avoid direct fire, but not the increasing rain of artillery and mortar fire. However, A Company's main Headquarters was caught in the open and unable to move. The rapidly increasing light enabled the enemy to bring down very effective fire.

The first attempts by A Company to clear Darwin Hill were unsuccessful and casualties began to mount. Casualties, dead or alive, were stripped of their ammunition which was re-distributed. Any soldiers armed with Sterling sub-machine guns threw them away and picked up SLRs from the casualties, or, better still, Argentine FALs which fired in bursts and provided more firepower. The Battalion mortars had run out of ammunition and the Harriers could not take off from the carriers because of mist at sea. However, the cloud base over Darwin and Goose Green, and, indeed, all of East Falkland, was high enough to allow the Pucaras to operate against the Battalion and the gun position at Camilla Creek House.

Several times, as A Company tried to close with the enemy, the guns of 8 Battery had to stop firing just at the critical moment for fear of hitting their own men. About 800 metres away to A Company's right, B Company was caught by indirect and direct fire on the open forward slopes overlooking

Boca House. The whole momentum of the Battalion's attack had ground to a halt on the bare, coverless ground. The casualties continued to increase and the ammunition stocks to dwindle.

By about 9.30 am Jones, forward with A Company, decided that this was the moment for direct intervention by him. With the utmost gallantry and disregard for his own life, he personally led an attack on an enemy slit trench and was hit by fire from another trench that he had not seen. He fell, mortally wounded. The position was now critical: A Company could make no headway, B Company was pinned down north of Boca House, the Commanding Officer was dying. Meanwhile D Company, whose Commander, Neame, had offered to assist A Company and had been ordered to stay where he was, were calmly cooking breakfast in dead ground to the rear of B Company, the kind of bizarre situation that is commonplace in war and will be only too familiar to anyone who has fought in a land battle. They were wisely following the experienced soldier's maxim, 'if in danger or in doubt, get the bloody brew-can out'. Support Company with Milans and GPMGs were also in the vicinity of D Company, having been sent there by Keeble, the Battalion second-in-command, on his own initia ıve.

When Jones fell, Major Keeble was with Battalion Main Headquarters. Jones's orders, in accordance with normal practice, required Major Rice, the Battery Commander of the supporting artillery, to assume command until Keeble, with a duplicate Tactical Headquarters, could move forward to take over. Rice, like all the battery commanders in the Brigade, was with the Commanding Officer's party and was caught up in the confusion on Darwin Hill, out of touch with the situation in the rest of the Battalion and in no position to carry out the orders. Keeble, therefore, ordered Crosland, commanding B Company, to assume command until he could reach him.

Keeble had three options running through his mind: first, reinforce either the left or right flank; second, go firm and ask for reinforcements; third, withdraw. He spent about thirty minutes on the radio trying to get the Company Commanders to give him an accurate picture of the situation forward. Based on what they told him, he chose to reinforce the right flank. He had given up his radio linking him to Brigade Headquarters to the Commanding Officer's Tactical Headquarters during the night. Therefore he decided to take forward Gullan, with his radio on a direct link back to me, and Gullan remained with Keeble for the rest of the battle. Keeble found him invaluable both as the most battle-experienced officer, apart from Crosland, and as a link with me at Brigade Headquarters. Gullan's commentary did not stop: 'Bit of a problem here — but we'll sort it out', this referring to Boca House.

The battle for Darwin Hill continued as Keeble moved forward and the Battalion came under air attack by Pucaras. At this moment a pair of Scout

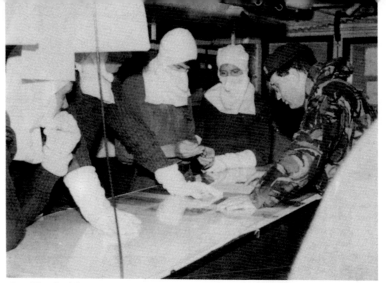

1. The decision to run into San Carlos Water made, Brigadier Julian Thompson checks on the fine details of the operation. On the Ops Room table are pictures of the objective. The rest of the group wear protective anti-flash gear, Air Raid Warning Red having sounded.

2. A Wessex helicopter brings another load of ammunition to Blue Beach at San Carlos. Previous loads stand waiting on the ground. An LCU brings further stores to the beach which are then brought inland by Marine and civilian tractors. In the foreground are the Beach Armoured Recovery Vehicle (BARV) and a Gemini inflatable boat.

3. Mirages and Skyhawks come in low over the ships in San Carlos Water. In this picture a Mirage flies low over the LSL *Sir Bedivere*. Fortunately the bombs it dropped failed to explode.

4. Bombs straddle, from the left, RFA *Resource*, MV *Norland* and HMS *Intrepid*. The period 21-25 May saw the Amphibious Group under intense pressure.

5. Elements of 2 Para move into their positions on Sussex Mountain over-looking the Amphibious Group in San Carlos Water. Once the Paras were in position they could dominate the southern approaches to the beachhead.

6. Surrender at Goose Green. Helmets and weapons lie in ordered lines just as their owners had dropped them when the Argentine garrison surrendered.

7. A Wessex and a Sea King helicopter wait to ferry the Marines of 42 Commando forward to Mount Kent some time on 31 May. The lead man and the last man carry 7.62 mm LMGs.

8. Mist shrouds the BV202s of HQ 3 Commando Brigade as they prepare to move out from Port San Carlos.

9. Lieutenant Lord Robin Innes-Kerr in his Scorpion tank south of Douglas Settlement. His Troop escorted the Brigade vehicles on their journey to Teal.

10. A 105 mm howitzer of 7 (Sphinx) Battery 29 Commando Regiment Royal Artillery is moved to Mount Kent by a Sea King Mk4 of 846 Naval Air Commando Squadron.

11. Marines of 42 Commando return to Mount Kent after a night excursion on to Mount Harriet. The Marine in the centre carries a Carl Gustav 84 mm anti-armour weapon, his colleague an SLR fitted with a night-sight.

12. A file of men from 45 Commando moves between Two Sisters and Sapper Hill. The lead man not only carries his SLR on his back but also the 66 mm LAW anti-armour weapon. Designed to deal with armour, it was mainly used to clear Argentine bunkers.

13. Men of 3 Para march through the outskirts of Port Stanley on 14 June.

14. Men of the old Naval Party 8901, now J Company, 42 Commando, re-enter Stanley after their abrupt dismissal by the Argentines some two months previously. Behind them the rest of 42 Commando follow them in.

15. Bullet and shrapnel holes pockmark a building in Stanley.
J and L Companies of 42 Commando finally find rest and shelter in the old seaplane hangar on the outskirts of Port Stanley.
Light shines through the holes, creating an unusual picture.
Two GMPGs lie on the ground with other pieces of equipment.

16. Outside the Falkland Islands Company warehouse the Argentines dump
their weapons. They are then taken to the camp at the airfield. The pile
consists mainly of Argentine-made 7.62 mm FN automatic rifles, but there
are also a number of light machine-guns and anti-tank weapons.

helicopters which had been shuttling ammunition forward to the Battalion and flying casualties back were summoned forward to casevac the dying Commanding Officer. They were bounced by the Pucaras, one of which shot down and killed Lieutenant Nunn, the pilot of one of the Scouts. His air gunner, sergeant Belcher, having survived cannon and machine-gun hits, which severed one leg and shattered the other, also survived the impact of the crash and lived. Lieutenant Nunn was awarded a posthumous DFC for his work that day. His brother-in-law, Captain Constance, Royal Marines, was Assistant Operations Officer in 2 Para's Main Headquarters and his elder brother commanded M Company of 42 Commando, now on South Georgia. There were many brothers and relatives fighting this war within the closely knit Royal Marines 'family'. Captain Niblett, the other Scout pilot, evaded the Pucaras by brilliant flying. His air gunner, Sergeant Glaze, was standing in the back of the Scout and by jumping from one side to the other could see out of the rear of the cabin and pass instructions to his pilot. The Pucaras ran at Niblett from every conceivable direction, at all heights, and at a variety of speeds, firing a combination of their deadly weaponry — rockets, cannon and machine guns. They defied all the expected tactics of fixed-wing attack which, although feared by the helicopter crews, had at least been anticipated and trained for. The Pucaras were able to slow down and mirror the helicopters' manoeuvres — they were a lethal enemy. Pucaras attempting to attack the gun position at Camilla Creek House were driven off by GPMG fire and Blowpipes — not the first or last time that the brave and aggressive British troops saw off or shot down those unpleasant and dangerous aircraft.

The fire pinning down B Company came from heavy and medium machine guns sited on a small hill to the south-west of Boca House, and from positions to the east of it. B Company Commander managed to get his company out of this fire, by working his two forward platoons into dead ground, although still on a forward slope, and pulling his rear platoon back from the ridge-line on to a reverse slope to join Support Company, now waiting to join them. However, they were still under indirect fire from mortars and artillery. Crosland then decided to use Milans from Support Company to engage the troublesome machine guns. This direct-fire, wire-guided weapon system enabled the company to stand back and slam the high explosive missiles with devastating accuracy into the bunkers, with hugely gratifying results. Neame, commanding D Company, with commendable initiative and eye for the ground, moved his Company along the shoreline below the low cliff and, supported by GPMGs on the ridge-line and by artillery fire, rolled up the enemy from the flank. The concentration of force broke the enemy's will to fight and they surrendered in large numbers.

By now A Company had taken Darwin Hill, supported by all the GPMGs available and using their 66mm LAWs to blast slit trenches. As one officer said, 'The "Toms" just put their heads down and went.' So by 11.10am, after nearly six hours, the battle for Darwin Hill was over, but not without grievous loss: the Commanding Officer, the Adjutant, A Company Second-in-Command and nine junior non-commissioned officers and soldiers were killed and several wounded.

Keeble ordered A Company to hold Darwin Hill, while C (Patrols) Company and one platoon of A Company moved through them to Goose Green. D Company was ordered to swing east from Boca House and seize the airstrip, while B Company moved to the west of D Company to capture the ground south of the settlement — in all a three-pronged attack, with A Company providing the necessary 'foot on the ground'. However, as the two platoons of C (Patrols) Company moved up and over the high ground overlooking Darwin and began the descent down the forward slope, a combination of artillery, mortar, machine-gun and anti-aircraft fire (in the ground role) was directed against the advancing troops. Little or no cover was available and 'it was hard to believe that this weight of fire could be maintained for long,' reported Livingstone, whose Commando Engineers were moving up with the infantry in every company of the Battalion. One engineer section had orders to 'spike the guns' when they were captured. This fire caused several casualties among C (Patrols) Company as they pressed forward towards the school house on the outskirts of the Settlement, while D Company were deflected from their route by a minefield and squeezed in towards the Settlement away from the airfield.

Lieutenant Barry thought he saw some white flags in the vicinity of the schoolhouse and received permission from Neame to arrange a ceasefire. Neame ordered his own company to stop firing. Barry and two NCOs went forward. The offer of a ceasefire was refused. Barry and his party turned to go. At this moment a machine gun from another company fired at the schoolhouse. The Argentines fired at Barry, killing him and his party. His platoon sergeant with the rest of the platoon overran the position, killing most of the enemy, although some of the occupants escaped, including the officer who had fired at Barry in the mistaken impression that the offer of a ceasefire was a ruse.

As C and D Companies reorganized, still under artillery fire, two Aermacchis attacked D Company, followed shortly by two Pucaras dropping napalm. Fortunately, both napalm canisters missed the rifle companies. One of the Pucaras was shot down by combined small arms fire from B and D Companies. One Aermacchi was shot down by Marine Strange of 3 Commando Brigade Air Defence Troop who stood up 'as though in a butt at a grouse drive' and shot it down with his Blowpipe. One aircraft crashed close by, drenching several men with fuel and napalm, which fortunately did not ignite. One man, lying face down, had his back pouches whipped off by part of the wing which scythed through the air. Keeble could see the anti-aircraft guns on the Goose Green peninsula firing at him and his men on the ridge line, keeping them all pinned down. There seemed no end to this battle and no answer to this fire, coming from well out of range of anything he could fire back, except his artillery, which was almost out of ammunition. At 3.25 pm, as the winter afternoon light began to fade, three Harriers arrived, having been prevented from taking part in the battle all day, by bad weather. The primary Forward Air Controller (FAC) with the Battalion, Squadron-Leader Penman, had damaged his ankle on the approach march. Keeble had ordered his radio team to link up with Captain Arnold, Royal Artillery, the NGFO. Fortunately all NGFOs are trained as FACs. With great skill, bearing in mind how close 2 Para were, having captured the airfield, he brought the first wave of two Harriers armed with cluster bomb units across the airfield and destroyed, or silenced, the air defence guns on the point of the Goose Green peninsula. He brought the third Harrier in from the north-east to attack with cannon. This silenced the fire not only from the anti-aircraft guns but from the other defenders of the settlement, including the Argentine artillery.

The violent blast of the cluster bombs, forty-seven to a cluster, rippling like a giant Chinese firecracker across the peninsula, broke the will of the Argentine defenders and tipped the scales in 2 Para's favour. Civilians released from the Settlement the next day reported that the enemy soldiers had sobbed and screamed in terror.

As the light faded 2 Para's companies started to go firm in the positions ordered by Keeble. When an enemy Chinook and six Hueys were reported disembarking troops about two kilometres south of Goose Green, Keeble ordered B Company to set up a blocking position on ring contour 100, south of the airstrip, and the enemy reinforcements were attacked by artillery. They were, it later turned out, the enemy reserve. He then returned to his main headquarters in the Gorse line south of Darwin. As he got back, utterly weary and not sure whether or not the battle was over, he said to himself, 'How the hell do I capture Goose Green?'

A commando engineer section wandered into a minefield, taking cover for the night in holes which they took for shell holes, but, they later found, had been made by anti-tank mines detonated by wandering cows. The morning light showed the trip wires and the sappers tip-toed out of the minefield, thanking their lucky stars.

Keeble reported back to me by radio that they had captured Darwin and had surrounded Goose Green. He asked for reinforcement and J Company of 42 Commando was warned to fly down at first light the next morning. I also agreed that Goose Green could be destroyed, if necessary, should the Argentines not surrender in the morning.

I went over to the BMA and Main Dressing Station in a rigid raiding craft for my usual nightly visit. The wounded were lying quietly in rows, waiting to be operated on, being operated on, or pale and dazed after surgery, while the doctors and medical staff worked around them. As always I was struck by the bravery of these young men, many with dreadfully torn bodies. I used the radio satellite telephone to speak to Northwood and brief them on the battle and ask that they apply pressure to get the hospital ship *Uganda* moved closer so that helicopter casevac could begin next morning to clear the dressing station of its wounded, ready for the next intake. Northwood immediately agreed, their only reaction being to help.

During the night a patrol from 2 Para made contact with the inhabitants of Darwin who told them that 112 civilians were being held captive in the village hall in Goose Green. Keeble's plan, to which I agreed, was to offer the Argentines the chance to surrender or be destroyed by artillery and air support. However, to make the threat credible the remaining guns of 8 Battery and much more ammunition would need to be flown down to join the guns already at Camilla Creek House. A tasking signal was sent to the Carrier Battle Group asking for a Harrier strike as a demonstration, clear of, but sufficiently near to, the Argentine Garrison to convince them that the British meant business and that, if the Garrison did not surrender, the next strike would be upon them. The Naval Gunfire Support Forward Observer with 2 Para would control the strike. The ultimatum was drawn up with the help of Bell, and at first light two Argentine prisoners were sent in bearing a message in Spanish which, translated, read:

To the Commander, Argentine Forces, Goose Green, from the Commander, British Forces, Goose Green Area. Military Options. We have sent a POW to you under a white flag of truce to convey the following military options:

1. That you surrender your force to us by leaving the township, forming up in a military manner, removing your helmets and laying down your weapons. You will give prior notice of this intention by returning the POW under the white flag, with him briefed as to the formalities, no later than 0830 hours local time.

2. You refuse in the first case to surrender and take the inevitable consequences. You will give prior notice of this intention by returning the POW without his white flag, although his neutrality will be respected, no later than 0830 hours local time.

3. In the event, and in accordance with the terms of the Geneva Conventions and the Laws of War, you shall be held responsible for the fate of any civilians in Goose Green and we, in accordance with those laws, do give you prior notice of our intention to bombard Goose Green.

Signed C Keeble

Commander, British Forces Goose Green Area
29 May, 1982

The Argentine Commander at Goose Green was warned that the two POWs would be carrying in this surrender ultimatum by using the Falkland Island radio link between Mr Miller of Port San Carlos and Mr Goss, the Settlement Manager of Goose Green. The arrangements for this were made by Brigade Headquarters during the night.

The night had passed slowly for the men of 2 Para lying out in the bitter cold, the reaction after battle setting in as the adrenalin ebbed away and the uncertainty about the morrow weighed in on them. During the darkness in appalling visibility Captain Greenhalgh RCT flew his Scout helicopter to collect some severely wounded Paras and Argentines, who, but for his gallantry and skill, would have died in the night. On his return to San Carlos Water over Sussex Mountain he asked for the ships to switch their lights on to guide him in. This they did and he landed safely at the FDS at Ajax Bay with his casualties. For this and other acts of gallantry he was awarded the Distinguished Flying Cross.

At Brigade Headquarters the level of activity in the Command Post had remained high as preparations were made for the following day — helicopters tasked, ammunition and fuel loads worked out, reports received and orders given to the other units in the Brigade who must still be commanded, despite the events of the day past and all that might happen on the morrow. 2 Para must be ministered to first, but 3 Para and 45 Commando, who had reached their first objectives at Teal Inlet Settlement and Douglas, had been without ration resupply for thirty-six hours. Their packs needed flying forward and there was the matter of artillery support, for both units were now forty kilometres or so away. The SBS reports were coming in, including, at 7.20 pm, that their patrol in Teal Inlet had made contact with 3 Para's forward company. The M and AW Cadre were moving to new locations and reports from D Squadron, which on the night of 28 May had completed its move to the landing site below Mount Kent, were coming in and needed assessing in preparation for the next night's move which would involve 42 Commando. 42 Commando asked if they could be relieved in their defensive positions, so that they would be able to fly forward to Mount Kent the next night. 'Tell 40 Commando to get a Company over to Green Beach Two by not later than 1300 tomorrow (9.00 am local),' is Chester's entry in the log in response to this.

The logisticians also wrestled with the problems caused by the need to keep as few ships as possible in the anchorage by day and delays caused by the air attacks. The lack of means to unload these ships when they came in during the night and the demands of fighting the Goose Green battle, resupplying 45 Commando and 3 Para well beyond the beachhead and completing the offload with the few craft and helicopters meant that many ships departed the anchorage before they were fully unloaded. As ships came in each night they were boarded by teams from the Logistic Regiment to check what they had on board. In some cases parts of their original loads had been cross-decked to other ships outside the TEZ without reference to the Commando Brigade, on orders from the Naval Staffs who had their own logistic problems. Then a race against time began, to get as much off the ships as possible before they weighed anchor and steamed out well before dawn, to be as far east as they could before daylight.

That night, with the possibility of an Argentine counterattack on Goose Green uppermost in everybody's minds and the chance that 45 Commando and 3 Para might be in contact at any moment if the Argentines reacted to their steady advance east, the evening logistic conference revealed grave shortcomings in the stock situation at the Brigade Maintenance Area: only eighty-three rounds for each 105 mm light gun; a total of thirty Milan missiles for the whole Brigade; no one-man ration packs; two days' supply of ten-man packs — totally unsuitable for carriage by marching troops; no hexamine for cooking — marching troops with the standard ration packs would be on cold rations and those with Arctic rations (the majority) would not be able to heat the water to reconstitute the dehydrated rations and would not eat at all; no spare clothing; three days' worth of medical stocks.

Extracts from the signal sent on 28 May by Wells-Cole are revealing:

After last-minute plea *Galahad* departure tonight has been delayed as she is not yet unloaded for future ops. Further she continues to hold some stocks that are essential to the force which must be offloaded.

Also understand *Percival* not coming in until 29 May. Plan was to load her with stocks for future ops as well as *Galahad*. However as *Elk* can not come in for another 24 hours we do not hold necessary stocks to fill *Percival* nor support the Brigade much longer without resupply — if position not improved we will grind to a halt.

The signal continues giving a full list of requirements.

The reference to loading the LSLs for future operations was to meet the Brigade plan to sail them round to Teal Inlet once it, and the high ground overlooking it, was secure, and set up a forward BMA. The Brigade had been attempting to achieve this since D + 3 and the forward planning by the logisticians was all to this end. Logistic resupply for a conventional land battle is difficult enough, but given the conditions in the Falklands and lack of means to move supplies it was, to quote Hellberg, 'a nightmare'. There was a feeling among the Brigade staff that this was not understood elsewhere.

My R Group, at short notice to move all day on 28 May, in case I needed to go down and take command in person at Goose Green, was stood by for a move from first light. The lift of the additional guns and ammunition began at first light. In the end so few helicopters were available that it took seven hours to fly in the three guns and re-stock the gunlines, a round trip of thirty-eight kilometres. So much for the pundits at home who talked so glibly of fast moves.

I was in continuous touch with Gullan by radio over the progress of negotiations down at Goose Green. At 9.05 am 2 Para sent a message to Brigade Headquarters saying, 'Args in area Goose Green and Darwin not to be fired upon without permission Call Sign 9 (Commanding officer 2 Para). Body of men emerging looking as though they're going to surrender'. This was followed on the Artillery net 'from NGFO 4 as at 1330 (9.30 am). Likely that garrison will surrender'. At 9.40 am Keeble briefed me that he had agreed a dignified surrender and handover. I had asked Gullan if he thought that it would help if I came down personally, but Gullan said no, Keeble was handling the situation perfectly well on his own. It was 2 Para's victory and I had no intention of stealing Keeble's limelight. At 10.01 am 2 Para sent: 'Three anti-aircraft guns in Goose Green. About to be ours!'

The Harriers were immediately re-tasked to attack enemy positions between Mount Kent and Mount Challenger in response to an SAS request. At 12.42 am a message was received over the artillery net in Brigade Headquarters: 'The Union Jack has just been raised over Goose Green Settlement.'

As we had agreed, and to keep the promise that the surrender would be dignified, I waited at my Headquarters to receive with due formality the Commander of the Goose Green Garrison, Air Commodore Pedroza, and see him into captivity, before flying down to Goose Green to congratulate Keeble and 2 Para on their brilliant victory. The battle had cost twenty British dead and forty wounded. Eleven hundred enemy were taken prisoner and the captured equipment included four 105 mm pack howitzers, two 35 mm anti-aircraft guns, six 20 mm anti-aircraft guns, six 120 mm mortars and two Pucara aircraft.

It was perhaps the most remarkable action fought by a British infantry battalion since the Second World War. Subsequently Jones has been criticised for going 'too far forward' and thereby 'getting himself killed'. In fact by going forward he did what many other commanding officers have done in the past, and should do in the future, in similar circumstances. My other commanding officers in battle were well forward from time to time, and had they been killed, no doubt, would have been similarly censured, wrongly: a commanding officer has to do what he has to do, even at the risk of his life. Jones found himself in the unenviable position of fighting a battle with inadequate support, and with time running out. The blame for that lay with the Brigade Commander, me. I should have given him the CVRT support he asked for, taken an additional commando or battalion down, and commanded what should have been a two-unit operation in person.

The battle was to have a profound effect on the conduct of the rest of the campaign. It signalled to the Argentines the determination of the British to succeed. It opened up the southern route to Stanley and, because the Argentines were convinced right to the end that the main attack would come from the south, it served to confirm their assessment, distracting them from what was actually the major thrust by 3 Commando Brigade from the north and west. The fighting over bare, open slopes in daylight had been costly. From then on, the brigade would if possible fight at night. The confusion of battle in the darkness would be offset by the greater skill of the marines and paratroopers, the better leadership and the intimate and flexible support made possible by our magnificent gunners. Finally, and an unforeseen bonus, the Argentine heliborne reserve had been drawn away from the vital areas of Mount Kent and taken prisoner with the rest of the Goose Green garrison. They were not, therefore, able to intervene during the highly risky three days when a light force of part of 42 Commando and D Squadron 22 SAS, with minimum support, was pushed forward forty miles on to Mount Kent.

Keeble was told to remain at Goose Green and consolidate his position, the order to withdraw after destroying equipment being rescinded. This was endorsed by Northwood later that evening when they were told that I intended that 2 Para should remain at Goose Green. For the present Keeble would keep J Company. Nobody knew for sure what force the Argentines had in Lafonia and a counter-attack was possible.

Meanwhile events had been moving on to the east of San Carlos and attention must be shifted to that direction. At about midnight that night, 29 May, I attempted to fly to Teal to see Pike and give him orders for the next phase, the advance towards Estancia. When commandos or battalions were moving on their feet without their Bandwagons in which the secure-voice radios were fitted, the Brigade Command Net had to be on insecure sets that could be monitored by the enemy. Giving further intentions over such a net was unwise, so any orders that had to be concealed from the enemy had to be given in person. Unfortunately a thick mist was down about halfway across East Falkland and the helicopter had to turn back. A first-light trip the next morning would be necessary.

CHAPTER SEVEN

Yomp East

While the battle for Goose Green was being fought, 45 Commando and 3 Para had been marching to Douglas Settlement and Teal Inlet, and the build-up of D Squadron on Mount Kent was completed on the night of 28/29 May, the night before the surrender of the Argentine Garrison at Goose Green. As has already been described, the fly-in of just D Squadron, starting on the night of 24/25 May, two days later than planned, had taken five nights to achieve. This in itself is an indication of the frustrations and delays caused by the bad weather at night and the lack of helicopter lift. Until the Mount Kent landing site could be properly secured, the wish of everybody from myself downwards and, we assumed, everybody in the chain of command above, to get on to the high ground overlooking Stanley, would be unfulfilled, but not for lack of trying by those on the ground. However, at last, on the night of 29/30 May all seemed set for the Tactical Headquarters of 42 Commando, with K Company, the Mortar Troop and three light guns, to be flown forward to the lower slopes of Mount Kent. The Commando had been ashore, but out of contact with the enemy, except for airstrikes, for over a week and everybody was straining at the leash to get into action. But soon after taking off in the helicopters, the snow flurries started and by the time the first wave had reached a position thirty kilometres short of Mount Kent, a full blizzard had reduced the visibility to a few yards. In the darkness, in white-out conditions, the helicopter pilots made several attempts to fly on. They even set down and waited, burning and turning, for the weather to moderate but, eventually, wisely decided to return to Port San Carlos and drop their passengers. It was an unnerving experience for the troops crammed in the dark bellies of the helicopters, almost deafened by the roar of the engines, not knowing what sort of reception awaited them at Mount Kent, if they even got there and did not crash into the mountain side, or fly into the ground before reaching the objective. The helicopters bucked and lurched in the turbulence of the near gale-force winds and anyone able to see out of the helicopters from the troop compartments was treated to glimpses of whirling snow in the blackness. Despite the disappointment of not reaching the objective, most felt relief at being back safely on the ground after a hair-raising two hours.

By this stage 45 Commando and 3 Para had been in their first objectives of Douglas and Teal Inlet for about 24 hours. 45 Commando had left Ajax Bay before first light on 27 May in LCUs bound for Port San Carlos, where they disembarked and started marching; each man was carrying about 120 pounds and some a good deal more. Even without his rucksack the average load of a marine or paratrooper was about seventy-six pounds. To begin with, Whitehead decided that his men would take rucksacks and not rely on helicopters to bring them forward. He knew that the helicopters would be busy supporting 2 Para and did not expect to see any until the Goose Green battle was over. On the voyage across from Ajax Bay to Port San Carlos, Captain Gardiner, commanding X Company 45 Commando, produced his mouth organ and played a few tunes. This seems to have been appreciated and he repeated the performance a number of times during the days that followed.

The first leg on the walk from Port San Carlos to Douglas Settlement was to New House, about twenty kilometres. Most people who took part in the march agree that this was the worst stage. The weather was not too bad, but the ground was very boggy with lumps and tufts of grass, which, even in daylight, made the risk of a sprained ankle an ever-present possibility and any sort of marching rhythm impossible. In places the ground was quite steep, but both the going and the steep hillsides faded into insignificance beside the crushing weight of the rucksacks. 'The Marines were magnificent,' wrote Gardiner. 'I was immensely proud of them.' Except for a short halt to brew up before last light, about 4.15 pm, the Commando kept going until it reached its planned harbouring-up area at New House at 10 pm. Marching in the darkness was worse than in daylight. For those at the back of the 'Commando Snake' of 600 men, bumping and stumbling through the night, life was extremely unpleasant.

At the harbouring-up area the Commando stopped to rest. Gardiner gave his Company the order to bed down without erecting bivouacs. (These bivouacs, 'bivvies' or 'bashas' were simply a waterproof poncho supported by a small stick and some rubber bungies.) 'This was a bad mistake,' wrote Gardiner. It rained heavily before dawn and the plastic bags, in which the Company's sleeping bags were fitted, did not keep the water out and the sleeping bags were soaked. The last citadel of morale is a man's sleeping bag; the comfort and resource it offers is unbounded. When the citadel is breached, morale can get pretty low, and that morning at first light it reached its low point, never to go so low again throughout the campaign. The Commando was to spend more uncomfortable and more bitter nights with wet sleeping bags, or without them entirely, but they hardened and got used to it. The men who survived that march stuck it out to the end and morale got higher as they moved east. They refined methods of living in this inhospitable place to such a degree that, by the end, they were like animals and almost preferred it out of doors. They could have lived in the wilds indefinitely in what they carried in their fighting order, often without rucksacks, and they resorted to all sorts of ingenuity to enable the essentials to be carried with the minimum weight. (1) 'Never let it be said that we had come to the end of our endurance by the time we had reached Stanley, or that the weather had beaten us,' wrote Gardiner in his diary. 'We could have gone on for ever.'

At first light the Commando covered the remaining twelve kilometres to Douglas Settlement in tactical formation with X Company leading, and the Reconnaissance and Surveillance Troops providing the reconnaissance screen. Expecting contact with the enemy, rucksacks were left behind and the Commando moved in fighting order only. The leading elements of 45 Commando reached the settlement at about 1 pm on 28 May. The enemy had fled. The immediate reaction of the people in the settlement was delight and to offer as much help as possible. On the march from New House, a farmer from the settlement who was driving his tractor towards Port San Carlos turned round and helped carry loads on his trailer. The enemy, who had vacated the settlement about two days before the Commando's arrival, were the same who had fled before 3 Para on D-Day. They had treated the settlers very crudely, vandalising houses and stealing valuables. The entire community had been locked in the schoolroom for four days.

The Commando dug in around the settlement and patrols were sent out to scout the surrounding area. The mortar troop, whose ammunition had been carried in four Bandwagons, set up their mortars to provide some immediate fire support if required. The Commando was well beyond the range of the supporting artillery at Port San Carlos. A large sheep-shearing shed was used for drying out. Rucksacks and rations were flown forward from New House the following day. The latter were particularly welcome because for many it was the first food for twenty-four hours. Many men started to build up small stockpiles of rations so that they would not be caught without them again. However, it was difficult for young men who had expended so much energy to resist eating everything and some men were constantly hungry. After the experiences of the last two days, the Commando quickly devised what they called heavy fighting order, enabling them to survive without helicopter lift to bring forward rations or sleeping bags, yet light enough to move and fight in. Light in this context is a relative term, because, loaded with ammunition, a man still carried seventy-eight pounds.

Having started out from Port San Carlos at 11 am on 27 May, after 45

Commando, 3 Para, moving on their own route, arrived at their lying-up position in the valley of the Arroy Pedro River, about nine kilometres short of Teal, at 11 am on 28 May. Their experiences on the gruelling twenty-four hour march had been the same as those endured by 45 Commando. 3 Para dropped off a rebroadcast team from Brigade Headquarters at Bombilla Hill on their way past. The purpose of this team was to enable Brigade Headquarters, still at San Carlos, to speak on the secure voice radio with 45 Commando and 3 Para until the Headquarters itself moved forward.

At the Arroy Pedro River the two columns of 3 Para made their rendezvous and lay up during the remaining hours of daylight in case of air attack. They were joined by their mortar platoon which had been lifted across country in two tractors and trailers driven by farmers from Port San Carlos. As soon as darkness fell the Battalion moved towards Teal Inlet Settlement. B Company, commanded by Major Argue, was deployed to the south-east of the settlement to cut off any escaping enemy. By 11 pm on 28 May the settlement was in 3 Para's hands. The first soldier to knock on the door of the Settlement Manager's house was greeted by the Manager, Mr Barton, in Spanish, who quickly and thankfully changed to English when he realized who the new arrivals were. Both 45 Commando and 3 Para had covered the distance to their objectives in less than half the time predicted by the locals.

3 Para was joined at Teal by the troop of Scorpions and Scimitars from the Blues and Royals which had landed with them on D-Day. This troop, number 4, had been ordered on 27 May to accompany the Battalion across to Teal, but could not set off until about four hours before dark on 28 May because of the fuel shortage in the beachhead brought about by LSL *Sir Lancelot* ditching her complete load of motor transport fuel when she was found to have an unexploded bomb on board. On 28 May the troop leader enterprisingly hi-jacked some fuel and his troop set off after 3 Para. This was the first, but not the last, time that the two troops of Blues and Royals were to demonstrate not only the remarkable ability of their light tanks to cross the soggy peat, but also the irrepressible spirit and initiative of their splendid crews. Picking up some 3 Para casualties from the line of march, 4 Troop motored on all night, being bombed at first light, rather ineffectually, before arriving triumphantly at Teal on the morning of 29 May.

On the evening of 29 May warning orders were given to 45 Commando and 3 Para to be prepared to continue the advance but not to move before first light the following day, 30 May. Both were given the objective of Estancia House. 3 Para, starting at Teal and therefore nearer, would get there first. My intention was then to pass 45 Commando through 3 Para to seize Long Island Mount. With Mount Estancia, Mount Kent, Mount Challenger and Long Island Mount held, the enemy in Stanley would be invested and 3 Commando Brigade would have unrestricted use of the many inlets of

Port Salvador which, like the fingers of an open hand, pointed towards the high ground dominating the approaches to Stanley from the west, north-west and south-west. I had tried to visit Pike and, if possible, Whitehead by helicopter that night, 29/30 May, to brief them both personally. But, as described in the previous chapter, I was forced to turn back by the same bad weather that stopped 42 Commando getting forward to Mount Kent. The next morning at first light I joined Major Cameron, the officer commanding the Brigade Air Squadron, who was briefing the crews for the trip. Major Cameron, a first-class pilot with a pooh-bear figure, a fund of stories and much courage and compassion, usually piloted me. By doing so he kept fully in the picture with what was in my mind and could see for himself what was happening throughout the Brigade, thus enabling him to brief his pilots so that the Squadron provided the best possible service to the Brigade. The forty-six kilometre flight would take between fifteen and twenty minutes; two Gazelles would go, the rear aircraft to cover the leader's tail and both flying a weaving pattern to enable a good look-out to be kept to the rear. Even flying low and fast, both aircraft would stand out like butterflies on a board against the bright, white grass below and thus be very exposed to attack by Pucara, Mentor or the armed Augusta 109. Once the Argentines knew that helicopters were shuttling regularly between San Carlos and positions west of Stanley it would surely be only a matter of time before the Argentine Air Force started to attack this line of communication and supply. Had they done so they would have wreaked havoc against helicopters unable to shoot back. They could have achieved this using the Pucara, Mentor and Augusta 109s already in the Falklands and without using any of their mainland-based fighters. Fortunately only one attempt was made, after the Goose Green battle, to disrupt the helicopter route, when two Sea Kings were spotted by a Pucara and an Augusta Bell 109 which gave chase, but broke away when the fleeing Sea Kings reached the vicinity of San Carlos and the protective Rapier. This was sufficient to stop all flying for the day. However, all this was in the future and my pilot for the trip, the large, cheerful rugby player, Colour-Sergeant Pulford, jokingly said, 'I hope we don't get a Yamamato job today,' referring to the Japanese Admiral shot down by the Americans in the Pacific in the Second World War because of a radio intercept which disclosed his flight path and destination. The quip was only half in jest and drew a reply warning him of the need to maintain security in conversations over the radios, which were all in plain language and vulnerable to intercept by the Argentines. The flight passed without incident, as did the return flight. This does not detract from the bravery of the light and medium helicopter crews who for the next two weeks were to fly this route and many others, with the ever-present threat, during daylight, of attack by the Argentine Air Force. Without the advantage of foresight they were not to know that the attacks would materialize only once more, and they pressed on, despite knowing that they had no defence against fighters and, particularly, the Pucara.

Pike and 3 Para were in good heart and impatient to be off. After giving them the order to advance, I returned to San Carlos Settlement. There I found that Major-General Moore had arrived and was in the process of being briefed by the Commando Brigade Staff in a cowshed by the Settlement Manager's house. Moore and his staff, having joined the liner *Queen Elizabeth II* at Ascension Island, sailed south towards South Georgia with 5 Infantry Brigade, commanded by Brigadier Wilson. Before *Queen Elizabeth II* went into Grytviken to crossdeck her troops to *Canberra*, Moore and Wilson with some of their staffs transferred to a destroyer and subsequently to HMS *Fearless* in order to get ahead to the Falklands with all despatch. Although thanks to the unsatisfactory communications fit on board *Queen Elizabeth II*, Moore had been out of touch and out of the picture for ten days, he appeared pleased with what he found and told me to continue with my plans. He said that 2 Para, at Goose Green, would come under command of 5 Infantry Brigade and that 40 Commando would be relieved in their positions on Sussex Mountain, Port San Carlos and San Carlos Settlement by a battalion from 5 Infantry Brigade when the Brigade arrived. This would allow 40 Commando to go forward to join the remainder of 3 Commando Brigade. A warning order to this effect was sent to 40 Commando telling them to stand by to hand over on the night of 31 May/1 June and to start making the preliminary moves to Port San Carlos, the intention being that 40 Commando would march to Teal Inlet. I was also told that the SBS and SAS would come under divisional command and would be tasked by them.

General Moore's arrival and his cheerful presence was most welcome because it allowed me to concentrate on commanding my Brigade. It was time for the Commando Brigade Headquarters to move forward and this we could now do without having to bother about how to take the Satellite Communications terminal or arrange for someone to fly back to Ajax Bay for the twice-daily situation reports to Northwood. This was now Divisional Headquarter's problem, and good luck to them we all thought as we happily made preparations to move forward to Teal Inlet the next morning (31 May), glad to be shaking the mud of San Carlos off our boots.

Meanwhile I briefed Whitehead (45 Commando) to leave Douglas and start advancing to Teal Inlet. He was told not to advance beyond Teal Inlet until ordered. 45 Commando started moving at 10 am on 30 May; their leading company arrived at Teal Inlet at 5.30 pm that evening and the Commando was complete in its new position by about 9 pm. It was on this leg on the march that the rumour spread down the length of the commando 'snake' that 'Galtieri was dead', but on investigation this turned out to be someone shouting 'Air Raid Warning Red'. After this it was always possible to raise a smile in 45 Commando by remarks such as 'Galtieri's in bed' or 'I'll have a Garibaldi instead', a reference to the choice of biscuits in the Arctic Ration packs. 'Air Raid Warning Yellow' was corrupted to 'Garibaldi plays the 'cello'. One of the Royal Artillery Forward Observer party with X Company 45 Commando snatched a five-pound brown trout out of a small stream during a ten-minute halt. They poached the fish when the Company arrived at Teal Inlet Settlement.

That night, 30/31 May, 42 Commando Tactical Headquarters, most of K Company, the Mortar Troop and three 105 mm light guns of 7 (Sphinx) Commando Battery were again flown forward to the landing site below Mount Kent. This time the move was a success, but was not without excitement because an Argentine Special Forces patrol chose this moment to wander into the area and was engaged by D Squadron 22 SAS as the first wave of helicopters arrived. D Squadron swiftly dealt with the Argentine patrol, but it provided some worrying moments for the helicopters crews as tracer criss-crossed the landing site. It was fortunate that I had ignored the views expressed by Northwood, that reconnaissance of Mount Kent before insertion of 42 Commando was superfluous. Had D Squadron not been there, the Argentine special forces would have caught the Commando deplaning and, in the darkness and confusion on a strange landing zone, inflicted heavy casualties on men and helicopters. The one Chinook had a hair-raising return trip when it inadvertently struck the water in one of the many creeks of Port Salvador when the pilot lost his vision during a snow flurry. The large helicopter skidded across the water for about 100 metres before the pilot regained control and lifted off the surface. He reached San Carlos without further incident, but not without some anxiety, because he was forced by the weather to fly at the height that enemy intruders might choose and his radio was apparently not getting through to warn the air defences not to fire. He switched on all his lights and hoped. He made it, but the aircraft was not available for further lifts that night while it was checked for damage.

By first light on 31 May K Company had reached the summit of Mount Kent to find the enemy had withdrawn. Vaux met Rose, the Commanding Officer of 22 SAS, on the summit and they ordered the three guns of 7 Battery to fire on Moody Brook Camp on the outskirts of Stanley. It was a triumphant moment. They could see Stanley laid out before them about eighteen kilometres away, the harbour and town looking exactly like the air photographs, taken years before, that they had studied for so long on the voyage south. The end really was in sight; but there was much to be done. Commando Tactical Headquarters, one rifle company, one SAS Squadron, six 81 mm mortars and three light guns with very little ammunition were sitting on a key piece of ground near, nobody knew exactly how near, six Argentine infantry regiments, supported by thirty-eight 105 mm guns and probably some 155 mm guns. The nearest British troops were 3 Para at least half a day's march away. The nearest guns, other than the three already forward, were sixty-five kilometres away, nearly four times the range of a

105 mm light gun. Except for Harriers in the ground attack role, the 200 or so Commandos and SAS men were on their own. They rapidly prepared positions and pushed out observation posts and patrols to give early warning of any Argentine moves.

One patrol from K Company, clearing the north-east slope of Mount Kent, found empty slit trenches, equipment and all the signs of a position abandoned in haste. They also found five Argentine soldiers whom they took prisoner. The Company sent several expeditions to this position to salvage food when their own rations failed to turn up for lack of helicopter lift. The significance of this deserted position only became apparent when 45 Commando set up a patrol base in the vicinity some days later. For the moment everyone thought that the previous owners had 'legged it' in the face of 42 Commando.

Knowing how thinly spread my men really were on the ground, I was furious when I was told that boastful remarks were being made back in England by those who should have known better to the effect that the British were now holding the high ground overlooking Stanley.

Also at first light on 31 May two other groups were moving, or preparing to move: 3 Commando Brigade Headquarters and the M and AW Cadre. The Commando Brigade Headquarters Staff and radio operators, with man-packed radios, flew forward to Teal Inlet Settlement and set up in the Settlement Manager's house, while our Bandwagons with the heavier radios, including the secure-voice sets, motored across country. The helicopter move was bedevilled by snow showers which delayed lift-off. The preceding night at San Carlos had been quiet, except for a high-level bombing raid by the Argentine Air Force, which caused no casualties, but merely startled the ground crews and pilots of one of the flights of 846 Naval Air Squadron when a 1000-pound bomb landed without warning about one hundred metres away.

Captain Boswell and nineteen of his men of the M and AW Cadre were champing at the bit at first light that morning because a Sea King helicopter, ordered to lift them off one hour before dawn, had still not arrived. The task that these men were about to undertake had originated in a report made on 27 May by Sergeant Stone's four-man patrol, also from the Cadre, sitting on Bull Hill. They had been in position since D-Day, 21 May, one of a number of Cadre patrols, the eyes and ears of the Commando Brigade, well forward on the route to Teal and Stanley. Stone came up on the radio in clear to Boswell back at San Carlos Settlement to say that this might be the last message from his patrol because two Argentine UH-1 helicopters were hovering right over his OP. Boswell could hear the sound of the helicopters over the radio as Stone spoke. Eventually, to Stone's and everybody else's relief, the UH-1s hover-taxied away, lifted and flew off in the direction of

Mount Simon. The summit of Mount Simon was in cloud, so Stone reckoned that they probably deposited their troops, patrols from a Commando Company of the Argentine Special Forces, on the lower slopes of the Onion or Mount Simon. Stone cancelled his order to his men to destroy their radios and codes and fight their way out.

However, the news that he sent back alerted the Commando Brigade Headquarters to the threat of Argentine Special Forces sitting on the high ground on the right flank of the approaches to Teal Inlet and beyond. The Argentine OPs would thus be in a position to do exactly what the M and AW Cadre were doing — report on any movement they saw on foot, in tracked vehicles or helicopters. The Commando Brigade was about to move towards Teal Inlet, so this threat to their security must be eliminated. Boswell was ordered to use the complete M and AW Cadre, less four patrols newly positioned or moving, to seek out enemy OPs on the high ground Mount Simon — Ball Mount — The Onion, fix their positions and clear them if he could, or at least find them so they could be taken out by other means. He regrouped his patrols and, by withdrawing three patrols from other tasks, adding his reserve patrol and his small headquarters, had, by 30 May, gathered nineteen men. He intended to start the insertion of his patrols on 31 May. But, on the evening of 30 May he received a message from Lieutenant Haddow's patrol. They had been marching to Mount Challenger from a position on Evelyn Hill overlooking Teal and now in the hands of 3 Para. They had been moving only at night and had been lying-up all day in an OP on the lower slopes of Mount Simon. Haddow said that he had just seen two UH-1s deposit a patrol of sixteen men at Top Malo House 400 metres from his own position and that they had also heard several other helicopters in the vicinity. Haddow asked for fighter ground attack to destroy the enemy in the house. But with only half an hour to nightfall, the request was refused and the weather the next day might not be suitable. Boswell was told to eliminate this Argentine patrol in the morning.

He attempted to make radio contact with his patrols on the ground, including Haddow's, to order them to meet him on his chosen landing site, having secured it first. But that night, for the first and only night of the campaign, he could not get through on the radio to any of his patrols because of atmospheric conditions. He therefore planned to arrive by helicopter about one hour before first light at a landing site about 1000 metres away and in dead ground from Top Malo House. He would then approach in darkness and assault at dawn. When, on the morning of 31 May, an hour late, the first helicopter arrived at the pick-up point at San Carlos Settlement, Boswell charged on board and angrily enquired if this was the helicopter for his task, to be told that it was for the move of Brigade Headquarters which had 'higher priority'. Fortunately the pilot in the aircraft Boswell had boarded was

Lieutenant-Commander Thornewill, the CO of 846 Naval Air Squadron, who, when he realized the importance of Boswell's task, summoned the correct helicopter forward. When it arrived, Boswell quickly briefed the pilot, who bravely agreed to the choice of landing site close to the enemy. The nineteen men then piled into the helicopter with their rucksacks loaded with sufficient rations for a week in the field without resupply. The overloaded helicopter took off and then, in Boswell's words, 'flew lower and faster than he had ever flown before' to deposit the Cadre on exactly the right spot after a forty-five kilometre flight — fine flying and typical of the pilots and aircrew of 846 Naval Air Squadron.

After dumping their packs on the landing site, the Cadre set off to a fence about 1,000 metres away. Here the seven-man fire group moved off to the left to a gate, about 150 metres from Top Malo House, from where they would support the assault group. The twelve-man assault group led by Boswell skirted round to the south-east of Top Malo House, remaining below the intervening crest line. As they moved round, the fire group commander, Lieutenant Murray, spotted some peat cuttings which would give the assault group an excellent covered approach. He sent Sergeant McLean after the fire group to tell Boswell. As Boswell approached the house he called his Section Commanders, Sergeant Doyle, Sergeant Stone and Colour-Sergeant Montgomery, up to him for a final check reconnaissance. As they lay looking at the target, Boswell realized that their dark uniforms on the snow-covered ground would be a give-away to an alert sentry. So far they had apparently not been spotted, despite fears that the enemy, being Special Forces, would surely have sentries out. Boswell cancelled the close reconnaissance and the whole assault group crawled forward, only too conscious that the ground over which they were moving was overlooked by a window in the upper floor of the building, like an eye watching them.

When Boswell judged they were close enough to the house and in full view of their fire group, he gave the order 'fix bayonets'. Sergeant Stone said, 'It's a bite, there's no one there'. Boswell fired a green mini-flare, the signal for the fire group to fire six 66 mm light anti-armour rockets at the house. As the first rocket was fired, an Argentine sentry moved to the window on the upper floor. Corporal Groves armed with a sniper rifle shot him. As the 66 mm rockets slammed into the house it burst into flames; Boswell and the assault group charged forward, halted, fired two 66s into the house and charged again. The enemy ran out of the house into a small stream bed about 50 metres away, firing as they ran. Sergeant Doyle fell, hit through the shoulder, and then Corporal Groves also fell, hit in the chest. The ammunition stacked in the house exploded as the assault group ran forward, causing them to recoil for a moment, while smoke from the burning building shielded them from the enemy lying in the stream firing at them. The fire fight went on for a few minutes as the assault group worked their way towards the enemy. Then the officer commanding the Argentine force tried to run off and was killed by two 40 mm rounds fired from M 79 grenade launchers by Corporal Barnacle and Sergeant McLean. The Argentines stood up and threw away their weapons. It was over. Five Argentines had been killed and seven wounded, the remaining five were taken prisoner. The Cadre had three wounded — Doyle, Groves and Stone. Haddow's patrol, who had watched the whole battle, came running forward waving a Union Flag as a recognition sign. They did not want to risk being shot by their own side in the excitement, with the adrenalin still flowing.

The whole operation had been a brilliant success, starting with good OP work and fieldcraft by Haddow's men, a good plan and briefing by Boswell, excellent flying by the pilot from 846 Squadron, canny use of the ground, bold and aggressive tactics and professionalism. It must be said that, despite being Special Forces, the Argentines did not have adequate sentries out, but that does not detract from the Cadre's achievement. Once again the better soldiers won. Unknown to the Cadre the assault had been watched by two other Argentine OPs who, having seen the treatment meted out to their comrades and imagining that it was their turn next, decided to call it a day. One OP stationed on the summit of Mount Simon walked into Teal Inlet where they were picked up by 45 Commando. The other walked from The Baby towards Lower Malo House and surrendered to 3 Para. Boswell, having sent out his and the enemy wounded and dead by helicopter, took his cock-a-hoop Royal Marines into Teal Inlet to be congratulated on their assault by me. The Cadre from the beginning of the land campaign had been giving sterling service by its patrolling, OP work and accurate passing of information and was to continue to do so for the rest of the war. It had now, on its own, caused the elimination of the Argentine Special Forces OP line which threatened the security of the Commando Brigade's right flank. That night, 31 May/1 June, L Company (Captain Wheen) and elements of Support Company 42 Commando, 2 Troop 59 Commando Squadron RE and the remainder of 7 Battery were flown forward to Mount Kent. An early load in with 7 Battery on the first day of the fly-in had been the gold-painted model Sphinx that always sat on the ammunition boxes at the Battery gun position. The members of 7 (Sphinx) Commando Battery were extremely proud of their Sphinx but also highly superstitious. It was deemed to be bad luck if 'she' was not on the Battery position. L Company and 2 Troop 59 Commando Squadron RE were immediately sent to Mount Challenger from where they could dominate the track from Fitzroy to Stanley. To complete the move forward of 42 Commando took two more nights of helicopter lifts: 1/2

June when Defence Troop and Surveillance Troop were flown forward, and on 2/3 June J Company, having rejoined their Commando from Goose Green, was also pushed out on to Mount Challenger.

By this time I had told 40 Commando to join the rest of my brigade all moving forward, and their advance parties were in the process of doing so. I made my intentions clear in my daily situation report to Divisional HQ, extracts of which are below:

2. 40 CDO RM. WARNING ORDER ISSUED FOR RELIEF OF UNIT POSITIONS AM 1 JUNE BY A BATTALION FROM 5 INFANTRY BRIGADE. 40 COMMANDO TO MOVE TO PORT SAN CARLOS IN RESERVE. [That is in reserve for 3 Commando Brigade, not anyone else, and to move forward - see next part of signal]
13. FUTURE INTENTIONS:
B. 31 MAY/1 JUNE. 40 COMMANDO TO BE RELIEVED. [ie by a unit of 5 Brigade]
D. 3 JUNE. LSL TO TEAL. 40 COMMANDO TO DOUGLAS OR TEAL.

Meanwhile 3 Para, marching mainly by night and lying up by day to avoid air attack or detection by enemy OPs and preceded by their Patrol Company, D Company (Major Butler), had secured Estancia House on the night 31 May/1 June. The Battalion took some prisoners on the way, stragglers from San Carlos, Douglas and Teal Inlet and the Special Forces, disheartened by the destruction of their comrades at Top Malo. A Company (Major Collett) then moved on to the dominating ground of Mount Estancia, followed early in the morning of 1 June by Battalion Tactical Headquarters. B Company (Major Argue) secured the southern shoulders of Mount Vernet, covering south across the valley separating Mount Kent from Mount Vernet. C Company (Major Osborne) occupied Mount Vernet. From some of these positions Stanley could be seen in the brief lulls between the driving rain, fog and snow showers as the weather turned increasingly foul, slowing down the rate of build-up of the Commando Brigade. It was not until 3 June that a second 105 mm light gun battery, 79 (Kirkee) Commando Light Battery Royal Artillery, could be flown forward to Mount Estancia. Both 3 Para and 42 Commando were in range of the Argentine artillery and particularly the 155 guns. Any movement by day on forward slopes or crest lines drew artillery fire. The paucity of helicopter lift available to 3 Commando Brigade resulted in so few shells being lifted forward that fire missions were limited to 100 rounds per battery per day, or about sixteen rounds per gun per day. Counter-battery and harassing fire against the Argentines was therefore tightly controlled and many opportunity targets could not be engaged for lack of ammunition.

Moore's original plan was that 3 Commando Brigade should take second priority to 5 Infantry Brigade in the allocation of medium-lift helicopters in order to allow the latter to get forward from San Carlos. However, reports brought back to Commando Brigade Headquarters on the evening of 31 May convinced me that the opportunity to build up the Mount Kent-Challenger-Estancia position must not be lost. Abandoned enemy positions had been found on the eastern slopes of Mount Kent by patrols from 42 Commando. The enemy must not be allowed to retake these positions and the key ground won by so much effort in sweat, scarce helicopters — and some blood — must not be put in jeopardy. I therefore asked Moore to fly forward to Brigade Headquarters at Teal Inlet early on 1 June. I put my case for speeding the build-up of my Brigade and Moore agreed, increasing the helicopter effort allocated to 3 Commando Brigade. Notwithstanding this decision and the arrival of more Sea King and Wessex helicopters in the Falkland Islands, there were still far too few to support two brigades. The frustrations caused by this lack of support showed in a signal sent to Divisional Headquarters by 3 Commando Brigade on 4 June which read:

1. Understand we only have one Sea King and one Wessex under opcon [operational control] tomorrow.
2. This allocation totally inadequate for current resupply tasks eg 2,100 rounds 105 ammo.
3. No shells, no attack!

The newly arrived helicopters, although very welcome and essential to the land forces, were flown by pilots many of whom lacked experience in the business of supporting a land battle. Some were taken straight from anti-submarine duties and indeed were flying anti-submarine Sea Kings in a ground support role. Several helicopter pilots risked being shot down because of map-reading errors which took them on to forward slopes in full view of the enemy. One such helicopter pilot landed the Commando Brigade Air Squadron Tactical Headquarters vehicle in a position that could be seen all the way from Stanley, let alone the Argentine forward positions. The vehicle and its crew were promptly and comprehensively shelled. The crew wisely withdrew, leaving the vehicle, which remained perched on a ledge high on the north-eastern slopes of Mount Kent, miles from any track, until the end of the war when it was lifted away by helicopter. The newcomers also had a disconcerting habit of landing close to Headquarters and parking alongside each other in neat rows. The battle-experienced 846 Squadron, the Wessex Squadrons and Brigade Air Squadron usually shunned the company of other helicopters on the ground, flew so low that they had to lift to clear the sheep fences, ceaselessly searched the sky for fighters and seldom made map-reading errors.

The Bandwagons of Brigade Headquarters motored across to Teal Inlet from San Carlos Settlement, escorted by 3 Troop of the Blues and Royals. The trip took seventeen and a half hours. Even the Bandwagons with their low ground pressure got bogged in time after time and the trip was painfully slow. It was described as being like the M4 westbound on a Friday evening. Having delivered their charges safely to Teal Inlet, 3 Troop motored off to Estancia House.

Teal Inlet Settlement was now bulging with troops. Slit trenches were dug all over the settlement, mainly for protection against air attack. But fortunately the weather was misty and the visibility only a few hundred yards. LSL *Sir Lancelot* slipped into Teal Inlet on 2 June bringing with her the first load of supplies for what was to become the 3 Commando Brigade Forward Maintenance Area (Forward BMA). She also brought the cheerful and most welcome figure of Seccombe. Supplies were landed by Mexeflote on to the beach at Teal Inlet and then dispersed into pits dug into the low banks at the back of the beach. The standard of dispersion and camouflage that could be achieved at Teal Inlet was far better than that at Ajax Bay. A Field Dressing Station was also set up at Teal Inlet to act as a link in the casualty evacuation chain between units forward and what had become the Main Dressing Station at Ajax Bay, now seventy kilometres from the front line. The quicker a wounded man was evacuated to a place where his condition could be stabilized before onward movement, the better his chances of survival. At the Regimental Aid Post up with each fighting unit, the best that could be done in the open, often under fire, was what might be described as Good First Aid. The Field Dressing Station was the first step at which surgery could be carried out and other steps taken to prepare the casualty for what might be a forty-minute, or even longer, helicopter trip to the Main Dressing Station and on to the hospital ship *Uganda*.

Helicopters played an indispensable part in the casualty evacuation system. In battle each commando or battalion in 3 Commando Brigade had at least two light helicopters under command. These would fly ammunition forward, sometimes right into the battle behind the leading companies and bring casualties back, either to the Regimental Aid Post, from where the casualty was taken out by a medium helicopter, or straight to the Field Dressing Station. The back seats of the Gazelles and Scouts were removed and boxes of machine-gun ammunition, 66 mm and 84 mm rounds, mortar bombs and Blowpipe missiles were piled in. On the return journey casualties would be sat or laid in the back. If conscious, they were usually invited to hold their own or their chum's saline drips. The bravery and unselfishness of the light helicopter crews was a byword throughout the Commando Brigade. Flying in appalling weather, often in darkness, there were very few occasions when they did not get through and they never refused a trip without trying it first.

45 Commando marched out of Teal Inlet after first light on 3 June and by midday on 4 June had arrived below Bluff Cove Park, south-west of Mount Kent (not to be confused with Bluff Cove), where they set up a Commando Patrol Base. I saw them march in looking remarkably full of high spirits. As always, it was like a tonic to see these tough, purposeful men, green berets above camouflaged black faces on which there almost invariably seemed to be a cheerful grin.

Captain Gardiner, of 45 Commando, summed up the situation thus:

We arrived as the wind stiffened and it started to rain but we didn't care because we were now 17 kilometres from Stanley and there was no way we were going back. It was curious that throughout the campaign, there was never any question about the justness of our cause and that we would win. We knew we were going to take casualties, possibly in considerable numbers. But while we would have all heaved a whoop of relief if they (the enemy) had surrendered, no man who was with the Commando for the advance on Stanley wanted to be anywhere else. One was with one's friends.

By 4 June 3 Commando Brigade, less 40 Commando still back at San Carlos, was deployed forward on the high ground Mount Estancia — Mount Vernet — Mount Kent — Mount Challenger. 3 Para had put in a probing attack on Mount Longdon in the afternoon of 3 June but had run into well-planned artillery fire and was ordered back. The Battalion established itself, with A Company forward, about four kilometres west of the Murrell Bridge just north of the Estancia — Stanley track. B Company was about 2,000 metres due west of A Company and level with Mount Kent, while C Company remained on Mount Estancia. Pike also set up a patrol base just west of the Murrell Bridge from which to mount patrols on his likely objective, Mount Longdon. He also held Mount Vernet with a patrol.

45 Commando were in a good central position to reinforce either 3 Para or 42 Commando in the event of an Argentine attack. 42 Commando, who had arrived first, were well established. There was much to do. The most important task was to patrol aggressively to find out exactly where the enemy were located in preparation for the forthcoming battle for Stanley. Hand-in-hand with this was the need to build up sufficient stocks of ammunition, particularly gun ammunition. I had decided with my gunner, Holroyd-Smith, that each battery should be stocked to a level of 500 rounds per gun. Ammunition was now coming into Teal by sea, but it had to be lifted forward from there by helicopter to the gun lines. The weather

at Teal Inlet, although not on Mount Kent, Estancia and Challenger, was improving. This caused a worry that the Argentine Air Force might put in an attack on the LSLs which lay unloading in the still waters of Teal Inlet; the low surrounding hills provided no cover at all. By 4 June the Rapier troop of four firing posts promised by Divisional Headquarters had not arrived. Although the Argentine Air Force had not been seen for several days by ground troops, there was, as far as 3 Commando Brigade knew, no reason why enemy aircraft should not appear at any moment — either fighter-bombers from mainland Argentine, or Pucaras and Mentors from Stanley and other airstrips in the Falklands.

The urgency to get some air defence around Teal Inlet was sharpened by a security breach emanating from the Press at home. Quite where they got this information from will probably never be known. It was certainly not leaking from correspondents with the Commando Brigade who would have put themselves at risk as much as anybody had they committed breaches of security. On 4 June I sent a signal to Divisional Headquarters part of which read:

Have just heard the BBC World News reported that quote Teal Inlet is HQ of Force attacking Stanley unquote I am absolutely fed up with hearing my plans broadcast on BBC News.

It is worth emphasizing that I now know that this BBC report, and the preceding ones, of which there were at least four others, all, without exception, originated from government sources in Whitehall, and not from the press with us in the Falklands. But if announcements like this did not bring the enemy air force, surely nothing would. By dusk on 4 June the Rapier Troop was still not complete and many anxious hours were to pass on 5 June before the long-awaited firing posts had arrived and were properly sited. The sore-pressed Divisional Headquarters was bombarded with signals from the Commando Brigade:

Lift of Rapier this location incomplete although assurance given yesterday to the contrary. Rapier this location non operational and short vehicles and vital stores. All launchers dumped on one site [from which they could not be moved without a helicopter to lift them].

And later in the day

Teal Inlet now plum target ... a successful strike could spoil our day and many more to come.

In fact the Argentine Air Force, for some unaccountable reason, did not attack Teal until the second-last day of the war. But the bombing of two LSLs at Fitzroy only four days after these signals were sent would be a sad reminder of the penalties that awaited those who let their guard drop. 3 Commando Brigade had seen what the Argentine Airforce could do. The new arrivals, which included Divisional Headquarters, had yet to find out. Divisional Headquarters patiently took these jabs on the chin and did a sterling job to provide the assets the two Brigades forward were shouting for. By now Brigadier Waters, a tough and resolute soldier and another friend from Camberley days, had arrived as Deputy Divisional Commander. It was good to see his round, cheerful face and to know that the excellent brain behind the large spectacles and benign expression was being brought to bear on the many problems facing us all in the Division.

On 2 June, I again asked for 40 Commando to be returned to my command, but to no avail. The Commando Brigade also lost both troops of CVRT to 5 Infantry Brigade, whose leading battalion, 2 Para, had flown forward to Fitzroy on 3 June. There was very nearly a disaster when the M and AW Cadre OP on Smoko Mountain reported an enemy Chinook landing troops at Fitzroy. The Commando Brigade Headquarters ordered two batteries of light guns to be prepared to fire on this 'enemy' because no warning had been received that friendly troops were in the vicinity of Fitzroy. The Argentines still had a Chinook helicopter and it was logical that they should reinforce Fitzroy by air since the track from Stanley to Fitzroy was dominated by 42 Commando on Mount Challenger. Fortunately a check with Divisional Headquarters revealed that it was 2 Para and calamity was averted.

Some years later I heard about 2 Para's adventures while they were away from my command. Moore had told Wilson to move his brigade along the southern route to Stanley via Goose Green. Keeble, still in command of 2 Para:

'Brigadier Wilson appeared in my headquarters and outlined a plan to march the Brigade forty miles from Darwin to Fitzroy, leap-frogging battalions, guns, and mortars. Although the terrain was better on this route than elsewhere in the Falklands, and there was a track traversable by lightly loaded landrovers, it would soon have been reduced to a morass by large numbers of heavily-loaded vehicles towing trailers and guns. I suggested we try something else. We had discovered that the civilian telephone line from Swan Inlet House, about ten miles to the east as the crow flies, might still be working to Fitzroy. My plan was to send Crosland and a large patrol from B Company in five missile-armed Scout helicopters to Swan Inlet House and see if the enemy were in Fitzroy.'

Wilson did not appear to support the idea, and departed. However, Keeble, Crosland and Captain Greenhalgh set to and prepared a plan based on what they had told Wilson. Two days later he returned, and said, 'Do it'. A stone through the window of the unoccupied Swan Inlet House and Crosland was on the telephone, discovering to his amazement that there were no Argentines in Fitzroy or Bluff Cove Settlements. That evening the surviving Chinook helicopter was busy moving Wilson's headquarters to Goose Green. Keeble asked for it to move his battalion to Fitzroy; Wilson agreed. When the pilot was briefed on the task, he replied that as darkness was approaching he was limited to two more sorties that day. He would, therefore, get only half the force to Fitzroy before nightfall. Keeble suggested doubling the load. The crew chief interrupted, reminding them that the peacetime load was forty men, at which a company sergeant-major yanked him off the tailgate of the helicopter, saying: 'That's one less'.

Eventually the pilot agreed to eighty men being crammed in, standing like commuters in a tube train in rush hour. There were no seats. In this manner A Company and a mortar detachment were lifted in, followed by B Company and battalion headquarters, escorted by Scout helicopters. The next day the remainder of the battalion moved up, and A, C and D Companies with battalion headquarters took up a position on a feature overlooking Bluff Cove, while B Company held Fitzroy.

The Commando Brigade had also lost the exclusive services of our own Logistic Regiment. 5 Infantry Brigade had come south with inadequate logistic support so an ad-hoc logistic support group was cobbled together by the Commando Logistic Regiment to provide a Forward BMA for 5 Infantry Brigade at Fitzroy, similar to that for 3 Commando Brigade at Teal. Hellberg protested loudly that his job was supporting 3 Commando Brigade, but I had no option but to let him go as the Force Logistics Co-ordinator. The Commando Logistic Regiment, organized to support three commandos and their supporting arms, having supported the Brigade enlarged by the addition of the two Parachute Battalions, now found itself yet further stretched, but coped magnificently.

Space does not allow a full analysis of the reasons for 5 Brigade's lack of logistic support. In essence they were caused by the muddled thinking that attended the deployment of the Brigade. This was in no way Wilson's fault, nor that of his staff. At root, it lay in the reluctance of the most senior officers in the Army to send it at all — symptomatic of their belief, declared at the earliest meetings, that the operation to re-take the Falkland Islands was impossible and doomed to failure. Once it was decided that they should go, their role was not clear. There was talk of garrison duties. Whereas it was absolutely clear to us already there that 5 Brigade was being brought in to fight.

Since then pundits have suggested that the deployment of 5 Brigade was unnecessary. This is the wisdom of hindsight. Had the enemy not surrendered when they did, had there been bloody and protracted fighting around and in Port Stanley, and given the Argentine strengths, there would have been plenty of work for two brigades. As it was, 2nd Battalion Scots Guards found themselves fighting one of the hardest battles, against probably the toughest Argentine unit, the 5th Marine Battalion.

Back at Port San Carlos the Commando Engineers had built a pumping and storage system to supply fuel to helicopters and Harriers. By the end of the war this fuel system was receiving and dispensing 50,000 gallons a day. It was built by 1 Troop of 59 Independent Commando Squadron Royal engineers left behind for the purpose when the remainder of the Squadron deployed forward with the commandos and battalions. In war there are never enough Sappers and the support given to the Commando Brigade by its Engineer Squadron, which included a Troop from 9 Squadron, was superb. The Harrier strip at Port San Carlos was built by 11 Field Squadron Royal Engineers, not part of 3 Commando Brigade, but under command until Divisional Headquarters arrived. They lost all their plant when *Atlantic Conveyor* went down but in true Sapper style built the strip nevertheless.

Macdonald, the Commander of 59 Commando Squadron, never seemed to rest. He was up with his forward troops then back at Port San Carlos to supervise work there, but always cheerful and positive, the more so the more difficult the situation. Fortunately he was not 'borrowed' by Divisional Headquarters, who had brought their own senior Sapper with them. Not did his Squadron have to support 5 Infantry Brigade because they had brought the balance of 9 Squadron with them.

The weather on the high ground, particularly Mount Kent and Challenger, was as bad as even the toughest old hands could remember it. Men were constantly soaked through by lashing rain or wet snow driven by a bitter wind; the temperature was always well below freezing at night and other than 'bivvies' built from ponchos there was no cover. On at least two nights on Mount Kent it dropped to minus twelve degrees Centigrade, measured on a thermometer issued to all Royal Marines Arctic Warfare Instructors, of which there were a number in K Company. A position even a few hundred feet lower on the side of the mountain made a difference of several degrees in the temperature and in the power of the wind. 42 Commando, who were to occupy the highest ground for twelve days, were in the worst position, but the others were not much better. Meanwhile the patrolling went on.

CHAPTER EIGHT

Probing

'The infantry night patrol — that great test of individual skill and leadership ... the paramount tactic in the struggle for information and initiative.'

General Sir David Fraser

The quality of the troops in 3 Commando Brigade was never more clearly demonstrated than by the events which took place in the days between the arrival of the Brigade on the Mount Estancia, Kent and Challenger positions and the opening battle for Stanley. The weather, as the southern mid-winter approached, was foul, with freezing nights, days of driving snow, sleet and rain, almost always accompanied by high winds. Visibility from the tops of the high features was often less than twenty metres and sometimes the wind was so strong that it picked men up and deposited them on their backsides a metre or two away. Occasionally the sun shone through and it was possible to dry out some kit, but most men were wet throughout this period and their feet in particular never dried.

From various points on the high ground in the Commando Brigade's possession it was possible to see the Argentine troops on Mount Longdon, Two Sisters and Mount Harriet. From time to time figures could be seen on the skylines and, if there was enough gun ammunition on the gun-lines, a few rounds of harassing fire would be directed at the enemy. But it was not possible to pin-point many defensive positions and bunkers, or the location and extent of minefields. All this would have to be done by patrolling, which would, in addition, have the aim of dominating the ground in between the opposing sides, and thus wresting the initiative from the enemy, or, as events turned out, forestalling any attempt on his part to gain it. The ground in between the Commando Brigade and the Argentine Army was bare of cover and could be crossed by patrols only at night, if they were not to be spotted the minute they moved onto the forward slopes and down into the broad valley that separated the high features occupied by the opposing forces. The distance between the main Argentine and British positions at this stage was 5-6,000 metres as the crow flies. Patrol routes would not be in straight lines and might involve a round trip of up to four times that distance to skirt minefields, take advantage of folds in the ground and to avoid using the same route too often. The ground everywhere was boggy and, like much of the Falkland Islands, criss-crossed by stone runs. These are 'rivers' of huge boulders, covered with slippery lichen which made crossing them a laborious business by day and difficult by night. These 'rivers' of stone could, in places, be thousands of metres long and several hundred metres wide. In the area where most of the patrolling took place they were usually about 2,000 metres long and 500 or so metres wide; but stone runs covered at least half the ground. Crossing one at night could take several hours and sometimes the stones would move and 'clink' loudly. The enemy had good night-vision equipment and when it was not raining, snowing or foggy, the light from the stars and particularly the moon, in the clear unpolluted air, lit up the white grassy landscape and patrols felt very vulnerable.

The tops of the high features were crowned with great, craggy castles of rock, which stood up like the spines of some vast prehistoric reptile. These crenellated bastions, with deep fissures, sudden sheer drops and great buttresses, provided excellent defensive positions, particularly when improved with rock walls or sangars. Few were less than 500 metres long and Goat Ridge, for example, was over 2,000 metres long.

The Commanding Officers in 3 Commando Brigade were warned that their objectives were likely to be Mount Harriet for 42 Commando, Two Sisters for 45 Commando and Mount Longdon for 3 Para. Each Commanding Officer now had to find out as much as he could about the objective and feed this information back to Brigade Headquarters, and at the same time work out how he would tackle the task when the time came. As soon as 42 Commando was established on Mount Kent and Mount Challenger, the Commanding Officer pushed a troop-strength observation post forward on to Wall Mountain. This was the minimum strength that Vaux considered necessary in such an exposed position. They took with them an artillery forward observation party, a mortar fire control party and a Forward Air Controller. At the time it seemed inconceivable that such a position should not be intolerable to the enemy and draw a determined response to dislodge them. The OP had a good view of the Argentine positions on the western part of Mount Harriet and of the Stanley to Fitzroy track which passed south of Harriet and about 1,000 metres south of their own positions on Wall Mountain. Any attempt by the enemy to use the track was thwarted by shell and mortar fire called down by the OP, who also reported that the area round the track was mined. Similarly the OP was able to hinder further attempts by the Argentines to extend the minefields, at least by day. Unfortunately such harassing fire had to be very limited to avoid using so much gun and mortar ammunition that the gun and mortar lines would never be stocked up for the forthcoming battle. The intention to build up the ammunition stocks to 500 rounds per gun in each of the five 105 mm gun batteries, a total of 15,000 rounds, would require 312 Sea King loads for gun ammunition alone.

The Wall Mountain OP reported that the Argentines had established a strong position on the western tip of Mount Harriet with dug-in positions, several bunkers and a number of machine guns. The enemy appeared to be sited to repulse any British advance along the track from Fitzroy. However, far more information about the enemy would be required before any attack could be mounted with a degree of certainty about the true strength and dispositions of the Argentines. Vaux reasoned that the low ground between Wall Mountain and Mount Harriet would be mined and was later proved to be correct. A direct assault on to Harriet from the west would not only have to cross this minefield, but from the siting of the position, would also fulfil what appeared to be the enemy's expectations. So the centre approach was out. A left hook was a possibility, but Vaux knew that 45 Commando had been warned that Two Sisters was likely to be their objective for the forthcoming brigade attack. He might therefore find himself straying into their territory if he chose a left-flanking approach, and the more he looked at it the less he liked it. A shallow left hook to keep clear of 45 Commando would have to cross the extensive stone runs that guarded the saddle between Mount Harriet and Goat Ridge. In any case that saddle looked to be an ideal killing ground; the enemy would do the killing while the assaulting troops attempted to cross it. A wider left hook, as well as risking entanglement with 45 Commando, would necessitate crossing the razor-backed, slab-sided spine of Goat Ridge before debouching on to the killing ground just described. Vaux decided to see if a right hook from the line of the Fitzroy-Stanley track was feasible. However, the minefields were more extensive than had at first been thought, as the first patrol from L Company found to its cost. A troop-strength patrol led by Lieutenant MacMillan was conducting a night patrol from Mount Challenger past Wall Mountain towards Mount Harriet when Marine Curtiss trod on a mine which blew off most of his foot. Corporal Cuthell picked up Curtiss, a fifteen-stone (95 kg) Royal Marines Colts Rugby player and carried him on his back out of the minefield. As the patrol withdrew, they were shelled. The patrol moved higher up the feature into the rock runs, hoping thereby to get out of the enemy defensive fire which they reasoned would be targeted on the more likely approaches. There they stopped so that Medical Assistant Hapworth could treat Curtiss before continuing to carry him back. It took the whole patrol seven hours to carry Curtiss across a distance of less than four kilometres. Helicopter casevac was impossible in the prevailing atrocious weather and the steep, boggy hillside, strewn with rocks, made the fireman's lift the only way of carrying him. As ill luck would have it, he was the heaviest man in the patrol.

The engineers from 59 Independent Commando Squadron commanded by Captain Hicks, with 42 Commando's own Assault Engineers, were then tasked to clear a safe route from the saddle between Wall Mountain and Mount Challenger southwards to the Fitzroy-Stanley track. The two teams worked side by side to clear a mine-free path about four metres wide while 5 Troop from L Company provided the protection. At first the thick mist, drizzle and darkness covered their activities. Suddenly the mist began to clear and the bright moon illuminated the patrol. It made their mine-clearing task easier, but, as they were well forward of any friendly troops by the time they approached the white surface of the track, they felt very exposed as they painstakingly probed each square foot of ground until they had covered the last 500 metres to the road. They were not spotted by the enemy and returned along the safe route which they 'fixed' by taking a bearing from a large dump of abandoned Argentine 105 mm artillery shells.

The following night Sergeant Collins from K Company set off to find a suitable route for a right-flanking attack by 42 Commando. Collins's small patrol, consisting of himself and three men, was supported by a back-up patrol of troop strength commanded by Sergeant Weston. After moving down the route cleared by the engineers, Sergeant Weston remained with two sections, while Collins went on, taking Corporal Roe's section with him. When he came level with the eastern end of Wall Mountain, Corporal Roe's section was about to drop off and go firm, while Collins and his three men continued eastwards, when Marine Patterson stepped on a mine which blew off his foot below the ankle. Collins, expecting an enemy reaction to the explosion at any moment, placed his three men out in a covering position, while he and Corporal Roe's section moved Patterson down to the Fitzroy-Stanley track. Patterson was extremely stoic and at times actually hopped along on one foot, being helped by the others because the rough ground made carrying him too difficult.

At this stage Weston appeared with his back-up patrol and Collins spoke to his Commanding Officer on the radio. Collins knew that it was important to try to continue with the patrol to find a way for his Commando, despite the possibility of a compromise, and Vaux impressed upon him the need to carry on. So Weston took Patterson back towards his own lines far enough to the west to be out of sight of the enemy and Captain Pounds, wearing night vision goggles, flew in a Gazelle of the Commando Brigade Air Squadron to collect Patterson and take him to the Field Dressing Station at Teal Inlet. It was a brilliant piece of flying, hover-taxiing in to pluck a wounded man from well forward of friendly positions. Sergeant Collins meanwhile, with his three men and without any back-up, continued towards the enemy, keeping to the south of the track. When they were almost due south of the western end of Mount Harriet's spine-back they were spotted and a large patrol moved down the hillside towards them. Collins led his patrol away, but as he did so he fell into a water-filled ditch and some of his patrol fell in on top of him, pushing him right under. Recovering quickly, he continued to lead his patrol south for a few more metres before turning them about and deploying into a skirmish line ready to receive the enemy patrol who were following up. As Collins's patrol went to ground, the Argentines followed suit.

They then began to shout to Collins's men in Spanish, perhaps thinking they were Argentine stragglers from Fitzroy or Goose Green and perhaps also warning them that they were in a minefield. Collins's men lay still and did not answer, the two patrols facing each other in what Collins described as a 'Mexican Standoff'. He knew that, if it came to a competition as to who could stick it out in the around zero temperatures, his men were going to win. After about an hour the Argentines began fidgeting and muttering and their Commander was snapping at them. A few minutes later they returned to the track and lined up like targets on a range. Collins's GPMG gunner got very excited, but restrained himself. The Argentines set off back to their own positions, perhaps not sure what they had seen, if anything, and possibly not in a mood to find out.

As they returned to their positions, Collins, watching through his Individual Weapon Sight on his SLR, could see them going back into their weapon pits. He had been unable to pick these out before among the rocks and shadows, but now he knew where to look he could identify them quite clearly. He was able to get a good idea of the lay-out of the position. By now the patrol had been out for eight hours and they must not be caught in the open by the onset of day, so Collins decided to return to Mount Challenger and report what he had seen.

The next day Vaux came forward to Mount Challenger and, having debriefed Collins, briefed him for another task — to try and find a route well south of the Fitzroy-Stanley track to a forming-up position (FUP) for the Commando on the south-east shoulder of Mount Harriet. That night Collins set out again, this time with a troop from J Company and a small party of engineers. When they reached the minefield the troop and the engineers remained, while the engineers did a reconnaissance to establish the extent of the minefield; Collins, Lieutenant Beadon and three men swung well south of the track. The going got increasingly boggy as they lost height and found themselves in an area of ponds and peat cuttings. They went south of a lake and then swung north to cross the track. At this stage Collins decided that the moonlight was so bright that he stood a better chance of success on his own. He also knew that he would move more quietly without his SLR, so he left it with the patrol. If there had been a pistol with the patrol, he would have taken it, but there was not. Armed only with a knife, he crawled slowly forward.

He got very close to the enemy and saw several Argentines moving about, and more defensive positions. He crawled along the low fence that ran generally north-east from the track to the south-east of Mount Harriet. It was marked on the map, but he was able to confirm that it was still there and subsequently tell his Commanding Officer. Collins then crept back to rejoin his patrol and led them back to Mount Challenger. As he withdrew back across the track to join his patrol he brought down some artillery fire on the position he had just left to catch anyone coming looking for him. It is a measure of the professionalism of everybody in the Commando Brigade that not only Collins, who was not a gunner, but also his radio operator, a Marine, were able to call down and adjust artillery fire at night. Sergeant Collins and his men had done splendidly and it is hard to over-emphasize what they achieved. On his first patrol one of the men with him had stepped on a mine close to the enemy, and he had subsequently been followed by an Argentine patrol. On each occasion he must have been sorely tempted to bow gracefully out of the contest on the grounds that his patrol had been compromised. That he did not, but went on to complete his task, and then on another night went in alone, in the bright moonlight, among the Argentine positions, speaks volumes for the tenacity and courage of this young Sergeant. He was subsequently to lead his Commando on their march round to their start line and take part in the attack with his troop. For the moment he and his men could return to L Company and their wet sleeping bags under their ponchos among the rocks, freezing bog and howling winds of Mount Challenger.

The next day a strong fighting patrol from K Company penetrated on to Mount Harriet, but this time from the north-west via Goat Ridge. The patrol discovered that Goat Ridge was unoccupied but was fired on several times by machine guns from the enemy depth positions on the north and east slopes of Mount Harriet. It was becoming clear that 42 Commando's objectives were held by at least two companies, well dug-in and well sited for defence. To glean this information had taken nights of patrolling by 42 Commando and their engineers, of which only three nights are described here. During the ten or so days which this patrolling and route-clearance took, 42 Commando occupied the highest ground in appalling conditions. Often the rifle companies would deploy working parties all night to porter rations and ammunition to forward positions. From time to time Argentine artillery, particularly 155mm guns, fired harassing tasks onto Mount Kent, Challenger and Wall Mountain. By this time the lack of helicopters to lift fresh water had forced the men of 42 Commando to use the brackish water in the peat bogs, to make their 'wets' of tea or reconstitute their dehydrated rations. As a result many had succumbed to diarrhoea or what came to be called 'Galtieri's revenge'. Meanwhile others in the Commando Brigade had also been patrolling and enduring.

Pike, Commanding 3 Para, having been warned that Mount Longdon was the most likely objective for his Battalion, set up a patrol base in the area of the Murrell Bridge, protected by 4 Platoon from B Company. The Battalion's patrols staged through this patrol base, reducing the distance that they had to travel to reach Mount Longdon and return to the main position each night. This enabled 3 Para's patrols to spend more time on the objective. The majority of the patrolling was done by D Company, the Patrol Company commanded by Major Butler, and was of a very high standard indeed. Several times strong patrols penetrated right into the middle of Argentine positions on Mount Longdon and brought back much valuable information. The apparent ease with which they repeatedly got right up to Argentine defensive positions and either withdrew unseen or, if spotted, despatched, or silenced opposition, misled me into believing that Mount Longdon would be taken quickly by 3 Para. I was far more concerned about Mount Harriet, in particular the extensive minefields guarding the feature, few of which were marked.

By 4 June the 3 Para patrol base at Murrell Bridge was attracting a considerable weight of Argentine artillery fire and clearly had been compromised, so Pike withdrew it. His patrols now had twice the distance to cover at night. Without the patrol base it was a sixteen-kilometre round-trip in a straight line from A Company's position to Mount Longdon. On occasions the patrols spent two or three nights out, withdrawing from the objective before first light, lying-up in hide positions between Mount Longdon and their own Battalion position, returning to complete their task on the following night.

Before 45 Commando, marching from Teal Inlet, arrived at their harbour area below Bluff Cove Peak, south-west of Mount Kent, the Commanding Officer arranged for his Reconnaissance Troop, commanded by Lieutenant Fox, to fly forward by helicopter to start patrolling the Two Sisters feature. The plan was that Fox should liaise with 42 Commando, who, at this stage, had K Company on Mount Kent, before he took his patrols forward of their positions. Careful briefing was required if a friendly-friendly clash was to be avoided. Taking a section of engineers from 59 Independent Commando Squadron with him, Fox reached the western end of the Two Sisters feature without being compromised and much useful information was acquired. The patrol approached Two Sisters by using the line of the Estancia — Stanley track as a guide, not walking along the track, but keeping to the south of it to avoid clashing with 3 Para. Their feet were continually submerged in the boggy ground and when the moon came up it seemed as clear as daylight. On two occasions the attached engineers probed for mines with their bayonets, but found none. The patrol took sixteen hours and covered about twenty kilometres, arriving back at the patrol base as dawn was breaking. On arrival they were warned for a similar task the following night.

By this time 2 Troop of X Company 45 Commando had relieved K Company 42 Commando on the summit of Mount Kent and the whole of 45 Commando was in its harbour area between Bluff Cove and Mount Kent. Fox's second patrol was even more successful than the first. He managed to hide his patrol, consisting of himself and eight men, in a rocky outcrop at the end of the Two Sisters feature. From here they were able to build up a picture of the enemy dispositions and the lie of the ground that subsequently proved to be vital to the success of the attack on Two Sisters. They eventually had to vacate their excellent OP when they were stumbled on by about twenty of the enemy. In the subsequent firefight a number of the enemy were killed. The remainder ran off, leaving their dead and dying, who were found when 45 Commando took the position five nights later. Calling for artillery fire to cover their withdrawal, Fox extricated his patrol. He was the only casualty with a flesh wound on one finger. Once again superior training, aggressive soldiering, the ability to think fast and, it must be said, calling for and getting artillery fire quickly, had won the day. The value of a worked-up and practised team was proving itself in this campaign as it had before.

Whitehead, with his usual foresight, ordered that his mortar troop set up a forward base to the north of Mount Kent in readiness for the forthcoming attack on Two Sisters. In this way his mortars would have the range to reach the objective. Mortar ammunition had to be pre-dumped, and this was done over a number of nights, carried forward by men from the rifle companies. Whitehead also ordered the setting-up of a patrol base on the north side of Mount Kent to reduce the round trip to the objective. On successive nights 45 Commando sent in fighting patrols to Two Sisters to harass the enemy. In doing so, the Commando ensured that they established a moral dominance over the Argentine soldiers, killing some most nights and preventing them from seizing the initiative.

Not every 45 Commando patrol was successful, but the majority were, particularly Lieutenant Stewart's patrol, consisting of his complete Troop, 3 Troop X Company, who during their patrol crossed 1,000 metres of open ground undetected, killed two enemy sentries and engaged the enemy on the western slope of Two Sisters. The patrol then conducted a fighting withdrawal, leaving several enemy dead, without any casualties to themselves.

45 Commando patrols and OPs had, by about 8 June, built up a good picture of the enemy dispositions on the western Sister but knew little about what he had on the eastern peak. However, between last light on 8 June and early on the morning of 10 June, some remarkable patrolling by the M and AW Cadre brought in information that not only gave a good idea of what the enemy had on the eastern Two Sisters, but also on Harriet, Tumbledown and Mount William. However, before describing this patrol, it is necessary to go back to 6 June and the series of decisions that culminated in the plan for the battle for Stanley.

By the evening of 6 June I believed that I had sufficient information on which to give orders for a brigade attack to be mounted on Mount Longdon, Two Sisters and Mount Harriet two or three days hence, still leaving time for confirmatory patrolling. Commanding Officers were sent a warning order summoning them to Teal for an Orders Group on the following day, 7 June. Before giving orders, however, I sought an assurance from Divisional HQ that 5 Infantry Brigade would be ready to support me once I started the attack. I reasoned that once my Brigade had penetrated the outer crust of the Argentine defences, the momentum of the attack must be kept going, the Brigades passing through each other in turn, taking the enemy out in 'digestible bites', preferably with a pause between each 'bite' to build up gun ammunition and move guns forward. The trick would be to avoid too long a pause between 'bites' or phases, preferably no longer than twenty-four hours and certainly not more than forty-eight. Once the outer crust was taken, British troops would be sitting on positions which the Argentines would have registered as defensive fire targets (DFs) for their artillery and mortars, and would be pounded. I also asked for another battalion to be switched to me provide a reserve for my attack, or, better still, 40 Commando, still languishing back at San Carlos, chafing and becoming increasingly bitter at being left behind. My request for 40 Commando was refused and Division could give neither an assurance that 5 Infantry Brigade would be ready nor a forecast of when they would. Headquarters 5 Brigade were having to cope with seemingly endless infuriating changes of plan caused by lack of shipping to move their units round to Fitzroy. No sooner had they given orders for one plan, than the shipping given to them would be changed, as Headquarters at various levels above them were told what they could or could not do with the various types of ships available.

The 3 Commando Brigade Orders Group was therefore told that orders for the Brigade attack would not be given that day. The likely objectives were repeated and orders to continue patrolling were given. I wanted to get on because the condition of my men was deteriorating in the inhospitable climate. 42 Commando, who had been on the highest ground for longest, was a particular worry. Although they were not complaining, on the contrary expressing their reluctance to be relieved in the strongest terms, it would only be a matter of time before the cold, diarrhoea and trench-foot in particular took their toll. The Orders Group broke up and left the Settlement Manager's house in Teal, where Brigade Headquarters had set up temporarily while our Bandwagons moved up to Mount Kent to be right up with the Brigade for the forthcoming battle. This took twenty-four hours, during which time the staff with our radio operators remained at Teal, because commanding from the Bandwagons on the move was unsatisfactory.

At this stage Divisional Headquarters intimated that they preferred to see an attack on a narrower front than that proposed by 3 Commando Brigade, leaving Mount Longdon untaken. Wilson and I were summoned back to Divisional Headquarters in HMS *Fearless* the following day, 8 June, expecting to be told what this new plan entailed. The meeting on 8 June turned out to be more of a council of war than an orders group. It was held in the planning room set up in HMS *Fearless* between the Commodore's cabin and the Landing Force Commander's cabin that I had thankfully bidden farewell to on 22 May. The meeting started with a briefing given by Captain Rowe, the GSO3 Intelligence from 3 Commando Brigade, who brought with him a map and operation order found by Lieutenant Shaw and a 45 Commando patrol in what had been an Argentine Command Post north of Mount Kent. The command post had belonged to the 12th Regiment, nominated as the strategic reserve, who had obviously left in a hurry to reinforce Goose Green and had gone into the bag there. The captured operation order had put this reserve at two hours' notice to move and, judging by the abandoned equipment, including sleeping bags and packs, left around the trenches, they had moved at even shorter notice, which accounted for all the kit and rations found by K Company, 42 Commando. This was the elusive strategic reserve that had been reported as being in at least three different places since early May. However they were no longer a threat and what was more interesting was a map with the operation order which showed the areas allocated to the infantry units defending Stanley. What it did not show was where, within regimental or battalion boundaries, the companies, headquarters, weapons and so forth were sited. Nor did it show the location and extent of the minefields.

Discussion then followed on what the Divisional plan should be. It became plain that the narrow front attack, leaving Longdon out, was gaining popularity, which did not make me very happy. The proposed attack seemed to be based on a thrust along the line of the Fitzroy-Stanley track, albeit that it included Two Sisters. 3 Commando Brigade had enough experience of fighting in the Falklands to know that moving and fighting over the rough, open terrain was a slow business, involving a high expenditure of ammunition, particularly gun ammunition. The mountain-top objectives were very restricting, allowing only enough elbow-room for, at most, one commando or battalion at a time. The battle was not being fought on the plains of North Germany by armoured units, so talk of narrow thrusts and swift follow-up to maintain momentum was academic. I strongly agreed with Rowe's assessment that attack from the direction proposed by Division would be along the line the enemy expected, had prepared for and had been confirmed by the arrival of 5 Brigade at Fitzroy, which he could see with his own eyes from Mount Harriet. The logistic line of communication to Teal could only be used by units on Two Sisters and Mount Harriet if Longdon was taken as well. The notion of shifting all logistic support to Fitzroy for both Brigades did not appeal to 3 Commando Brigade, because bad weather on the Smoko Mountain — Mount Challenger range would prevent helicopters from flying from the Commando Brigade's gun areas around Mount Kent and Mount Estancia to and from Fitzroy. Later we resisted pressure from the senior doctor at Division to close our Brigade Field Dressing Station at Teal and amalgamate it with the one at Fitzroy. We were subsequently proved right when at one stage in the battle the weather was such, that the only Field Dressing Station in the whole Division that could be reached by helicopter was at Teal. Finally, securing Longdon was crucial to the 3 Commando Brigade plan to attack Stanley from the west and north-west, and, by taking Two Sisters and Harriet as well, the enemy would not know from which direction the next punch was coming. There would be plenty of room to deploy the five gun batteries forward and the logistic lines of communication would be out of sight to the enemy, enabling the gun lines to be restocked and casualties to be evacuated before the next phase or 'bite'.

However, before the meeting could be brought to any conclusion and plans agreed, a message arrived saying that the LSLs *Sir Galahad* and *Sir Tristram* had been bombed in Fitzroy and there had been considerable casualties. Clearly there were to be further delays and the meeting broke up. The 3 Commando Brigade team returned to Mount Kent in our helicopters, flying low and fast across the bare, yellow landscape — the helicopters weaving and all occupants, passengers and crew watching out for Pucaras for the twenty-five or so minutes it took to complete the seventy-kilometre trip. On arrival at my Headquarters I directed that planning continue on the assumption that the plan would be in three phases. In the first phase 3 Commando Brigade would secure Longdon, Two Sisters and Mount Harriet, but, if possible, the Brigade would exploit forward on to Mount Tumbledown and Mount William and Wireless Ridge in the event that the enemy broke and ran away. Phase two would be to secure Wireless Ridge, Tumbledown, and Mount William, if not already done in phase one. Phase three would involve attacking Sapper Hill and the high ground south and south-east of Stanley on a one-commando/battalion-front from a westerly direction, passing commandos and battalions through each other in succession. The time separation between phases and which Brigade was to take on phases two and three was open to question; but the outline in my mind was as has been just described.

There was, however, one important gap in the information available to 3 Commando Brigade which Rowe, as Intelligence Staff officer, had realized must be filled if at all possible before the Brigade attack. Little was known about the ground formed by the triangle from the eastern end of Two Sisters, the eastern side of Mount Harriet and Mount Tumbledown. Rowe, having been frustrated in all his requests for air photographs, knew that the only way to find out would be to get a patrol into a position to observe this ground, preferably by day. The most skilled patrollers in the Commando Brigade were the M and AW Cadre. After discussing the problem with Chester and myself, Rowe had summoned Boswell, the Cadre's Commander, on 8 June, and tasked him to get the information. Boswell briefed Lieutenant Haddow and Sergeant Wassell to take their patrols, a total of eight men, including the two leaders, to Goat Ridge that night. They were to stay in a hide on Goat Ridge during the following day and return the next night. Their tasks were to report on enemy strengths and dispositions on the north-eastern side of Mount Harriet and the south-eastern side of Two Sisters. Boswell arranged that the two patrols should go out with a troop-strength fighting patrol from K Company 42 Commando, led by Lieutenant Townsend. This patrol was tasked with checking Goat Ridge for enemy before swinging south on to the Harriet feature from the north-east. By this time the co-ordination of the patrolling in the Commando Brigade had been well refined, thanks to Chester's idea of instituting a 'Patrol-Master', a task carried out by Major Gullan. He knew exactly what patrols were going out, their routes and tasks and, by consulting with the Brigade Intelligence Staff and other agencies, such as artillery and engineers, was able to minimize the chances of inter-unit patrol clashes and could task patrols to a Brigade plan.

The combined patrols left the eastern end of Mount Challenger after last light on 8 June. When they reached a point about 300 metres from the western end of the Goat Ridge spine-back, Haddow's and Wassell's men halted and waited for the K Company patrol to move south towards the north-east slopes of Mount Harriet. They saw the K Company fighting patrol engage an enemy heavy-machine-gun position with an 84 mm round before withdrawing. The Argentine fire directed at the K Company patrol, as it conducted a fighting withdrawal, was heavy, most of it passing over Townsend's men's heads and striking around the M and AW Cadre men lying by the Goat Ridge spine-back. Haddow and Wassell noted where the fire was coming from for future reference. When all was quiet again the

Cadre patrols started moving. Haddow's men worked along the north side of the narrow spine-back, while Wassell took the south side. Each patrol spent the whole night carefully creeping forward and searching the rocks and ground. They found a well-worn track that connected Mount Harriet and Two Sisters and, even though it was dark, discovered that there were strong enemy positions on the reverse, or eastern, slopes of Mount Harriet and Two Sisters. This confirmed Rowe's suspicion that Divisional Headquarters was underestimating the strength of the positions, hence his wish to get a patrol into the middle of the enemy to 'eyeball' the ground.

Wassell and Haddow met at the eastern end of Goat Ridge and decided to find an OP position in which they could spend the day and observe. The spine-back was so narrow that finding a position on the eastern tip was difficult and they eventually settled for one about half-way back along the ridge. The two patrols operated as one team armed with two M79 grenade launchers and two sniper rifles, as well as their personal weapons. Haddow and Wassell sat under a rock, back to back all day, Haddow facing south and Wassell facing north. The remaining six men hid under another rock about twenty feet away, providing flank and rear protection for their two leaders. Deep in the middle of the Argentine positions, Haddow and Wassell were about forty metres away from the track connecting Two Sisters and Tumbledown, which the Argentines were using as a route for administration and casevac for the positions on Two Sisters. Daylight revealed the enemy positions on the eastern slopes of Two Sisters and Mount Harriet. From their OP they could also see the enemy positions on Mount Tumbledown and Mount William. Lieutenant Haddow and Sergeant Wassell each spent the day drawing a sketch map showing the positions they had seen. These included a large command-wire-initiated demolition consisting of barrels dug into the ground on the eastern end of Two Sisters, with wires leading back to a firing point. Assaulting troops would take heavy casualties if they were on or near these large 'mines' when they exploded.

The patrol remained all day watching the Argentine soldiers moving about in what were reverse-slope positions to the Commando Brigade OPs on Wall Mountain, Challenger and Kent, but were clearly visible to the OP in the heart of the position. About three hours after dark the patrol withdrew and moved back to Mount Challenger and thence to 42 Commando's Tactical Headquarters between Challenger and Mount Kent. Here they briefed the second-in-command, Sheridan, on what they had seen, before going on to Brigade headquarters to speak to Rowe and Gullan, the Patrol-Master. Wassell was then sent to brief 45 Commando. The information they brought back caused both Whitehead and Vaux to make alterations to the plans they were hatching in anticipation of being told to attack Two Sisters and Mount Harriet. The grid references of enemy positions that Haddow had seen on

Tumbledown and Mount William were passed to 5 Infantry Brigade. This patrol was remarkable in what it achieved, bringing back a wealth of information that was to save many lives, including locating the large command-detonated mine on Two Sisters. Wassell and Haddow led their men away after the debriefing, brewed up, cleaned their weapons and crept into their 'bashas' for a well-earned sleep. They would have one more important task to carry out before the campaign was over, but, in the meantime, they had more than earned their rest.

Meanwhile, on the morning of 9 June, General Moore had come forward to 3 Command Brigade Headquarters and told me that he agreed with the plan to weight the attack on the north and west because Division now had intelligence that the Argentines expected the main attack would come from the south-west and would be 'looking' in that direction. Longdon would therefore be included in the first phase attacks and the Commando Brigade would be reinforced, not by 40 Commando, who I had asked for yet again, but with 2 Para and 1 Welsh Guards. The latter would have two companies of 40 Commando under command to replace two of their own companies, who had lost most of their equipment when *Sir Galahad* had been bombed at Fitzroy. Divisional Headquarters was about to issue an operation order which detailed 3 Commando Brigade to carry out phase one (Harriet, Two Sisters and Longdon); 5 Brigade would capture Tumbledown and William in phase two, while 3 Commando Brigade captured Wireless Ridge; finally, in phase three 3 Commando Brigade would capture all the high ground south of Stanley, starting with Sapper Hill.

An earlier idea favoured by some in Divisional Headquarters to fly forward a battery of light guns and a protection party, consisting of a rifle company from 40 Commando to a position north of Mount Low, was not to go ahead. The idea had been born out of the wish to bring artillery fire on to Stanley airport, which the Argentines were still using every night to fly in supplies by C-130 transport aircraft and presumably to evacuate casualties. The airport was out of range of all the 105mm light gun batteries in both Brigades. 3 Commando Brigade Staff had never liked the idea which smacked of foolhardiness and was based on an SAS report that there were no enemy troops or OPs between Mount Vernet and Mount Low. We, sceptically, did not believe the report, and it was just as well that our view prevailed because a strong Argentine patrol surrendered to Captain Rowe on Mount Round on 15 June, having been there since early June (1). Helicopters attempting to fly in and then supply a battery and a company north of Mount Low, well outside the Brigade boundary, would have been seen by the enemy OP on Mount Round and probably shot down by ground fire or fighters and Pucaras sent for the purpose.

As soon as Moore had left, the warning order went out summoning

Commanding Officers to another Orders Group for the following day, 10 June, at Brigade Headquarters. Here I gave the order for the Brigade night attack. 3 Para was to capture Mount Longdon, exploiting forward on to Wireless Ridge if possible; 45 Commando was ordered to capture Two Sisters and exploit forward on to Mount Tumbledown if possible, while 42 Commando was to capture Mount Harriet and be prepared to follow up 45 Commando through Tumbledown on to Mount William. The main objectives were Longdon, Two Sisters and Mount Harriet, but I did not want to cramp my Commanding Officers' initiative if the attacks went well and the enemy folded without much of a fight.

At the Orders Group were two new faces — the Commanding Officers of 2 Para and 1 Welsh Guards. Lieutenant-Colonel Chaundler had joined 2 Para at Fitzroy, having been parachuted down to the Carrier Battle Group at sea. He was a large, cheerful and confident man who had been a student at the Army Staff College when I had been there as a member of the Directing Staff. He had coped well with the difficult business of taking over a battalion that had already won its spurs and he was firmly in the saddle. Lieutenant-Colonel Rickett had weathered the heavy casualties to his Battalion at Fitzroy, which were not of his making, and was quietly determined that the Welsh Guards would now proceed to settle the score.

Chaundler was told that 2 Para would remain in reserve during the forthcoming attack and was to move down the centre line between 45 Commando and 3 Para, but behind them, ready to reinforce either unit on my orders. Chaundler's most likely objective, however, if all went to plan, would be Wireless Ridge, which he would attack by hooking round to the north of Mount Longdon so as to approach it from the north. Rickett was ordered to secure 42 Commando's Start Line for their assault on Mount Harriet and to be prepared to support them if necessary.

After the Orders Group the Commanding Officers chatted together and drank the hot soup that the ever-meticulous Chester had ordered, before dispersing to their commandos, battalions, regiments and squadrons to give their own orders and prepare.

About this time, unknown to 3 Commando Brigade, a little scene was being played out that was to cause much amusement when we heard about it after the war. A Harrier pilot flying over Pebble Island reported on his return to his carrier that he had seen two Argentine helicopters on the airstrip raided by the SAS weeks before. The sighting was included in the daily situation report from the Carrier Battle Group to England. The day before, an SBS patrol had been landed on Pebble Island to look for a land-based Exocet missile and its radar, that was thought to be situated somewhere on the island. The patrol was working its way along the island, moving by night and lying up and observing by day. They had three hills to check on the way and, to ensure that enemy observation posts were not missed, progress had to be slow. To his surprise the Officer Commanding the SBS received an angrily worded signal from Northwood asking why the SBS had not also reported the helicopter's presence on the airstrip. The answer was quite simple. They were three hill crests and fifteen kilometres away from the airstrip on a straight line and had neither seen nor heard the helicopters, which is not surprising since they were the same distance from the airstrip as Windsor is from Battersea heliport. On the part of Task Force Headquarters, in their bunker 8,000 miles away, it was a case of 'big hands on little maps' — again.

CHAPTER NINE

Night Battle

On the morning of 11 June the Commanding Officers of 42 Commando, 45 Commando and 3 Para gave orders to their assembled O groups for the attack that night. All the Commanding Officers had models made of the terrain, using whatever lay to hand — lumps of peat, pieces of canvas, rifle slings and twigs — to assist in putting across their plans for one of the most complex of military operations, a night attack. After the Commando and Battalion O groups the Company Commanders dispersed to prepare their own orders and give them to their companies. In all cases these company orders were followed by rehearsals and the necessary preparations before battle. One Company Commander described these hours in his diary:

Before last light we conducted rehearsals on a nearby crag conveniently similar to our objective. We then relaxed and ate a meal. We moved off, all 150 of us, about one hour after last light. The Chaplain [Wynne-Jones] came with us. He brought up the rear with extra medical stores. I was sufficiently apprehensive to say to him quietly as we gathered to do our final checks, 'Pray for our souls Vicar'. 'I won't need to,' he said, 'I won't need to.' His presence had a curious effect. The Company did not have many who would have professed allegiance to any formal religion. But to have this man of God in our midst was a wonderful source of comfort. How much of it was his personality and how much was the idea that his presence somehow lent an air of legitimacy and respectability to our endeavours, I do not know. All I can say is that his presence was most beneficial and the Marines thought the world of him. He told me afterwards that he had chosen to come with my company because he reckoned we would take the most casualties.

While the final preparations were going on throughout the Commando Brigade, 2 Para was flying in by helicopter to rejoin us. As they arrived at their harbour area below Bluff Cove Peak, I went to welcome them back to the Brigade. They seemed glad to be back and even more happy that they

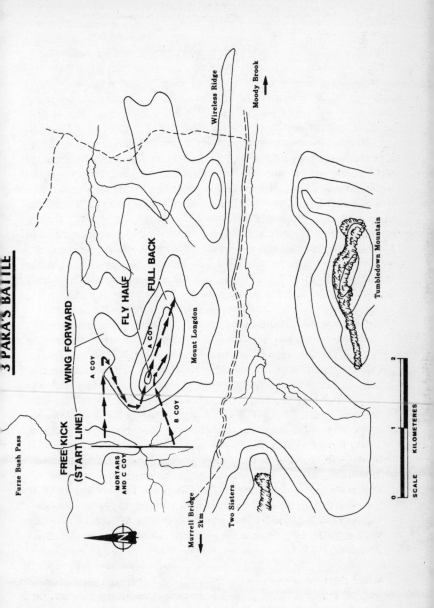

3 PARA'S BATTLE

Furze Bush Pass

FREE KICK
(START LINE)

WING FORWARD

FLY HALF

FULL BACK

MORTARS
AND C COY

A COY

A COY

B COY

Mount Longdon

Wireless Ridge

Moody Brook

Tumbledown Mountain

Murrell Bridge

2km

Two Sisters

SCALE   KILOMETRES

0   1   2

N

were not to attack the Argentine positions on Sapper Hill or Mount William from the south-west from their positions at Fitzroy, which they had thought would be their task. By last light most of the commandos and battalions in the Brigade were moving to start the attack, 2 Para, as the Brigade reserve for the northern part of the attack, being the last to go, at 7 pm.

The battle began with 3 Para assaulting Mount Longdon on the left flank of the Commando Brigade. We now know that the enemy consisted of B Company of the Argentine 7th Infantry Regiment reinforced by marines with eight .50 machine guns. The Battalion had been given an H-hour, the time when the leading companies cross the start line for the attack, of 8.01 pm. Because it was dark by about 4 pm at that time of year, this should allow the approach to the objective to be made in darkness, but the moon should be up soon after 8 pm, giving some light for fighting through the objective. The timings for 42 Commando, 8.30 pm, and 45 Commando, 9 pm, were selected by me for the same reason. I planned that, by allowing three-quarters of the night for fighting through, the objectives would be secure by dawn. In this way our assaulting troops would not be exposed to the fire of the Argentine heavy machine guns in the coverless terrain in daylight. Furthermore, it avoided the traditional dawn assault which I thought the Argentines might expect. I expected that the superior training and quality of our troops would enable them to overcome the opposition in their well-prepared, mountain-top positions. I was not disappointed.

Pike's plan for 3 Para, like those for the two Commandos, was, like all good plans, simple. The three rifle companies and Battalion Tactical Headquarters, led by guides from D (Patrols) Company, would approach the objective in darkness, taking about three hours. The long, narrow summit of the Mount Longdon feature, covered with rocks, allowed enough room for only one company to fight along it at one time. Pike decided that he had no option but to attack Longdon end-on from the west. Outflanking movements were not feasible because of extensive minefields to the south of the mountain and known enemy positions on Wireless Ridge to the east. The ground around Mount Longdon was open in every direction for at least 1,000 metres, so an approach, even by night, would be hazardous. Pike selected the stream running north to Furze Bush Pass as his Start Line, a good choice because it lay at ninety degrees to his axis of attack on to the objective and was easily recognizable, even on the darkest night. He gave it the nickname Free Kick. The western summit of Mount Longdon was nicknamed Fly Half, the eastern summit Full Back and the spur running north from the main feature Wing Forward. It is hard for sailors and airmen, still less the average civilian, to imagine how much information commanders at all levels in an infantry battle at night have to carry in their heads. The commanding officer orchestrating the show is not sitting in a warm well-lit operations room, surrounded by staff, powerful radios and radar displays showing the positions of friend and foe; or even in a relatively warm armoured command vehicle with an on-board satellite navigation system giving him a constant read-out of his position. He is walking, crouching, running, lying, probably in pouring rain, under fire, trying to update his mental picture of the battle by conversations on a low-powered man-pack radio and going to see for himself if he can. The flashing of torches to read maps or look up codes can be unwise. Nicknames would enable the Battalion to refer to key features on the radio without the time-consuming and, in the dark in the middle of the battle, almost impossible business of using code. The Argentines, listening to the radio conversations, would eventually work out the nicknames for each position, but, with luck, it would take them most of the night to do so. Most commandos and battalions used this dodge, as did Brigade and Division.

B Company was to assault the Longdon Summit ridge (Fly Half and Full Back) while A Company seized the spur running north (Wing Forward). C Company was to be in reserve for this phase, while fire support teams, equipped with machine guns and Milan anti-tank missiles, under the command of the Officer Commanding Support Company, Major Dennison, would remain on the Start Line (Free Kick) until called forward. The Battalion's mortar platoon was to move independently and set up a base-plate position behind the Start Line. The ammunition resupply and casualty evacuation teams, under the command of Major Patton, the Battalion second-in-command, were to move in Bandwagons and requisitioned civilian tractors. Once Longdon was secure, it was Pike's intention to exploit forward on to Wireless Ridge with both A and C Companies, to meet my wish that assaulting units should press on if the opportunity occurred. Such an exploitation by 3 Para would only be possible if Mount Tumbledown, which dominated Wireless Ridge, was also taken. This was 45 Commando's exploitation task and, as we shall see, could not be achieved that night.

Major Argue, commanding B Company 3 Para, decided that 6 Platoon would clear the southern slopes of Mount Longdon, while his Headquarters with 4 and 5 Platoons would clear the northern slopes. The move of B Company to the Start Line went well initially, until the Fire Support Group, moving to their positions, cut across the B Company column. Part of 5 Platoon and all of 6 Platoon got separated from the Company and did not meet up again for thirty minutes. There was a further delay caused by the time it took to ford the Murrell River. Argue therefore decided to make up for lost time by assaulting from further south than intended and well to the right of A Company. Nevertheless, both Companies crossed the Start Line at 8.15 pm, only fourteen minutes late.

A few minutes later the Battalion reported that it was still very dark, with no moon up yet, but soon it started to rise, silhouetting the jagged rocks on Mount Longdon and illuminating the bright yellow grass. Argue ordered his platoons to move in closer to the rocks to gain as much cover from them as possible. As the platoons shook out into assault formation the left forward section commander of 4 Platoon trod on an anti-personnel mine. This alerted the enemy, who started firing at both A and B Companies. The battle was on, about one hour after the Battalion crossed the Start Line. The fighting lasted until just before daybreak, about ten hours of what someone described as 'gutter fighting', conducted often at close quarters with grenade, rifle and bayonet and 66 mm LAW, with support from guns, naval gunfire, mortars and machine guns. It was a battle in which junior officers, NCOs and private soldiers fought with courage, tenacity and aggression.

6 platoon occupied the western summit of Mount Longdon without fighting, although they grenaded some enemy bunkers on the way up. But they missed one bunker with at least seven enemy in it, who fired into their backs as they advanced through Fly Half, causing a number of casualties. As they lay pinned down by this fire they also found themselves under fire from enemy shooting at 5 platoon who had fought their way up on to the ridge from the other side and had now made contact with 6 platoon. 4 platoon, moving on the left of 5 platoon, became intermingled with 5 platoon and both platoons moved over the top of the western summit on to more open ground sloping away to the east. They could see the eastern summit in the distance when both platoons came under fire from a company defensive position, the nearest platoon of which apparently contained a 105mm anti-tank-gun, at least two medium machine guns (GPMG) and one heavy machine gun (.50 inch), as well as a number of snipers with night sights. It was a classic reverse slope position, sited to catch attacking troops moving down off a crest line.

Lieutenant Bickerdike, the commander of 4 platoon, was wounded in the thigh and his signaller hit in the mouth by the first burst of fire. The platoon sergeant, Sergeant McKay, immediately took command. The signaller continued to man his radio until relieved later on. Sergeant McKay decided to take out the heavy machine gun which seemed to be the key to the position. The weapon was sited in a sangar and protected by several riflemen. Sergeant McKay quickly gathered some of 4 platoon, mainly Corporal Bailey's section, and assaulted the sangar. They were met by a hail of fire. Corporal Bailey and a private soldier were seriously wounded, and Private Burt was killed. Despite these losses, McKay continued to charge the enemy position alone. On reaching it, he despatched the enemy with grenades, thereby relieving the pressure on 4 and 5 Platoons, who were now able to re-deploy. McKay was killed, his body falling into the sangar. For this action he was awarded the Victoria Cross, posthumously.

However, a second heavy machine gun continued to fire on B Company Headquarters with 5 platoon. Argue, hearing that Bickerdike had been wounded and Sergeant McKay was missing, sent Sergeant Fuller forward from Company Headquarters to take command of 4 platoon, now without its platoon commander and platoon sergeant. Fuller gathered 4 platoon and, with fire support from Corporal McLaughlin's section of 5 platoon, attacked the heavy machine-gun position. Although they cleared several enemy positions on the way, they could not reach the machine gun and were halted after taking five casualties. Corporal McLaughlin's section also tried to reach the machine-gun position, but he too was forced to withdraw.

Argue decided to withdraw 5 platoon and the remnants of 4, regroup his Company and, after giving the enemy a good dose of artillery and machine-gun fire, conduct a left-flanking assault on the enemy position. The gunners as usual were reacting splendidly and bringing fire down within fifty metres of where 4 and 5 platoons were lying, keeping the enemy neutralized while the company sergeant-major of B Company, Weeks, organized the withdrawal of the remnants of the two platoons. Lieutenant Bickerdike and his signaller had not given up the fight, despite their wounds, and were firing from where they lay, helping to cover the withdrawal of 4 and 5 platoons.

Pike had by now arrived and was with Argue. The Battalion's mortars were 'bedded in' at the Start Line and Major Dennison, commanding Support Company, had brought forward the machine guns to the western summit of Mount Longdon. Meanwhile the 105mm guns pounded the enemy, assisted by several salvoes of naval gunfire.

Argue took the remnants of 4 and 5 platoon, organized into three sections, and retraced the route along which they had just withdrawn, before putting in the left-flanking attack. As soon as artillery fire on to other targets lifted further east, and after going forward about thirty metres, the composite platoon came under heavy fire. Lieutenant Cox and Private Connery fought their way forward with grenade, 66mm LAW, bullet and bayonet, killing a number of the enemy. The fire died away. It seemed for a moment as though the enemy had folded at last; as Company Headquarters moved forward, however, they came under fire again. Clearly the enemy in this area were not finished yet. Pike decided that B Company had sustained such heavy losses that he would pass A Company through to continue the battle.

A Company, after crossing the Start Line, had heard the anti-personnel mine exploding to their right and had then seen the enemy shells falling on Mount Longdon. To begin with the Company were in dead ground as they advanced towards Wing Forward, the spur jutting north from Mount Longdon, so the bullets from the firefight on the mountain went over their heads. As soon as they emerged on to the top of the ridge they came under fire from the same enemy on the eastern end of Mount Longdon that was causing B Company so much trouble. The Company went to ground among convenient peat banks which afforded some protection from direct fire, but little cover from the increasingly accurate mortar and artillery fire being directed on them and C Company in reserve. Although initially the mortar and artillery fire was a pre-planned defensive fire task the enemy soon adjusted the fire right on to the Company. The Company had to stop firing back at the enemy, which they could see through their Individual Weapon Sights (Night Sights) because of the close proximity of B Company to the enemy position.

Pike, realizing that A Company could not advance from where they were, ordered them to pull back and move round the western end of Mount Longdon, pass through B Company and take the eastern end of the feature (Full Back). Still under artillery and small arms fire, the Company moved round to the rocks at the western end of Longdon and halted there, while the Company Commander moved forward to find Argue and be briefed. It became clear that an attempt to outflank the northern side of the feature would prove too costly, so A Company would fight along the ridge in an easterly direction.

As soon as the artillery, directed by Lieutenant Lee, the FOO, and the GPMGs under Captain Freer, A Company second-in-command, started giving covering fire, 1 platoon moved forward, working its way through the enemy positions. Clearing systematically to avoid leaving any enemy behind to shoot them in the back, A Company, sometimes crawling, sometimes rushing, bombed and bayonetted its way forward. The supporting fire had to stop; it was becoming a hazard to A Company. As the Company worked forward, the enemy could be seen withdrawing from the ridge, an encouraging sight, while 1 and 2 platoons started to clear the numerous positions with fixed bayonets. As soon as the eastern end of Longdon was secure, 3 platoon was pushed forward to hold the long narrow slope leading down to Wireless Ridge and the remainder of the Company reorganized and began digging in. When daybreak came, the heavy morning mist hid the position from Tumbledown, so that the enemy artillery fire was inaccurate. But it became increasingly more accurate and heavy as the mist cleared and the day wore on. Clearly there would be no question of going forward on to Wireless Ridge yet. That would be 2 Para's task.

The centre of 3 Commando Brigade's three-pronged attack had also gone well. Whitehead's plan for his attack on Two Sisters was good and simple. Although from a distance the Two Sisters feature looks like a pair of sharply pointed little pimples, in fact it consists of two peaks and five formidable rock ridges. The north-eastern peak has a spineback about 500 metres long on its crest and another about the same length directly to the east. The south-western peak which, at 316 metres, is a few metres the taller of the

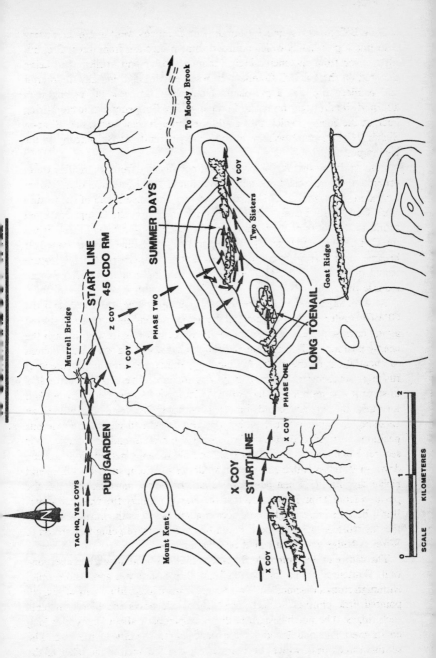

two, has three rocky spinebacks in line ahead, running east-west, covering about 1,500 metres in all. The whole Two Sisters feature is well guarded by rock runs and the steep 250-metre climb from the valley floor is bare and easily covered by observation and fire. Two Sisters was held by B Company of the 6th Argentine Infantry Regiment and a very strong reinforced C Company of the 4th Argentine Infantry Regiment. The bulk of the 4th Regiment were on Mount Harriet.

Whitehead decided that X Company would attack the south-western peak and its three rock ridges (nicknamed Long Toenail). This would be followed by Z Company assaulting the western ridge on the north-eastern peak (nicknamed Summer Days) and finally Y Company assaulting the eastern ridge on the same peak. X Company's attack was planned to start at 9 pm, followed, about two hours later, or when ordered by Whitehead, by Z Company and Y Company. The fire plan was to be 'silent', meaning that artillery and mortars were available on call, but were not to be fired until the enemy engaged the Commando. X Company was to take 40 Commando's Milan Troop with them to provide fire support for their own attack and then, if necessary, to shoot in the other two Companies. 45 Commando's Milan firing posts had all been destroyed when Ajax Bay had been bombed on 27 May and their Milan Troop converted to machine-gunners and 84mm MAW gunners.

45 Commando, but without X Company, left their positions between Bluff Cove Peak and Mount Kent at 10 am for an assembly area to the north of Mount Kent, where Whitehead had earlier established a patrol base. This would cut down the distance he would have to cover in darkness to about 6,000 metres before reaching his Start Line about 800 metres south-east of the Murrell Bridge (nicknamed Pub Garden). X Company was to march due east over the saddle between Mount Kent and Mount Challenger, following a route taken by one of their own fighting patrols a few days before. Their Start Line was the line of the stream running due north from the base of Wall Mountain to Murrell Bridge. Whitehead hoped that by starting his attack with X Company the enemy's attention would be concentrated on the south-western peak (Long Toenail), while he, with two companies, approached the north-eastern peak from a different direction, the north-west.

However, X Company's march, starting at 5 pm, after dark, took nearly six hours instead of the three that Gardiner, the Company Commander, had calculated. His reconnaissance team did not pick the best route for a company of men loaded down, not only with their own kit and ammunition, but also with the Milan firing posts and forty Milan missiles, each weighing thirty pounds. One man knocked himself unconscious falling down a cliff, but the Company second-in-command managed to resuscitate him and he carried on. As the Company got further and further behind the time when it should have arrived at its forming-up position for the attack, Gardiner decided to break radio silence and tell Whitehead what was going on. By the time X Company had reached the forming-up position, two and a quarter hours late, they were very tired — before the real work had begun. Gardiner explained the problem on the radio to Whitehead who to his great credit, put no undue pressure on Gardiner, merely saying:

'Carry on as planned, I will do nothing until I hear from you.' As a result of his patience and understanding, Gardiner was able to turn to his troop commanders and say, 'Put the last six hours right behind you, make your final preparations in your own time and when you are completely ready, let me know and we will go.' Ten minutes later the 150 men of X Company were as good as new and began their assault at 11 pm.

Meanwhile, Whitehead with his Tactical Headquarters, Y and Z Companies, were just short of their forming-up position south-east of Murrell Bridge, with Z Company leading. On the way they had seen the fierce firefight of 3 Para's assault on Mount Longdon to their left front. Y and Z Companies arrived at the forming-up position five minutes before the time Whitehead had planned — excellent timing. Marching hard, it had taken five hours to cover the five-kilometre journey — exactly in accordance with the planned rate of advance for large, formed bodies of men at night over this rough terrain. Whitehead decided that as soon as Y and Z Companies were ready, he would move forward out of the forming-up position and not hang about in what was likely to be an enemy defensive fire task for artillery and mortars. He also decided that getting phase two under way was more important than waiting for X Company to secure its objective. The final approach to, and the forming-up position itself, had already been secured by Lieutenant Fox's Reconnaissance Troop. When each Company Commander arrived in the forming-up position he went forward with Fox to orientate himself on the ground. As Captain Cole, commanding Z Company, was lying on the lip of the fold in the ground that constituted the forming-up position, an enemy artillery defensive fire task came crumping down just to his front. The whole area was well lit not only by moonlight but by the 3 Para battle on Longdon, about 3,000 metres to their left rear and by 42 Commando's battle on Mount Harriet about 5,000 metres to the south of where the two officers lay.

By this time X Company had begun their advance from their Start Line, led by Lieutenant Kelly's 1 Troop. His objective was the western third of the spineback on the south-western peak of Two Sisters (Long Toenail). Gardiner watched his leading troop crossing the open ground with his heart in his mouth, hardly believing that they would not be seen. To the left of Kelly's troop he could clearly see the support section moving under the command of the company sergeant-major. This team had been specially formed for the attack and was armed with seven light machine guns and a number of 66mm LAWs. Its task was to move parallel with each assaulting troop in turn, but to keep about 200 metres to the north, ready to give fire support from the left flank. Kelly radioed back that there was no opposition on his objective. Gardiner then sent off 3 Troop, commanded by Lieutenant Stewart, through 1 Troop. Stewart reported his objective clear and asked permission to exploit forward, which was approved. About half way up the 1,500-metre-long feature he ran into opposition from two machine guns, one a heavy machine gun, on the top of the ridge. Any attempts to close with them drew fire from riflemen hidden on the right-hand side. He tried moving up the left-hand side of the spineback, but came under fire from the north-eastern peak of Two Sisters (Summer Days).

Gardiner pulled 3 Troop back and ordered mortar and artillery fire before sending in 2 Troop. He then ordered the Milan to fire over their heads at the enemy. 2 Troop, under Lieutenant Caroe, was ready, but although the mortars had fired a few rounds, they could not fire any more because their base plates and half the length of the tubes had disappeared into the soggy ground. There was no artillery available; it was engaged on other targets, but Lieutenant Caroe took his men up the hill regardless. The enemy started firing a 105mm anti-tank gun and enemy artillery fire was falling round the company. Caroe's men picked and clambered their way round, up and over the rocks towards the enemy. Among the steep, house-sized boulders and crags it was like fighting in a built-up area. 2 Troop battered their way to the top, to be temporarily forced off by the enemy artillery firing defensive fire tasks on to the objective. They returned, however, and secured the objective, killing or driving off the machine-gunners who had stayed to fight it out with X Company.

At about half past midnight, while X Company were still fighting through their objective, Whitehead ordered Y and Z Companies forward, Z on the left and Y on the right. Just before they moved off, Argentine artillery firing a DF task came crashing down just forward of the Start Line. Whitehead thanked his good fortune that he had not ordered the advance to begin a few minutes earlier. Had he done so, both Companies would have been in the beaten zone of the DF task. Cole, commanding Z Company, expected a repeat of the enemy artillery fire at any moment as they started their 1,500-metre advance uphill. The going was hard over bog, rock runs and tussock grass, and the Company net still maintaining radio silence. The objective was clearly skylined and maintaining the axis of advance was easy. The advance went so well and the enemy on the eastern Two Sisters (Summer Days), possibly distracted by X Company's battle on the western Two Sisters (Long Toenail), appeared not to have noticed Y and Z Companies closing with them. So Whitehead decided to revert to his first plan and ordered Y and Z Companies to go to ground and wait for X Company to secure their objective.

Corporal Hunt, a section commander in 8 Troop, the right forward troop in Z Company, was scanning through his IWS, as were all who were equipped with them, and spotted enemy movement on the skyline above them. Lieutenant Dytor, his Troop Commander, crawled forward to Hunt and together they located several more positions, including an enemy machine gun which turned out to be a .50 heavy. Dytor ordered his section commanders to hold their fire and sent his Troop Sergeant back to tell Cole what he had seen. At that moment a flare thrown by the enemy fizzed and bounced over the ground in front of Z Company. Dytor shouted to his Troop to engage the enemy, while the enemy fired back with .50 inch heavy machine guns, FALs and GPMGs. Fortunately Y and Z Companies were still lying down because most of the enemy fire went over their heads. Had Whitehead not ordered both Companies to halt to await the completion of X Company's attack, they would have been badly caught by the heavy fire from the Argentinian defensive positions above them.

Cole turned to Lieutenant Baxter, his artillery forward observer, who immediately called down the pre-planned artillery fire on the western end of the Company objective. Enemy mortar bombs began to fall round the rear of Z Company. Dytor, realizing that his Troop must not remain pinned down, stood up and started running forward shouting 'Zulu Zulu', the Company battle cry. As he ran he heard his section commanders shout 'Move now' and, taking up the cry of 'Zulu Zulu', the whole Troop skirmished forward and then went to ground where the slope was concave and enemy fire was going over their heads. Cole ordered 7 Troop forward and told his leading troops to fire on the objective to their front and not across each other. As well as the artillery fire being brought down on the enemy, the mortar fire controller with Cole called down mortar fire beyond the objective and then 'crept' it back right on to it. Meanwhile the leading troops kept up a steady fire with GPMGs, 84 mm MAWs and 66mm LAWs to win the firefight. By now the whole company was shouting 'Zulu Zulu'.

Y Company, on Zulu's right, and unable to go forward without becoming involved in Zulu's battle, found it difficult to support Zulu by fire because of the folds in the ground. While they lay there, the enemy mortared them, causing several casualties including two of the three troop commanders, Lieutenants Dunning and Davies. Their troop sergeants, Davidson and Gracie, immediately took over. Major Davis, commanding Y Company, could see the Battery fire missions coming down on the .50 inch heavy machine guns firing at Zulu Company. These guns were well protected because no sooner had the shells stopped bursting than the heavy machine guns opened up again. Whitehead, moving on Z Company's right, ordered

Y Company, who were to his right rear, to swing slightly right and come up alongside him. When Y Company had come up to the position ordered by Whitehead, Davis ordered one of his 84mm MAW teams to move out to his right front to open up the angle between it and Z Company and engage the heavy machine guns. This they did, knocking out at least one, although the 84mm rounds went uncomfortably close to their own Commanding Officer's head. Whitehead was up with the leading Troop of Zulu Company.

Cole then ordered 8 Troop to advance to seize the crest line while 7 Troop provided covering fire. Still shouting 'Zulu Zulu', 8 Troop charged forward clearing the enemy as they went and, arriving on the crest, were immediately fired on by a machine gun well to the south of them. The Marines fired back but were stopped by Dytor, concerned that they were firing towards X Company. Whitehead who was well forward, to say the least, appeared at that moment by Dytor and told him to carry on with the task given him by Cole, to clear the southern side of his Company objective.

8 Troop skirmished forward again, taking a newly acquired .50 inch heavy machine gun with them. Clearing enemy positions as they went, they arrived at the limit of their objective, while Lieutenant Mansell's 7 Troop did likewise on the northern side of the rock ridge. 9 Troop in the rear of Z Company had been reduced to two sections by enemy mortar and artillery fire, so Cole ordered them to remain in reserve. By about 2.45 am Z Company had secured its objective, two and a half hours after crossing the Start Line.

Y Company then moved forward between the peaks of Two Sisters, X Company having by now secured the south-western peak. They then swung to their left and, as they debouched on to the slope leading down to the easterly rock ridge, came under heavy fire from their objective. Dytor, reorganizing on his Company objective, could clearly see the enemy fire which was coming from positions immediately to his front and about 200 metres away. He at once started to move his Troop forward with their .50 heavy machine gun, three GPMGs and three Bren LMGs to engage this fresh target. But he was stopped by Whitehead who told him to leave it to Y Company, rightly assessing that an inter-company clash might ensue in the dark and confusion if Dytor's men encroached on Y Company's objective.

Y Company advanced, two troops up, along the south side of the eastern spineback. All the time they were very conscious of the large, wire-controlled mine reported by Haddow and Wassell. They crossed a number of wires as they cleared their objective under sporadic shell-fire, but set off nothing more formidable than a booby-trapped rifle. At the eastern end of the spineback they were held up for a moment by an enemy machine-gun post, but a section took it out with a 66 mm LAW. Davis then thought he saw an enemy mortar or gun position 500 metres east of his spineback and sent forward a section under Corporal Siddall to recce and report back. Bombardier Holt, with a radio, went with them in case they needed artillery support. As they approached they heard Spanish being spoken. Siddall and Holt continued forward on their own and saw four enemy but no guns or mortars. Siddall killed one and, with Holt, brought in the other three as prisoners.

As the Commando was reorganizing, the Argentine artillery fire, mainly 155mm, started falling on the positions the enemy had just lost. The triumphant Marines took cover among the deep fissures in the rocks while shells exploded round them. The mist crept in at about this time, but neither this nor the barrage of 155s kept Sergeant Menghini of 3 Commando Brigade Air Squadron from flying in his Scout helicopter in the darkness to the dim green torch light marking the landing site where 45 Commando's casualties were being collected.

At first light clearance patrols brought in several more prisoners. The strength of the position became evident as daylight came. In one of the many natural revetments caused by the formation of the rocks there were four 81mm mortars, piles of ammunition and empty mortar-bomb containers.

45 Commando had done very well; the combination of good control, fitness and the proper use of fire power had enabled them to take this formidable position with light casualties. Their Commanding Officer's calm voice on the radio had been like a tonic to all who heard him and he was always where he was needed at the right time to bring his influence to bear. He had handled the Commando skilfully and never lost his grip on his night battle among the rocks and spinebacks.

At 4.30 am on 12 June Whitehead reported that the Commando was secure on all its objectives and, speaking to me on the radio, told me that he was making preparations to exploit forward on to Mount Tumbledown as instructed. To Whitehead's annoyance, I ordered him to go firm on Two Sisters and not assault Tumbledown. There were several reasons for making this decision. By the time 45 Commando had reorganized for the next attack daylight would be only two or so hours off and it would take the remaining hours of darkness to cover the 5,000 metres from Two Sisters to Tumbledown via Goat Ridge, the best route. Daylight would find the Commando starting its attack over open ground against a well-prepared position where the heavy machine guns would inflict many casualties. In any case 42 Commando had not yet secured Goat Ridge, a prerequisite to 45 Commando moving on to Tumbledown. Finally, the 105 gun batteries were running low on ammunition and no naval gunfire support would be available in daylight. Indeed, HMS *Glamorgan*, who had bravely remained later than ordered to support 45 Commando, had paid the penalty for overstaying the time — she was hit by a land-based Exocet missile when she cut across the

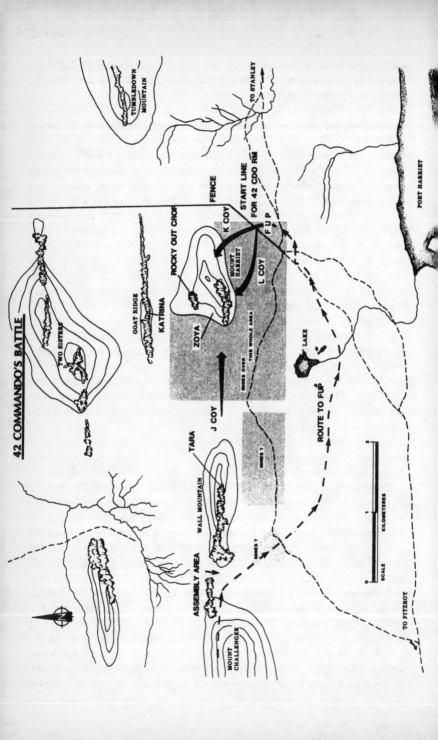

Exocet danger area in a bid to get away to the east before daylight. An attempt at Tumbledown, in daylight and without proper support would be unnecessarily expensive in casualties.

On the Commando Brigade's right flank, Vaux, commanding 42 Commando, had opted for a bold plan which involved assaulting the enemy battalion position from the rear. The wide outflanking movement required to implement his plan would only be possible because of the excellent patrolling by 42 Commando over several days and the pin-pointing of enemy reverse-slope positions by his own patrols and the M and AW Cadre. Vaux decided that K and L Companies would march south from the western end of Wall Mountain, cross the Fitzroy-Stanley track and then go south-east until they had reached a point about 1000 metres south of the track before swinging in a north-easterly direction and crossing the track again to a forming-up position on the south-east shoulder of Mount Harriet. Using the fence, which ran north-east from the Fitzroy-Stanley track, as a Start Line, K Company would assault the eastern end of Mount Harriet, followed sixty minutes later by L Company assaulting the western end. Once Harriet (Zoya) was secured, K Company would assault Goat Ridge (Katrina). J Company was to be in reserve, but also had the task of creating a diversion from a position on the eastern end of Wall Mountain (Tara), aimed at attracting the enemy's attention away from the outflanking movement by K and L Companies. Finally, again to distract the Argentines and to keep their heads down, I allowed 42 Commando to shell Mount Harriet before H-hour, unlike the other two attacks which started silent, i.e. without preliminary bombardment. 4th Argentine Infantry Regiment on Mount Harriet included two strong rifle companies, and with its reconnaissance platoon, heavy mortars, Regimental Headquarters and other headquarters cooks and bottle washers was equivalent to a small battalion.

In preparation for the attack on Mount Harriet, Vaux moved the whole of J Company on to Wall Mountain. He set up his assembly area and established his mortars at the western end of the feature. Soon after last light, about 4.15 pm, on 11 June, K and L Companies moved forward to the assembly area from Mount Challenger where they had been preparing for battle and conducting rehearsals. At the assembly area they dropped their rucksacks and moved off along the route previously cleared by the Sappers. 12 Troop of J Company, led by Lieutenant Beadon, who had been with Sergeant Collins when he pioneered the route, went ahead as soon as darkness fell to mark the route and drop off two Milan sections, one immediately south of Mount Harriet and 800 metres from the spineback ridge, the other on the Fitzroy-Stanley track south-east of Harriet in case the Argentines decided to send in their Panhard armoured cars while the Commando attack was going in. This track was the only surfaced 'road' outside the immediate environs of Stanley and Panhards could motor along it, although they would be unable to deploy off it. 12 Troop from J Company also had the task of meeting up with a reconnaissance patrol from the Welsh Guards who had been tasked with securing the Commando Start Line.

At 5.30 pm, just over an hour after last light, K Company, led by Sergeant Collins, set out from the assembly area, followed about an hour later by L Company. The separation between the two Companies was deliberate to avoid the risk of both being caught out on the same piece of open ground on the six-kilometre march to their Start Line. About an hour's march behind L Company was the Porter Troop of thirty-four men formed from Headquarter Company. Their task was to carry forward the six tripods and dial sights (SF kits) for K and L Companies' GPMGs and 10,000 rounds of ammunition. In this way ammunition would be immediately on hand and the GPMGs on their tripods ready to beat off an Argentine counterattack once Harriet and Goat Ridge were taken.

On two occasions, as K Company was moving round to the forming-up position, the Argentines fired mortar illuminating flares and the men froze, expecting artillery and mortar fire to follow. L Company was held back by the Commanding Officer so that they would not be illuminated. There then followed a delay because 12 Troop and the Welsh Guards reconnaissance patrol missed each other in the darkness and did not link up for nearly an hour, delaying H-hour. Just before this J Company fired flares and their own and captured enemy weapons from the eastern end of Wall Mountain at the enemy opposite them on Mount Harriet, hoping to deceive the Argentines into believing that a large-scale patrol clash was taking place on their own doorstep.

The delay in marrying up with the Welsh Guards meant that the moon was now higher and brighter than anticipated, so K Company used the peat cuttings, found by Sergeant Collins, to provide a covered approach. When K Company arrived in the FUP, Captain Babbington, the Company Commander, collected his Troop Commanders and went forward to the Start Line to orientate them and look at the objective through binoculars. The ground showed up remarkably clearly and he was able to point out the Company axis of advance and their troop objectives. They returned to the Company and at 10 pm crossed the Start Line for the 800-metre approach to the objective. They covered 700 metres without being sighted by the enemy. Then, about 100 metres from the rock ridge, 1 Troop engaged some enemy moving in the rocks. 2 Troop dashed forward as ordered and started to clear the right-hand side of the Company objective. It took them about three-quarters of an hour to fully clear a very craggy position which included four 120mm mortars. One of the Section Commanders, Corporal Watts, was killed capturing this key position which could have caused considerable trouble had it not been taken out so quickly.

Babbington then passed 3 Troop through 2 Troop up on to the ridgeback and, with 1 Troop moving along the low ground to the south of them, both Troops started working westwards, engaging machine guns, snipers and riflemen, all in bunkers. As the two troops fought their way forward, keeping each other informed on the radio, Corporal Ward of 3 Troop reported being held up by snipers and machine guns. Immediately Corporal Newland of 1 Troop said he could see the enemy position that was causing the trouble and could approach it from below. Corporal Newland left his section and, going forward alone, climbed a rock slab twenty feet high. Peering round a rock, he realized he was about to assault nearly half a platoon of enemy. Putting a full magazine on his SLR, he tossed in two grenades, charged, and single-handed killed all those who survived, or so he thought. Corporal Ward, coming in from another direction, shouted 'sixty-six' to warn Newland that he was about to fire a LAW. Newland withdrew a few metres behind a rock. Immediately after the 'sixty-six' had slammed into the position, Newland went forward again. He was greeted with a burst of fire from an Argentine soldier's FAL which wounded him in both legs. In Newland's words, 'The Argentine soldier died rather quickly'. Newland, being unable to move because of his wounds, lit a cigarette and, propping himself against a rock and, using the radio, calmly directed 3 Troop towards another machine-gun position he could see further on. His clear directions were of great assistance to Lieutenant Heathcote, commanding 3 Troop, and his two forward section commanders, Corporals Ward and Eccles, in clearing their troop objective.

The handling of the Company by Babbington, at night, in the confusion of battle, was a masterpiece. The officers, NCOs and marines worked like a well-drilled football team as they fought their way forward to the crash of the 66mm LAWs and 84mm MAWs, the crump and flame of their own artillery and mortar fire and that of the enemy. Babbington described it after the battle:

Throughout the early stages I, with my Artillery Forward Observation Officer (FOO) and Mortar Fire Controller (MFC), remained out on the open hillside in order to see more clearly what was going on. All my sections were on the Company radio net which meant I was getting up to date situation reports from my section commanders (by listening to them reporting to their troop commanders) so leaving the troop commanders to get on with directing their own fights. It also allowed section commanders to direct mortar and artillery fire as the FOO and MCFs were by my side. At one stage the FOO was controlling simultaneously 81mm mortar illuminating, a naval gunfire and an artillery fire mission on two targets within 100 metres of us. Enemy fire was fairly heavy, mainly heavy machine guns and automatic rifles. They were using a lot of flares which was to our advantage in indicating their positions.

As soon as his Company was firm on the east end of the ridge, Babbington moved forward with his Headquarters between 1 and 3 Troops as they cleared along the ridge to the west. About halfway along the Company objective, 3 Troop set fire to an Argentine sangar with a white phosphorus grenade. The flames acted as an aiming point for Argentine artillery which started to fall all round the Company, causing casualties, including the Company second-in-command, Lieutenant Whitely.

At about this time L Company, having crossed the Start Line, came under heavy fire from enemy on K Company's objective. L Company retaliated with GPMGs, but some of their fire was too close to K Company for comfort. Fortunately no casualties were sustained by K Company during the few minutes of heated exchange on the radio which eventually stopped the fire. By now prisoners were beginning to come in, subdued and shocked by the battle. Porter Troop came into its own bringing forward ammunition and SF kits and taking back prisoners and casualties.

L Company's task was to clear and secure the western end of the Mount Harriet feature. Starting after K Company, surprise had been lost and so L Company came under effective fire from heavy machine guns within 200 metres of crossing the Start Line, taking three casualties almost at once. Captain Wheen, commanding L Company, called for Milan to fire at the machine-gun positions. This proved effective. The Company had to clear six medium machine-gun positions and at least four sniper teams equipped with night sights before reaching the end of its first objective, the western end of the Harriet spineback. This involved a fighting advance of about 600 metres and, as each position took a separate troop or section attack to deal with it, it took about five hours to cover the distance from the Start Line. The Company found that it was best to keep skirmishing forward throughout this advance, because going to ground for any length of time meant sitting in the middle of the enemy artillery defensive fire tasks that inflicted eleven casualties. As the Company arrived at the Western end of Mount Harriet they found large numbers of Argentines wishing to surrender. In the darkness there appeared to be about fifty of them, although when daylight arrived many more appeared.

Wheen reorganized his Company, sent the prisoners to the rear and then ordered 5 Troop to move forward to the Company's next objective, an enemy position in a rocky outcrop about 500 metres due north of the western end of Harriet. Before they moved, however, Wheen concentrated all his machine guns, less those with 5 Troop, fifteen guns in all, on the ridge. As 5 Troop moved forward down the slope to the rocky outcrop, they came under heavy fire from their objective. Wheen pulled them back and then hit the enemy with mortar, artillery and machine-gun fire before ordering 5 Troop forward again. They dashed forward with great determination and winkled out about six enemy; the remainder fled into the mist.

L Company was ordered by Vaux to press on to Goat Ridge, while K Company remained on the western end of Harriet. Time was getting short and Vaux wanted to be firm on both features before first light and the expected Argentine counterattack materialized. Vaux and his Tactical Headquarters led J Company directly on to the Harriet feature from the eastern end of Wall Mountain. He did not wish to waste time taking them along the route followed by K and L Companies. They sprinted through the minefield with 'their fingers crossed and if they could have managed it, their toes as well'. The most dangerous moment for an attacker is often just after he arrives on an objective and in the euphoria, or exhaustion, or both, relaxes and is then hit by a counterattack which knocks him off the hard-won position. The well-trained troops in 3 Commando Brigade speedily prepared themselves to receive such an attack, but, except on one occasion, the Argentines did not mount counterattacks, although it is only with the wisdom of hindsight that we know this now. They did, however, resort to the other expedient of those who have lost ground, which is to shell and mortar their recent positions. L Company found Goat Ridge unoccupied, although, before they arrived, they saw about fifty enemy running up the side of Tumbledown and called down artillery fire on them. Vaux consolidated his Commando with L Company on Goat Ridge and the rocky outcrop, K Company on the western end of Harriet and J Company on the eastern end.

The dawn found all 3 Commando Brigade's objectives secure. With the daylight enemy shelling intensified. It was particularly heavy on Mount Longdon, overlooked by Argentines on Mount Tumbledown who could adjust the fall of the shells. But 155s and 105s also fired regularly on Two Sisters and Mount Harriet. Cole, commanding Z Company 45 Commando, described the col between the twin peaks of Two Sisters as 'looking like a field which had been ploughed by giant moles'; it was covered by the big 155 shell craters. The weather provided its usual variety; soon after dawn the mist on Two Sisters, Harriet and Longdon gave way to bright, frosty weather while at Brigade Headquarters, at the base of Mount Kent, it was snowing. I had been in touch with my Commanding Officers through the long night on the radio, and, after listening to a situation report from the redoubtable Gullen with 45 Commando, stepped out of the Command Post into a grey dawn with snowflakes whirling down. As I stood outside I could hear the crump of the incoming artillery on the hills my Brigade had just secured. The big 155mm shells were distinctive among the smaller 105mm shells and 120mm mortar bombs, each sounding, as someone so aptly said, as if thousands of crates of bottles had been dropped all at once on to a concrete road. The sooner the next phase took place the better; the less time my men would have to spend sitting under the Argentine artillery fire.

However, the night had been an unqualified success, thanks to the magnificent efforts of the Marines and soldiers and the spirited leadership of their officers and NCOs. At Brigade Headquarters the busy night had been further enlivened by reports of a high-level bombing threat by Argentine Canberras and indications from the artillery mortar-locating radar, Cymbeline, that the Argentines were mounting a helicopter counterattack on the eastern slopes of Mount Kent just as the Brigade attack was going in. The former threat was highly probable; indeed Canberra bombers had plastered the area round 3 Para's tactical headquarters some nights before. The latter threat looked highly unlikely, but there was an outside chance that Cymbeline had picked up a helicopter assault aimed at Brigade Headquarters, perhaps a desperate gamble mounted by Argentine Special Forces, if they had pinpointed the Headquarters from the radio traffic emanating from it. Such an attack, while the Headquarters was commanding a night battle, would be most unwelcome. There was nothing that could be done except beat it off when it came. Neither threat materialized, although Cymbeline 'saw' another wave of helicopters later that night.

2 Para, who had been following down the centre line between 3 Para and 45 Commando, were ordered to swing north and dig in on reverse slopes to the north-west of Mount Longdon and await further orders. The Welsh Guards withdrew from their exposed positions south of Mount Harriet about 400 metres to the west, where at least they would be out of sight of Mount William, dug in and waited for orders. 2 Para had had a frustrating and tiring fifteen-kilometre march through the night, as the Battalion 'snake' stopped and started, expanding and contracting like a concertina so that men who had to walk fast or almost run to keep up one minute then found themselves waiting for what seemed like hours the next. By now several soldiers in the Battalion had 'Galtieri's Revenge', common throughout my Brigade. Puritabs sterilized the brackish water but did not remove the sediment which inflamed the gut. Men having stopped to drop their trousers galloped after the column which, having momentarily halted, continued when the reason became all too apparent. Some men in the Brigade found it more convenient to dispense with underpants and cut a slit in the seat of their trousers.

The Battalion could see the battles on Longdon and Two Sisters to their left and right front and could hear the shells from the British batteries firing in support whooshing overhead.

On all the captured positions prisoners were being collected and clearing patrols winkled out those who wished to surrender and despatched those who declined to do so. Everywhere there were mountains of equipment, weapons, ammunition, food and filth. Sanitation had clearly not been a strong point in the Argentine Army and its soldiers defecated wherever it took their fancy. Throwing oneself down when incoming shells were heard could be a messy and smelly business anywhere on an Argentine position. Dytor, sitting in the dark on his captured objective, decided to celebrate victory by eating a Rolo. Finding that they tasted strange, to say the least, he realized to his horror that his gloves and the Rolos were covered with Argentine ordure.

The Argentine rations, however, were good. As Gardiner wrote:

> We found a prodigious amount of ammunition, weapons, food and equipment on the position. As it turned out, it was as well there was so much there. Our bergens again failed to turn up and it froze that night. Without the Argentine blankets and other clothing, we would have been extremely uncomfortable. Almost everybody gorged themselves on enemy rations. They were pretty good and clearly there was no shortage. A notable advantage they had over ours was the 20 fags and tot of whisky they each contained.

Perhaps the most highly prized item among the spoils of war was a pair of the excellent Argentine boots to replace the sodden, leaking footwear which was all most men in the Commando Brigade possessed. So eager were some individuals to get a pair of decent boots that they did not wait to see if their owners were dead before removing them, as Lance-Corporal Koleszar of K Company, 42 Commando, found when two apparently dead Argentines leapt to their feet when he tried to remove their footwear.

On Mount Harriet 42 Commando found themselves with over 300 prisoners, including the Commanding Officer of the Argentine 4th Infantry Regiment and several officers. This gave the lie to later Press reports that all the officers ran off leaving their conscript soldiers to be slaughtered or surrender like sheep. On Mount Harriet, as elsewhere, the Argentine officers and senior NCOs fought hard and on several occasions towards the end of the battle, tried to prevent their men surrendering by firing at them. The only solution was to kill the officers or senior NCOs in question before accepting the surrender of the remainder. Mount Harriet had been held by the better part of the 4th Infantry Regiment and it was a remarkable achievement by 42 Commando to overcome a defensive position held by an equal or even greater number of men with so few casualties to themselves. The key factors in the Commando's success were surprise and the superior training and fighting qualities of the Marines, NCOs and officers. After the battle the Commanding Officer of the 4th Argentine Infantry Regiment, in a conversation with the RSM of 42 Commando, WO1 (RSM) Chisnall, paid tribute to the night-fighting skill of the Commando. But he added that if his own soldiers had had as many night vision goggles it might have been a different story, implying that every man in 42 Commando had a pair. The RSM replied that none of the Commando had them, but would shortly be equipped with those taken off their prisoners.

From the number of bunkers and quantity of abandoned equipment found on Two Sisters, it was evident that the position had been held by at least a reinforced company, and possibly two companies, many of whom had fled once the machine-gun positions were overcome. Unlike the Harriet battle where the direction of 42 Commando's assault had blocked most escape routes and only about fifty Argentines got away, 45 Commando had of necessity to assault from the flank and frontally, so the enemy were able to run off the back of the position. 45 Commando took forty-four prisoners, among them an officer who spoke good English. The Adjutant of 45 Commando, Captain Irwin, a keen polo player, gave him a cigarette and asked him if he played polo and if he knew the Argentine officer who had been at the British Army Staff College the previous year. The answer to both questions was yes, and furthermore the Argentine officer in question was on General Menendez's Staff.

'In that case' asked Irwin, 'if Menendez had a Camberley-trained officer on his Staff, what on earth was the Argentine Army doing conducting its defensive battle in such an unprofessional manner?'

'He must have been asleep during the lectures,' was the rejoinder from the Argentine Officer.

Like many British officers that morning, Whitehead could hardly believe his eyes when he saw the inherent strength of the natural fortress his men had taken. His only spoken comment was, 'If we'd had a Company up here, we'd have died of old age before it was captured.'

On Mount Longdon the scene that greeted the eyes of the weary but triumphant soldiers of 3 Para was the same as that on the other two mountain objectives taken by 3 Commando Brigade.

Pike remembers that morning:

'The misty scene as dawn broke will perhaps be the most haunting memory of this long cold fight. The debris of battle was scattered along the length of the mountain, encountered round every turn in the rocks, in every gully. Weapons, clothing, rations, blankets, boots, tents, ammunition, sleeping bags, blood-soaked medical dressings, web equipment, packs — all abandoned, along with the 105 RCLs, 120mm mortars and .50 inch Brownings that had given us so much trouble during the darkness. The enemy dead lay everywhere, victims of shell, bullet and bayonet. The sour odour of death lingered in the nostrils long after many of them had been buried, for it was a slow job, and eventually the task was abandoned when their artillery and mortars started again... . Standing among the shell holes and shambles of battle, watching the determined, triumphant, shocked and saddened faces of those who had lost their friends on this mountain, the Iron Duke's comment was never more apt: "There is nothing half so melancholy as a battle won — unless it be a battle lost".'

Wherever he could, Pike pulled his men back on to reverse slopes, out of sight of Tumbledown. This was not always possible and on several occasions men were pinned down in the open by the fire directed from Tumbledown, causing a steady trickle of casualties.

All that day and the next the positions on Harriet, Two Sisters and Longdon were shelled by the Argentines. Everybody had become expert, by the 'whoo-eer' noise of the incomer, at telling how far away the shell would land. The shorter the noise, the closer the shell. Meanwhile preparations for the night and next day were going ahead throughout the Commando Brigade. By the time darkness fell it was clear that no attacks were to be mounted by either Brigade that night and everybody settled down for another night under the stars.

'That evening, as I was giving my instructions for the night,' recounted Gardiner, 'a figure appeared out of the darkness on our position. We were somewhat edgy and were naturally extremely amused to hear a shout out of the gloom in a strong Welsh accent: "Hello X Ray Company, it's the Vicar and I've forgotten the bloody password."'

CHAPTER TEN

'Capture Port Stanley'

3 Commando Brigade, having secured Mount Harriet, Two Sisters and Mount Longdon, now had to wait for 5 Infantry Brigade to capture Mount Tumbledown and Mount William before mounting the next full Brigade attack in its turn. However, there was one operation which I aimed to carry out at the same time as 5 Brigade's attack. This was to capture Wireless Ridge as a preliminary to launching my Brigade round the southern side of Port Stanley from a Start Line on the north-east shoulder of Mount Tumbledown, to take the Argentines on Sapper Hill and other positions south of Port Stanley in the flank and rear. The operation to capture Wireless Ridge had to be timed to coincide with 5 Brigade's assault on Tumbledown. The latter overlooked Wireless Ridge and, if still held by the enemy, would have made any battalion position there untenable.

At first the intention had been for 5 Brigade to mount its attack on the night 12/13 June and we were informed accordingly during the morning of 12 June. Later in the day I returned to my Headquarters from visiting my commandos and battalions to find General Moore and Brigadier Wilson there. They informed me that Wilson had, quite rightly, asked for and been given more time to prepare for a night attack over ground which his Brigade had not previously seen. The services of the M and AW Cadre were immediately offered to 5 Brigade to lead the assaulting battalions to their start lines. I had Haddow and Wassell in mind for this task, as both had first-hand knowledge of the route to the eastern end of Goat Ridge, which Wilson's Battalions were to follow, and of some of the enemy positions on Tumbledown and Mount William, following their successful patrol a few nights previously. The offer was accepted.

The Wireless Ridge operation, to be carried out by 2 Para, was therefore postponed, which was fortunate because the liaison officer, Gullan, carrying the orders for the operation to the Battalion, was badly delayed. The orders could not be transmitted by radio because the secure speech net was not working to the Battalion. There was no question of sending a message about future intentions on an insecure radio. So the

Battalion was making some frantic preparations for the attack at short notice when the postponement message arrived hard on the heels of Gullan.

After a quiet but bitterly cold and clear night, the morning of 13 June brought beautiful, sunny, almost springlike weather, provided one kept out of the wind. Everybody in 3 Commando Brigade was in good form and morale was high. The clatter of helicopters ferrying gun ammunition and moving the batteries forward seemed incessant. Sometimes an importunate helicopter, from one of the newly arrived squadrons, judging by the radar dome on its back, would land near Brigade Headquarters, perhaps mistaking it for one of the gun positions, to be angrily waved away by the imposing figure of Seccombe, waving his walking stick and cursing them roundly for risking compromising the position of the Headquarters. An O Group was summoned to be at Brigade Headquarters in the early afternoon, but fortunately, subsequently postponed for two hours while changes were made to the orders.

In the early afternoon, just when the Brigade Orders Group should have been in full swing but for the postponement, four Skyhawks roared in over the ridge to the east of Brigade Headquarters. Although Air-Raid Warning Red had been received earlier, few ground troops took any notice of these warnings any more. I was strolling over to my helicopter to go off to visit the commandos and battalions. Hearing the jets, I looked up and saw the stubby fighters tearing in with the flashes from their cannons winking below their wings. Like most people without a suitable weapon to fire back, I hurled myself behind the nearest rock. The Blowpipe operators and GPMG gunners stood their ground and fired back, but to no effect; Seccombe stood and waved his stick. The 400 kg bombs on their small retard parachutes seemed to float slowly down, before exploding in a series of earth-shaking explosions, showering peat and rock and metal splinters around the Headquarters and 2 Para's mortar and machine-gun platoons who were situated nearby.

At the moment of the attack Rowe was in the Brigade Command Post showing Chester the first set of air photographs to be received. They were poor quality and pretty useless. Nevertheless Rowe had painstakingly arranged them in order but had not yet numbered them. As the Skyhawks roared in and Rowe and Chester took cover, Rowe said, 'Whatever you do, don't mix up these photos.' Chester, in his normal, calm way, stacked them neatly on the floor of his Bandwagon before going out to find a trench.

All but one of the fighters made two passes, a total of seven attacks. Although five of the bombs exploded, leaving two unexploded bombs to be dealt with, the only casualty was a man with mild concussion, whose trench had been a few metres away from one of the bombs. It was a very lucky escape, because the furthest bomb was only fifty metres away from the

Headquarters. The soft peat had absorbed the blast and most, but not all, of the flying splinters. Three light helicopters were damaged, one badly enough to be out of action for the rest of the war. The briefing tent where the Orders Group should have been assembled, but which was empty at the time because of the delay in preparing orders, was shredded with splinter holes and many of the legs of the camp stools within were chopped off or mangled. The casualties inside would have been heavy, probably wounding or killing most of us, including all the Commanding Officers and key Staff Officers in 3 Commando Brigade.

The position of the Headquarters had clearly been compromised. The previous night I had said that the Headquarters had been in one position too long, but the Staff had pooh-poohed the idea of moving. They were now in full agreement that a move was in order. In fairness to them I should say that most of the Bandwagons were stockpiled in Norway and for lack of shipping space the Brigade Headquarters had only half its normal allocation of these vehicles. The Headquarters was not, therefore, able to carry out its normal routine for moving which involved placing out a duplicate set of Bandwagons and radios in the new location and only moving the Staff when all was ready. Consequently, in this campaign, moves of the Headquarters were taking a long time to complete and communications were severely disrupted in the process. With a battle pending, the communications had to work properly so we had not moved. To ensure that we would have at least some communications now that Main had to move, my Tactical Headquarters was deployed and tucked away in a small gully about 500 metres away from the old site while the Main Headquarters moved. Until Main Headquarters was properly established again, my Tactical Headquarters would have to remain static to ensure good communications. I would be unable to deploy my Tactical Headquarters forward and would be able to operate forward with only my R Group and man-pack radio sets. The going, combined with the onset of darkness, was such that the Main Headquarters was not established in its new position until well into the next morning. By which time events had moved very fast indeed.

When the Orders Group finally gathered in a little hollow near the Tactical Headquarters there were a few quips from the assembled company about Brigade Headquarters' recent experience. Nothing appeals to the fighting man's sense of humour more than the thought of Staff Officers flinging themselves to the ground to avoid bomb or bullet – the more senior the headquarters and the further back it is, the funnier the joke.

Lieutenant-Colonel Chaundler, having appeared at the Orders Group as bidden, asked to be excused to return to his Battalion to continue preparations for his attack on Wireless Ridge that night. The Welsh Guards, having been under command, were reverting to 5 Brigade for their attack, but their second-in-command attended the Orders Group because they were to come back under my command at 8 am the following day, 14 June. By this time 3 Troop of the Blues and Royals, with their Scorpions and Scimitars, had rejoined the Commando Brigade and had been sent off to join 2 Para for their attack.

The orders given by me were for the night 14/15 June, i.e. for an H-hour thirty hours hence, and assumed that 2 Para would have secured Wireless Ridge by that time and that Tumbledown would also be in British hands. The attack was to be in four phases, and the mission I gave to my Brigade was simply 'to capture Port Stanley'. In phase one 3 Para was to advance and secure the Esro Building, but not to exploit further than the eastern edge of the old racecourse. In phase two 45 Commando was to advance and seize Sapper Hill from a Start Line north-east of Tumbledown. Phase three would see 42 Commando securing the positions immediately south of Stanley, passing through 45 Commando on Sapper Hill. Phase four would involve the Welsh Guards passing through 42 Commando and attacking and seizing the positions south-east of Stanley which would cut the road to the airport. The 105 mm light gun batteries would be flown as far forward as possible before the attack so that the whole objective area and the whole of the airport beyond would be well within range. Until this was done, only the western end of the airport peninsula was in range.

The plan followed the directive from Division to avoid fighting in the town itself if possible, in order to minimize civilian casualties. However, I knew this would probably be impossible and had plans to change the direction of the attack if necessary, which I kept to myself. Brigade Tactical Headquarters would move to join 2 Para on Wireless Ridge during the day of 14 June and the battle would initially be commanded from there. H-hour was set for midnight 14/15 June, but the fighting would go on until daylight and this time would not stop at the onset of day. Wireless Ridge would provide a good observation post from which I could see what was going on. There were few questions and the Orders Group dispersed.

3 Commando Brigade was destined to capture Port Stanley but not quite in the way I, or anyone else in the Brigade, foresaw. Although I knew about the various moves being made to persuade the Argentines to surrender, I dismissed them as worth a try but nothing more. No one in the Brigade had agreed with the views being bandied about at quite senior level in Britain before the Brigade sailed that the Argentines would run away when the British appeared; there was even less reason to believe that they would now. The Commando Brigade confidently expected to fight all the way to the airport isthmus; after that the Argies might see the sense of giving in. If not we would bottle them up and pound them to pieces until they changed their minds. The battalion and commando Order Groups that passed on the orders

were given to what one Commanding Officer described as 'coldly confident men, determined to do even better next time — if that were possible'.

When Chaundler returned to his Battalion he found that he had to make a rapid change of plan, because a feature north-east of Longdon thought to be held by 3 Para contained enemy; a hill (ring contour 100) on the left of the Battalion's axis also contained enemy; the hill (ring contour 250) north of Wireless Ridge was more heavily defended than he had thought and finally the enemy positions on Wireless Ridge extended further to the east than had been at first appreciated. A short altercation between 2 and 3 Para then followed as to who did hold the contested feature and was settled by 2 Para having it comprehensively shelled without complaint from 3 Para.

Chaundler's new plan was for a four-phase, noisy, i.e. with preliminary bombardment, attack. In phase one D Company would capture the feature north-east of Longdon, nicknamed Rough Diamond. In phase two A and B Companies would attack ring contour 250, nicknamed Apple Pie. In phase three D Company would attack Wireless Ridge, nicknamed Blueberry Pie, from the west supported by fire from A and B Companies. In phase four C Company, Patrols Company and 2 Para, would attack ring contour 100. The fire support for the attack included two batteries of artillery, the mortars of both 2 Para and 3 Para, 3 Troop the Blues and Royals, HMS *Ambuscade* to provide naval gunfire support, the Milan Platoon and Machine Gun Platoon.

The Wireless Ridge position was held by 7th Argentine Infantry Regiment. We now know that C Company held Rough Diamond, A Company held Apple Pie, and that Wireless Ridge itself, 2 Para's Phase Three objective, was occupied by a reinforced company and the Regimental Headquarters. A Company of the 3rd Infantry Regiment occupied a position just south of Wireless Ridge, astride the track about one kilometre west of Moody Brook Camp.

Gullan, my personal liaison officer with 2 Para, flew back to my Headquarters with the new plan and then returned to the Battalion bearing with him fresh intelligence of a minefield in front of Apple Pie and that Wireless Ridge was held by two companies not one. He arrived to find the Battalion in its forming-up position, having moved at last light, 4.15 pm. Chaundler decided that it was too late to change anything at that stage and to press on. It started to snow.

At 9.15 pm on 13 June the supporting fire started raining down on D Company's objective, Rough Diamond, and at 9.45 pm D Company, supported by fire from the Scorpions and Scimitars and the machine-gun platoon, crossed the Start Line. The Company found a few enemy dead on the objective, but the majority had withdrawn. As D Company reorganized in the position, the Argentines began to fire 155 mm airburst, so Neame, the Company Commander, advanced for about 300 metres to get clear of the

2 PARA'S BATTLE FOR WIRELESS RIDGE NIGHT 13/14 JUNE 1982

Furze Bush Pass

2 PARA

D COY
PHASE 1

C COY

B COY

A COY C COY
PHASE 2

Ring Contour 250

APPLE PIE

ROUGH DIAMOND

Mount Longdon

3 PARA

D COY

PHASE 3

BLUEBERRY PIE

Wireless Ridge

Ring Contour 100

PHASE 4

Hearndon Water

Moody Brook Camp

Stanley Harbour

Esro Building

Tumbledown Mountain

2 SCOTS GUARDS

SCALE
0   1   2
KILOMETERES

enemy's defensive fire task. Then, with Farrar-Hockley's A Company on the left and Crosland's B Company on the right, the two Companies crossed their Start Line. As they approached their objective, Apple Pie, the enemy could be seen running away, shocked and terrified by the storm of fire from shells, mortars and machine guns. The Battalion found several radios still switched on. Any opposition was quickly silenced, but the main problem was the speed with which the Argentines shelled their old position and kept it up for the next nine hours. Chaundler decided to bring forward C Company's attack on ring contour 100 on the Battalion's left flank, which was found clear but with all the signs of having been abandoned in haste.

D Company moved to its next Start Line at the western end of Wireless Ridge, while the CVRT, Milan Platoon and the Machine Gun Platoon moved up to join A and B Companies on Apple Pie to provide support for D Company. The first part of the ridge was taken unopposed, while suppressive fire was brought down on the eastern end by the CVRT, Milans and the Machine Gun Platoon. As D Company moved to assault the second part of their objective they encountered considerable resistance. During the close-quarter battle for this objective a fire mission was called down which landed directly on D Company, resulting in casualties. The enemy conducting a fighting withdrawal from bunker to bunker, suddenly broke and ran, chivvied off the ridge by fire from the CVRT and pursued by D Company. Once again, as D Company reorganized, the enemy defensive fire tasks began to rain down, as well as small arms fire from Tumbledown where the Second Battalion Scots Guards were still fighting their gallant battle. In the darkness the enemy who had been chased off by D Company could be heard regrouping further along the ridge and in the area of Moody Brook.

As dawn broke on a freezing morning about forty Argentines put in a counterattack on D Company. The small arms ammunition in the Company had all but run out and even 105 mm gun ammunition was getting low, so the order was given to fix bayonets and have grenades ready. But a short fire mission from the artillery and mortars and small arms fire from D Company repulsed the attack.

By this time the Scots Guards, after a tremendous battle, had captured Tumbledown. They had been led to their Start Line, a fence east of Goat Ridge, by Lieutenant Haddow of the M and AW Cadre, who had also briefed the forward Company Commander and Platoon Commanders on the enemy positions he had seen on 9 June. He left the Battalion on their Start Line and then walked back to meet Sergeant Wassell who was to lead 1/7 Gurkha Rifles forward for their assault on Mount William. Haddow waited for Wassell at the Scots Guards' Regimental Aid Post, had a cup of tea and a cigarette and watched the Tumbledown battle.

During their busy night the 2 Para battle went so smoothly under the hand of its Commanding Officer that Brigade Headquarters was not called upon to intervene except to try to bring artillery fire, at 2 Para's request, on to the 155 mm guns which the Battalion thought that they had pinpointed. In the event they did not have the right positions, although 29 Commando Regiment fired at the grids given. 2 Para fought a model all-arms battle. 3 Troop of the Blues and Royals played a major part in the victory achieved at such low cost. The Scorpions and Scimitars had stood up to the test brilliantly, as had their crews. The image-intensifier sight had proved invaluable in acquiring targets, despite the moon being obscured by falling snow. This and the weight of fire these light tanks had been able to lay down to suppress enemy machine guns and 105 mm anti-tank guns, continuing firing after the artillery and mortars had to lift, enabled the battle to be won so quickly. What a difference they would have made at Goose Green.

There were only two crises, neither of them of 2 Para's making. At one stage, while 2 Para's battle was in full swing, a radio message came through to the SAS liaison officer at Brigade Headquarters. A party from G Squadron 22 SAS in rigid raiders, provided and driven by the 1st Raiding Squadron Royal Marines, had taken casualties after an abortive attempt to conduct a raid on the fuel depot on the north arm of Stanley Harbour. They had been illuminated by a searchlight from the Argentine hospital ship in Port William and well and truly brassed up by air defence guns firing in the anti-boat role. They now needed casevac urgently. Somebody in the Command Post was heard to mutter, 'Bloody Special Forces; the whole world has to stop for them, I suppose.' Fortunately for them they landed up with 2 Para who took care of them until they could be evacuated.

The second crisis occurred while both 2 Para's and 2 Scots Guards' battles were still going strong and one of the gun batteries which had started the night with about 500 rounds per gun was down to around eight rounds per gun on the position. More ammunition was requested, but at first the Sea King pilots were understandably reluctant to fly in the darkness and in the snow showers until Major Cameron and some of his pilots from the Brigade Air Squadron led them to the battery position in their Scout helicopters.

The weather did not stop an Argentine C 130 landing at Stanley airport that night, as on most previous nights. This was reported by 2 Para on the Artillery net, saying that they could see the lights of Stanley Airfield and the C 130 landing. Major Armitage at Brigade Headquarters tried to bring fire to bear on the runway. When told, correctly, by the battery closest to the airport that it was out of range, Holroyd-Smith roared, 'Tell them to cock the bloody guns up and have a go' — a fire order that would probably cause the instructors of gunnery at Larkhill to pale with horror! The outburst was a reflection of the frustration felt by the whole Brigade that the air blockade was not effective. The battery fired but, as expected, it did not hit the aircraft. If the Argentines had not surrendered the next day, the batteries would have moved forward and the guns of 29 Commando Regiment would have imposed the air blockade for good.

At first light I was impatient to go forward to 2 Para who were reporting the enemy retreating eastwards in large numbers and asking permission to advance. But Brigade Tactical Headquarters was in the middle of a snow blizzard and nothing could fly. The weather then cleared and I was about to get off, but was summoned to meet General Moore at Wilson's Tactical Headquarters by the rocky outcrop between Goat Ridge and Mount Harriet. I protested, but the order was repeated. On arrival I was met by Wilson and we stood for a moment watching the Gurkhas go in on Mount William while waiting for General Moore. A few rounds of Argentine artillery fell, but some distance off. Wilson said they had been shelled at intervals throughout the night. I told General Moore what my plans were for the coming night and a short discussion followed over the matter of whose command the Welsh Guards would come under for the forthcoming battle. Wilson said that he intended taking Sapper Hill with the Welsh Guards. I reminded Moore that I had already given the Welsh Guards their tasks for the following night, which did not include Sapper Hill, which was 45 Commando's objective, and, furthermore, he had a copy of the orders. It was my understanding that the Battalion would revert to my command that morning. It was agreed that the Battalion would be under 3 Commando Brigade for the next night's battle and their objective would be the one already given them. Having settled this point, I left as quickly as possible and flew to see 2 Para, accompanied by Rowe, my Intelligence Staff Officer.

Leaving the helicopter north of A Company on Apple Pie, we walked forward to Wireless Ridge in order to find Chaundler, who was with his forward Company. To begin with we could not find him and stood looking through our binoculars at the scene before us — Moody Brook almost at our feet, Stanley away to our left and Tumbledown to our right. Rowe then reminded me that we were skylined and had better take cover. Conscious that standing about on the skyline in other people's positions is an unfriendly act because of the fire that it draws on the owners of the real estate, we threw ourselves down behind a rock and continued studying the ground and searching for enemy positions. Almost at the same time a voice, instantly recognizable as a Company Sergeant-Major shouting at idle soldiers, roared: 'Don't stand about on the skyline, you stupid bastards; the bloody war isn't over yet.'

Chaundler appeared soon afterwards. I stood up and watched as the Argentines fired what must have been one of the last artillery fire missions on the north side of Tumbledown. The shells crashed down, throwing up smoke and peat. The thought went through my head at that moment that the Argentine fire was coming down exactly on the position my commandos would be forming up in that night. I made a mental note to see if the route could be altered slightly to avoid the defensive fire task.

Chaundler told me that he had seen the enemy running away in large numbers from Moody Brook, Mount William, Tumbledown and Sapper Hill. Nevertheless the Argentine artillery was still effective, as had just been demonstrated. I told him to take his Battalion and advance as far as the spur above the Esro Building on the very edge of Stanley. I would go back to my Tactical Headquarters and get the rest of the Brigade moving. Rowe and I returned whence we had come to find our helicopter which seemed to take hours to appear. While we waited we saw three Scout helicopters fly in behind Wireless Ridge, line up and hover-taxi forward to fire their SS11 missiles at an Argentine artillery position across the valley. They stayed too long savouring the prospect of hitting such a juicy target, because artillery shells and anti-aircraft fire started dropping around them and they broke off abruptly and flew off low and fast. We both laughed because the fleeing helicopters reminded us of cheeky little boys that have been caught thumbing their noses at the village policeman over the garden wall.

On the return journey to Brigade Tactical Headquarters I received a message from Divisional Headquarters that I was to go forward and take charge of the pursuit into Stanley. This suited me because it was exactly what I intended doing. At Brigade Tactical Headquarters I spoke to General Moore on the secure voice radio and suggested that the Welsh Guards stay with 5 Brigade because they were still on the 5 Brigade radio net and therefore more easily gathered up by Wilson since speed was now of the essence, despite the agreement earlier that morning that the Battalion should revert to me. I also told General Moore that I was about to give orders to my Brigade to advance and that all units had been brought to thirty minutes' notice to move. This was approved. As quick radio orders were being prepared for the whole Brigade a message came from Division that the Argentines were surrendering and that fire was not to be opened unless the British were fired on first.

At that moment the Brigade Air Liaison Officer, Lieutenant-Commander Callaghan, Royal Navy, reminded everybody in the Command Post that an airstrike on Sapper Hill with cluster bombs had been ordered and was due in a few minutes. With the Argentines surrendering the last thing that was wanted at this stage was a massacre of the enemy. Fortunately Wing-Commander Trewerne, Royal Air Force, was forward in Brigade Tactical Headquarters; he grabbed the radio and stopped the strike as the aircraft were coming in.

Telling Chester to give orders to the Brigade to advance, 2 Para, 42 Commando and 3 Para to Stanley and 45 Commando to Sapper Hill, I left by helicopter to rejoin 2 Para, taking Holroyd-Smith, Rowe, Marine Mcguire with a radio and Corporal Dean for close protection. The other key member of the R Group, Macdonald, was forward with 2 Para already. It was with jubilation that we stepped out onto Wireless Ridge to join the tail of 2 Para moving down into Stanley. As the R Group stood looking at 2 Para snaking their way down the hill past Moody Brook and into Stanley, a message came over the radio from Brigade Headquarters that Divisional Headquarters said there were now 'white flags over Stanley'. After a good look at the town through binoculars no one in the R Group could see any white flags and to this day Chaundler and Rowe say there were none. Holroyd-Smith thought he saw something resembling a white flag but Marine Mcguire's only comment was: 'It looks more like someone's knickers on the line'.

2 Para moved along the road into Stanley, led by the Scorpions and Scimitars of 3 Troop Blues and Royals, the leading vehicle flying the Regimental Flag and all four CVRT carrying men of the Battalion. They passed an abandoned Argentine gun position containing at least a regiment's worth of 105 mm pack howitzers. The mud lay thick everywhere and among it abandoned equipment, vehicles, guns and a few dead Argentines. There seemed to be red crosses on many of the larger buildings. There was little sign of any live Argentine troops at the western end of the town. As the R Group marched in orders were received from Division that no British troops were to advance beyond the eastern end of Port Stanley racecourse. This was quickly relayed to 2 Para who looked set to keep going until they reached the airport.

By this time 3 Para were hard on the heels of 2 Para and 45 Commando were marching hard for Sapper Hill, breaching their way through a minefield en route. When 45 Commando arrived on Sapper Hill they found the Welsh Guards with A and C Companies of 40 Commando arriving by helicopter, having been ordered there by 5 Brigade.

The two Companies of 40 Commando had joined the Welsh Guards on 11 June in time to watch the attack on Harriet by 42 Commando, and then spent a couple of days in reserve under 5 Brigade. During this period the Welsh Guards had a frustrating time, including being caught in an extensive minefield, which caused two casualties in C Company, 40 Commando. On 14 June, the day of the surrender, the Battalion, having been told that they would not be moving before 3 pm as part of 3 Commando Brigade's attack, then received orders from 5 Brigade, with whom they remained, to move forward by helicopter to a forming-up position south-west of Mount William and attack Sapper Hill. C Company, 40 Commando, moved first to secure the forming-up position, followed by A Company. Unfortunately the pilots of the helicopters carrying 7 Troop made a map-reading error and landed them three kilometres further forward than intended, on Sapper Hill instead of the lower slopes of Mount William. The enemy opened fire, wounding two Marines slightly. In the subsequent battle several Argentines were killed before the remainder surrendered. At this stage news of the cease-fire was heard and the Welsh Guards moved quickly to occupy Sapper Hill.

This unilateral move by 5 Brigade without telling anybody had potential for a major 'blue-on-blue', a euphemism for shooting at one's own side. Sapper Hill was 45 Commando's objective; this was known to Divisional Headquarters. Perhaps Wilson, smarting at having lost the earlier argument over who was to have the Welsh Guards under command, was determined to take Sapper Hill himself. As 45 Commando advanced up Sapper Hill they were surprised to find it already occupied by the Welsh Guards. Luckily it was daylight and the visibility was good.

By 1.30 pm 45 Commando was starting to dig in on Sapper Hill, they and the Welsh Guards providing a stronghold on a key feature overlooking the town, should the Argentines decide to change their minds. All of 29 Commando Regiment's guns were ordered to remain loaded and laid on targets at the eastern end of town and the narrowest part of the airport isthmus as a precaution should any hard-liners among the Argentine Army decide not to accept the surrender, in particular the regiment on the airfield peninsula and units at the eastern end of Port Stanley who had not yet been involved in the fighting.

As unit after unit heard the news that a surrender was likely, the sense of joy and relief hardly knew any bounds. Gardiner described it thus:

> As we were advancing up Sapper Hill, rumours started filtering through about a surrender. Later in the evening, we heard for sure that it was all over and that the Belgians had beaten them 1-0 in the World Cup. I need not describe my feelings. I think it was the inner warmth supplied by that knowledge that kept me going that night. It was the bitterest of the War and the most uncomfortable of my life, and I slept not a wink.

The Brigade R Group stopped by 2 Para's Headquarters which was setting up in an extraordinary-looking wooden bungalow which, it later transpired, had apparently been brought in from Argentina and erected for the use of the Argentine Air Force Headquarters Officers. Pausing to congratulate 2 Para in being first into Stanley, the R Group, now joined by Seccombe, who had appeared as if by magic, continued on into town, past Government House to the Secretariat. Here, this rather down-at-heel crew with little visible sign of rank anywhere, was challenged in excellent English by a large, smart Argentine Military Police Officer. When identities were established he asked if the Brigadier wished to see the General. On being told that, although General Moore had not yet arrived, there were two British Officers already with General Menendez, I declined the invitation to join them. Guessing who the British Officers were and not wishing to provide a distraction which might disrupt the rapport being established in the negotiating procedure, we turned on our heels and left. It was an uncanny feeling to be walking around surrounded by so many armed Argentine soldiers.

Meanwhile 42 Commando, who had been flown forward from their Mount Harriet/Goat Ridge positions to the north-east shoulder of Tumbledown, had started walking into Stanley. I met them and told them to go firm at the western end of town. They moved into the old sea-plane hangar and a large building opposite. The sea-plane hanger allocated to L Company was like an abattoir, having been used by the Argentines as a field dressing station and mortuary. Amputated limbs had been tossed on to the roof of a small shed within the hanger, as L Company discovered when the frozen pools of blood melted and dripped on to them when they lit braziers to warm themselves up. The dead Argentine soldier in a wheelbarrow was easily wheeled away.

After a few words with Robert Fox of the BBC and Jeremy Hands of ITN, we saw 42 Commando into their unsavoury accommodation and 2 Para and 3 Para into some deserted houses and the racecourse grandstand. Two matters then remained for the R Group to sort out before nightfall: first a quick orders group to the Commanding Officers to tie up arrangements for the night and second, if possible, a home for the night. Brigade Tactical Headquarters with our rations and sleeping bags was miles away on the wrong side of a minefield and it would take all night to negotiate a way through, losing a Bandwagon blown up on a mine in the process. By this time both Chester and Gullan had appeared. Gullan with his usual initiative had persuaded Crosland, commanding B Company 2 Para, to allow the Brigade R Group to use the top floor of one of the houses he had requisitioned. Somehow the radio orders summoning the orders group became garbled in transmission because both Whitehead and Vaux who decided to hop the short distance by Gazelle were decanted, in turn, into the garden of Government House under the startled eyes of the Argentine soldiers still guarding it.

Sitting in the dark bedroom of the requisitioned house by the light of torches, orders were given to the Commanding Officers of 42 Commando, 45 Commando, 2 Para and 3 Para, tying up inter-unit boundaries and areas. There was still no news of a formal surrender, so everyone was ordered to remain alert and be prepared for the unexpected. We heard that General Moore was to fly to Stanley sometime that night, but that was all. The first firm news of the surrender came to the R Group some hours later when one of the radios was switched to the BBC World Service and we first heard the terms of the surrender from a news flash broadcast from London 8,000 miles away describing events that had just taken place in the Secretariat building 800 metres down the road from where the R Group sat in the darkened house. It was an emotional moment.

Gullan located some plastic bottles of Argentine red wine and, repairing to the kitchen, we found the happy soldiers of B Company Headquarters 2 Para brewing up a huge stew of liberated Argentine rations in a communal pot over the peat-fired Rayburn stove. An invitation to join them was issued and soon all present were dipping their spoons into the pot, for most the first food for over twenty-four hours.

So it was all over. There were prisoners to be collected, disarmed and guarded until they could be returned to Argentina. There were minefields and booby traps to clear which would cost two more lives and several more men a foot. But there would be no more fighting and no need to re-embark in ships to assault West Falkland, which would have been necessary if Menendez had not been persuaded to order the capitulation of all Argentine troops on all the islands of the group. So with luck all of the young men now alive in my Brigade would go home alive, the soldiers of B Company 2 Para lying asleep in heaps all over the house we shared, so that every square inch of space was covered in bodies, still clutching rifle or machine gun, only sentries alert: the gunners of 29 Commando Regiment Royal Artillery, asleep beside their now silent guns, only the gun sentries awake, one at each gun, ready to fire the loaded pieces on to the targets on which they were laid; 45 Commando shivering with cold on Sapper Hill; 42 Commando among the rats and debris of the sea-plane hangar; 40 Commando about to go to West Falkland; 2 Para and 3 Para in deserted houses, sheds and the racecourse grandstand in the west end of town; the Sappers who had taken part in every attack; my logisticians working through the night, as always, preparing loads at Teal and Ajax Bay for the morrow; Major Armitage missing and with a broken back being kept warm by his driver, Gunner Inch, lying out in the dark and snow all night by the wreck of their Bandwagon, destroyed on a mine when it became separated from my Tactical Headquarters in a snowstorm (Major Armitage would be skiing within a year); Corporal Lockyer my staff car driver who came south at his insistence, without his staff car, but with his rifle, who should have been in the back of Major Armitage's Bandwagon and dead, but at the last moment had replaced another Bandwagon driver. He, and about five thousand others like him in my Brigade, had done what we had come 8,000 miles to do.

Notes

CHAPTER ONE

Units in 3 Commando Brigade Royal Marines

Brigade Headquarters
Two Troop B Squadron RHG/D The Blues and Royals
29 Commando Regiment Royal Artillery
   7 (Sphinx) Commando Battery
   8 (Alma) Commando Battery
   79 (Kirkee) Commando Battery
   148 (Meiktila) Commando Forward Observation Battery (1)

And:

   29 (Corunna) Field Battery, 4 Field Regiment Royal Artillery Battery
      Commander and OP parties 41 Field Battery, 4 Field Regiment Royal
      Artillery
   T (Shah Shujah's Troop) Air Defence Battery (2)
59 Independent Commando Squadron Royal Engineers (complete)

And:

   2 Troop 9 Parachute Squadron Royal Engineers
   One team 49 Explosives Ordnance Disposal Squadron, 33 Engineer
      Regiment
   One Explosives Ordnance Disposal Team RAF
40 Commando Royal Marines
42 Commando Royal Marines less M (3) Company but plus J Company
45 Commando Royal Marines
2nd Battalion The Parachute Regiment (2 Para)
3rd Battalion The Parachute Regiment (3 Para)
Special Boat Squadron Royal Marines
D and G Squadrons 22 SAS
Mountain and Artic Warfare Cadre (M and AW Cadre) Royal Marines

3 Commando Brigade Air Squadron Royal Marines (complete)

And:

One Flight 656 Squadron Army Air Corps
3 Commando Brigade Air Defence Troop Royal Marines (complete)

And:

Two sections 43 Battery, 32 Guided Weapons Regiment, Royal Artillery
605, 611 and 612 Tactical Air Control Parties Royal Marines (4)
613 Tactical Air Control Party
3 Commando Brigade Headquarters and Signals Squadron Royal Marines

And:

Satellite Communications Detachment Royal Signals
1 Raiding Squadron Royal Marines
Commando Forces News Team
Commando Logistic Regiment Royal Marines
Postal and Courier Communications Unit Royal Engineers
Elements Transport Squadron
Medical Squadron
 Surgical Support Teams
 Parachute Clearing Troop
 Commando Forces Band
Ordnance Squadron
Elements Workshop Squadron
Force Reinforcement Holding Unit
Field Records Office

Notes:

1. Provides the Observer Parties to control Naval Gun Fire Support and liason teams aboard the firing ships.
2. Rapier Battery.
3. M Company detached to Operation PARAQUAT, the re-capture of South Georgia. The nucleus of J Company was formed from men (in NP 8901) captured when the Argentines invaded the Falkland Islands, re-patriated to England and who volunteered to return, led by Major Norman, commander of NP 8901. The balance of J Company was formed from men from Support Company and Headquarters Company 42 Commando Royal Marines.
4. To control air strikes.

CHAPTER TWO

1. The Landing Craft Utility (LCU) was the 'work-horse' of the waterborne part of the campaign. Designed to carry two main battle tanks or about a company of infantry, it is commanded by a Colour Sergeant Royal Marines and has a crew of five. Four LCU were carried in each of the two Landing Platform Dock (LPD), HMS *Fearless* and HMS *Intrepid*.

2. a. The ships were:

   HMS *Fearless* — LPD
   LSL *Sir Geraint* — Landing Ship Logistic (LSL)
   LSL *Sir Galahad* — Landing Ship Logistic
   LSL *Sir Percival* — Landing Ship Logistic
   LSL *Sir Lancelot* — Landing Ship Logistic
   HMS *Hermes* — Harrier and helicopter carrier with one company of
      40 Commando RM embarked. This company was transferred to
      Canberra at Ascension. *Hermes* then sailed ahead with Woodward
   RFA *Resource* — Fleet Stores Ship
   RFA *Stromness* — Fleet Stores Ship
   RFA *Fort Austin* — Fleet Stores Ship
   SS *Canberra* — Civilian Liner (Ship Taken Up From Trade [STUFT])
   MV *Elk* — Civilian Ferry (STUFT)

   b. Later, at Ascension, the Amphibious Task Group was joined by
   Atlantic Conveyor — Container Ship (STUFT)
   MV *Norland* — Civilian Ferry (STUFT)
   MV *Europic Ferry* — Civilian Ferry (STUFT)
   HMS *Intrepid* — LPD
   LSL *Sir Tristram* — LSL

   c. For the passage South from Ascension, the landings and subsequent operations, escorts were added to the Amphibious Task Group and came under Commodore Clapp's command.

CHAPTER SEVEN

1. The essentials, 'and all else is folly', were, according to one Company Commander:

   2 Days' rations in jacket pockets plus the wherewithal to cook them
   Torch
   Maps
   Spoon

Spoon
Water sterilizing tablets
Weapon
Ammunition
Weapon cleaning box
1 Water bottle
Pick or shovel
Waterproof trousers and jacket
Poncho
Duvet suit including boots
Sleeping bag
Spare socks
Gloves
1 small tent pole and six pegs
3 rubber bungies

CHAPTER EIGHT

1. Captain Rowe the GSO3 Intelligence of 3 Commando Brigade RM tells the story: 'On 15 June, 1982 [after the Argentine surrender], I was minding my own business in the Secretariat building [the government administrative building in Stanley requisitioned by 3 Commando Brigade Headquarters as a command post] when Colonel Baxter [the head logistician at Divisional Headquarters] appeared and grabbed me and told me of the OP and "asked" if I would go and accept its surrender. I was allocated an Argentine Huey helicopter for the task. The pilot was drunk and aggressive and the co-pilot not so drunk and aggressive. With the exception of an Iranian air assault in the Dhofar, it was probably the most dangerous flight of my career so far. The weather was foul and we had to land twice to sit out blizzards. However, with me doing the map reading — they did not have a map — we eventually found the OP.'

INDEX

AS12 missiles, 29

Aermacchi M339s, 36, 80

air attacks, Argentine, 57, 58, 59-60, 66-7, 68, 79, 80, 84, 91-2, 94, 147-8

air control, battle for, 33, 61

Air Defence Section, Number 1, 44

Air Defence Troop, *see* Headquarters and Signals Squadron

Ajax Bay, 32, 38, 66, 71, 72, 159; plan to land at, 43, 52, 53; SBS at, 51; storage of ammunition and supplies at, 60, 63; Satellite Communication Terminal at, 71, 92; attack on BMA at, 73; Field Dressing Station, 63, 73, 83; Main Dressing Station, 100

Ambuscade, HMS, 150

ammunition and supplies, 40, 60-1, 63, 99, 100, 101; shortage of, 77, 78; unloading problems, 84; captured Argentinian, 143; *see also* rations

Amphibious Task Group, 10, 15, 17, 19-26, 70, 189; D-Day Operation, 49, 54; Operations Room, 54

Antelope, HMS, 67

Antrim, HMS, 17, 28, 29, 57

'Apple Pie', 150, 152, 154

Ardent, HMS, 51, 58, 64

Argentine Air Force, 35, 50, 58, 61, 64, 68, 91-2, 94, 101, 102, 119

Argentine Army, xviii, 106, 107; artillery and equipment, 35-6, 143; estimated strength of, 19, 27, 35-6, 72; surrender, 155, 157, 158-9

Argue, Major M.H., 90, 98, 125, 127, 128

Armitage, Major B., 153, 159

Army Air Corps, 656 Squadron, 19

Arnold, Captain K.D., 81

Arrow, HMS, 75, 76

Arroy Pedro River, 90

Artillery Regiment, *see* Royal Artillery

Ascension Island, xv, 12, 14, 15, 43, 45; 3 Commando Brigade at, 15-26, 27, 52, 55; General Moore at, 23, 92

Atlantic Conveyor, MV, 68-9, 70, 105, 189

Augusta A 109A helicopters, 36, 91

BBC newsreels, 48

BBC World Service, 73, 102, 159

Babbington, Captain P.M., 138, 139, 140; quoted, 139

Baby, The, 97

Bailey, Corporal, 4, 126

Baldwin, Major W.D.H., 9, 24-5, 41

Ball Mount, 95

Band of Commando Forces, 11

Bandwagons (BV202s), ix, 64, 67, 86, 89, 94, 125, 147, 148, 159; motored to Teal Inlet, 99; moved to Mount Kent, 115

Barnacle, Corporal, 97

Barry, Lieut, 80

Barton, Mr (Manager Teal Inlet Settlement), 90

Baxter, Lieut J.S., 133

Bay Brook Valley, 64

Beachhead, The (map), 39

Beadon, Lieut C.J.A., 110, 137

Belcher, Sergeant, 79

Bell, Captain R.D., 43, 51, 57, 73, 82

Berkeley Sound, 23, 24

Bickerdike, Lieut A.J., 4, 126, 127

Boca House, 73, 75, 78, 79, 80

Boswell, Captain R.J., 7, 25, 94, 95-6, 97, 117; quoted, 96

Boultby, Staff-Sergeant, quoted, 59-60

Blowpipe missiles, 6, 35, 53, 61, 79, 80; air defence sections, 44, 75, 147

Blue Beach One, 43, 52, 53

Blue Beach Two, 43, 50, 52, 53, 64, 73

'Blueberry Pie', 150

Blues and Royals, The, 11, 25-6, 40, 90; at Teal, 90; 3 Troop, 44, 99, 149, 150, 153, 156; 4 Troop, 90

Bluff Cove, xviii, 113

Bluff Cove Peak, 100, 112, 122, 130

Bombilla Hill, 72, 90

Brenton Loch, 35, 64, 67

Brigade Command Net, 86